THE
CRYSTAL
HEALER
VOLUME 2

THE CRYSTAL HEALER

VOLUME 2

HARNESS THE POWER OF CRYSTAL ENERGY

PHILIP PERMUTT

CICO BOOKS
LONDON NEW YORK

Published in 2018 by CICO Books
An imprint of Ryland Peters & Small Ltd
20–21 Jockey's Fields   341 E 116th St
London WC1R 4BW   New York, NY 10029

www.rylandpeters.com

10 9 8 7 6 5 4 3 2 1

A CIP catalog record for this book is available from the
Library of Congress and the British Library.

ISBN: 978-1-78249-654-0

Printed in China

Editor: Marion Paull
Designer: Emily Breen
Photographer: Roy Palmer
Illustrators: Tiffany Lynch and Trina Dalziel

Commissioning editor: Kristine Pidkameny
Senior editor: Carmel Edmonds
Art director: Sally Powell
Production controller: David Hearn
Publishing manager: Penny Craig
Publisher: Cindy Richards

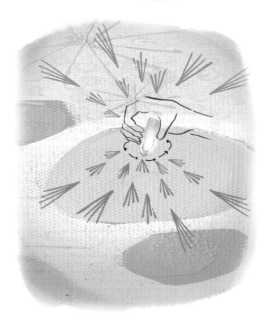

SAFETY NOTE
Please note that while the descriptions of the properties
of crystals refer to healing benefits, they are not
intended to replace diagnosis of illness or ailments, or
healing or medicine. Always consult your doctor or other
health professional in the case of illness.

CONTENTS

INTRODUCTION

The first book in this series, *The Crystal Healer*, was essentially a record of my journey with the Stone People—crystals, gems, rocks, minerals, and stones. Colloquially, I like to call them all crystals. This is what I do, and I've been working with crystals, clients, customers, and students almost every single day for over a quarter of a century—healing myself and clients, buying and selling around the world, teaching and learning with my students, and writing about these amazing crystal beings. *The Crystal Healer* was originally published in 2007. At some time in the now distant past, the possibility of a "Volume 2" had been mooted. I wrote other books in the meantime, including *The Complete Guide to Crystal Chakra Healing* and *The Book of Crystal Grids*, but finally, here is the second volume. There was never going to be enough room within the pages of a single volume to cover all the available crystal knowledge. There isn't the room in two volumes, or three or four or … So, I apologize right at the beginning for my omissions and look forward to sharing them with you in the future!

There is so much more that I wanted to reveal to you: diverse ways of working with crystals, some ancient and some new; topics either not covered or just touched on in the original book that I wanted to expand, such as crystal grids (see *The Book of Crystal Grids*); and crystal colors and shapes (see pages 24–30). In an updated edition of *The Crystal Healer*, I included a new section on "How Crystals Work," adding then current developments in quantum research to our layman's understanding. I have included more information on this subject

here, giving us a better image of the way we interact with crystals and how they affect our inner world.

Your feedback from *The Crystal Healer* was that you loved the Crystal Finder's 250 crystals organized by color, with clear photographs, descriptions, and healing properties. There are 250 "new" crystals in this book, arranged in exactly the same color-coded format. Many of these crystals are included because they have become more widely available and some are newly discovered since the first book.

I am passionate about our relationships with crystals and understanding the messages that crystals carry: how they "talk" to you and how you "listen" to your crystals and stones. To this end, I've written an entire section on crystal communication (see pages 19–23). Here is where I explore the possibilities of adding to our personal well-being in ways we cannot see or expect. Crystals will look beyond the dimensions we see in, touch our heart, and bring healing to our soul.

I am sharing my passion for crystals with you in these pages and I hope a little of it rubs off and encourages you to take the next step on your crystal journey. Whether that's holding a crystal or visiting a crystal store for the first time, going to a local workshop, training as a crystal healer, or becoming a Crystal Master Teacher to pass on your knowledge of the Stone People to others, I hope these words can help you to heal and will inspire you.

CHAPTER 1

WORKING WITH CRYSTALS

In this chapter, we look at how crystals work and how we work with them, including communicating with them and understanding how different colors and shapes can affect their energy.

WHAT ARE CRYSTALS?

I'd like to begin by explaining that to me, and used throughout this book, the term "crystal" is not limited to the scientific definition but includes all of the mineral kingdom, the Stone People—crystals, minerals, rocks, stones, and gemstones, as well as mineralized shells, fossilized animals, and petrified plants.

Crystals are beautiful in both their appearance and their feel. They're fun to work with, and have no ill side effects. Even if sometimes their effect can feel uncomfortable as we release thoughts and emotions we don't want to face while they are bringing balance to our energy system, they do only good.

Most of the crystals we work with are created in the Earth's surface. A few are created in the depths of outer space, but these are basically the same minerals—just without air spaces between the molecules, since they really are formed in the vacuum of space; and a few are produced from natural crystals and minerals by man.

Minerals are natural, consistent solids with precise atomic arrangements. They are usually formed from inorganic processes. Rock contains minerals. When it is melted, the mineral particles are able to "find each other" and come together, so that when the rock cools, crystallization occurs and minerals are formed. Similarly, minerals can be dissolved in water, whether groundwater (that is the water between underground soil and rocks) or the oceans. Crystallization happens when the water is cooled or when it evaporates. The minerals formed are the building blocks of the crystals, rocks, and gemstones of the world.

A crystal must have an exact crystalline form to its atomic arrangement and a specific color. However, these may vary, especially color—not only from one specimen to another, but within the same crystal. Each mineral has a relative hardness, as described by Mohs Scale, which is one of the identifying features of all crystals.

CRYSTAL ENERGY

People talk about crystal energy, but what is it? How do crystals affect and interact with your energy and, ultimately, bring healing? Well, the first place to look is where, and how, we feel the energy when we work with crystals.

You may have noticed that I like the phrase "we work with crystals"; I've written it over and over in every one of my books. It's an expression that, taken literally, starts to explain how crystals work. It's a partnership. It's an exchange of energy; they give and take, we absorb and release. It happens throughout our being but the principal energy route is through our chakras, and especially the seven major chakras—your energy hot spots.

THE CRYSTAL CHAKRA SET

CHAKRA	ASSOCIATED CONCEPTS	ASSOCIATED CRYSTAL	
Crown	Spirituality, connection to universe, imagination, awareness, optimism	Amethyst	
Brow	Mind, ideas, thoughts, dreams, psychic abilities	Lapis lazuli	
Throat	Communication, expression, responsibility, freedom, leadership	Blue lace agate	
Heart	Love, safety, trust, adventure, relationships	Malachite	
Solar plexus	Physical center, personal power, emotions	Citrine	
Sacral	Connection to other people, creativity, energy, confidence	Carnelian	
Base	Survival, health, abundance, connection to Earth, moving forward in life	Red jasper	

LOCATING THE CHAKRAS

Crown chakra—on the top of the head

Brow chakra (also known as the third-eye chakra)—in the center of the forehead, above the eyebrows

Throat chakra—in the center of the throat

Heart chakra—in the center of the chest

Solar plexus chakra—behind the soft cartilage at the bottom of the breast bone

Sacral chakra—just below the belly button. Try placing your thumb on your belly button with your palm on your tummy—your sacral chakra will be under the palm of your hand

Base chakra—at the coccyx at the base of the spine

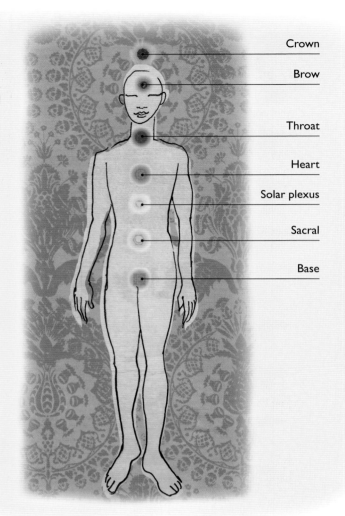

Crown

Brow

Throat

Heart

Solar plexus

Sacral

Base

CLEANSING CRYSTALS

Whenever we add energy, such as when we work with crystals to heal ourselves, there is a release of energy. We take in helpful energy and expel energy that hinders us. This is the reason why it is so important to cleanse your crystals regularly (see opposite). They are picking up energy from you, collecting it, and will release it sooner or later. You don't want to start picking up your own problems from your crystals! And if you're working as a crystal healer, it is imperative to cleanse your crystals; if you don't, they will pick up the energy released from one client and pass it on to the next!

Tingsha, also known as Tibetan cymbals, can be used to cleanse crystals.

✳ My preferred way to remove any unwanted energy stuck to my crystals is with sound. I like to work with tingsha (Tibetan cymbals) to create a sonic vibration that essentially shakes the crystal on a molecular level—the vibration literally jiggles off unwanted energy. You can also sound a Tibetan bowl, chant, or drum to create a similar cleansing effect.

✳ Another recommended way of cleansing crystals is under running water (not suitable for water-soluble crystals). A natural spring, stream, or river is ideal, but tap water will suffice. Hold the crystal in the flow of water for a minute or two. It may need longer if it hasn't been cleansed for a while or if it's been working hard.

✳ Sunlight is cleansing but beware of leaving quartz, especially crystal balls, in direct sunlight, because it will focus the sun's rays and can be a fire risk. Also, some crystals, such as amethyst, may fade with long-term exposure to direct sunlight.

✳ The moon is capable of moving oceans, so it should be no problem for the lunar body to move the energy of a small crystal. Leave your crystals in the moonlight overnight; they especially like the full moon and new moon.

✳ Sage smudge sticks, traditionally used in Native American ceremonies, are excellent cleansers. It is the smoke of these that is cleansing, so waft the smoke over your crystals. Conventionally, the smoke is directed with a feather because feathers carry our prayers and wishes to spirit. Hold something underneath your smudge stick to catch any falling embers; this is usually a seashell, such as abalone, to represent water and complete the embodiment of the four elements:

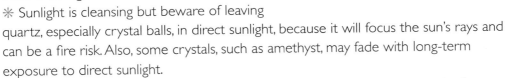

    sage herb = earth
    feather = air
    smoke = fire
    shell = water

The inclusion of these aspects enhances the ritual of the cleansing process, adding an extra dimension.

Whichever method you choose, and there are many others too, be sure to cleanse your crystals with your mind clearly focused on what you are doing. Concentrate on your intent, and take your time; cleansing is not something to be rushed.

CRYSTAL ELIXIRS

The healing effects of crystals can be experienced by drinking water in which a crystal has been immersed—this is known as a crystal elixir. Elixirs can be effective in the treatment of various conditions, as detailed in Chapter 4. However, some crystals should never be made into elixirs—these are clearly indicated by "No elixir" in Chapter 3.

MAKING AN ELIXIR

Start by cleansing the crystal you will be working with (see previous page). Place the crystal in a glass or other container of water. It is preferable to use distilled or mineral water from a pure source, but tap water will do. Cover the container and/or place it in the refrigerator and leave overnight. Throughout this process, focus your intention on what you want the elixir to do. Some people like to enhance elixirs by placing them in the light of the sun or the moon or surrounding them with quartz crystals. The next morning, the elixir will be ready. It can be drunk or applied topically over the next 24 hours. Try preparing some quick elixirs and seeing what effect they have on you. Take three different crystals (for example, quartz, amethyst, and rose quartz), and place each in its own glass of water. Also have a glass of plain water as a control. Leave the glasses of water to stand for 20–30 minutes and then taste each one. Usually, quartz tastes fresher than the plain water, amethyst tastes noticeably metallic, and rose quartz is slightly bland. Don't worry if you experience different tastes, as we can all describe our sensations in our own way.

THE THEORY

The world is not solid and nothing in it is solid either, including you and me, crystals, and even the laptop I'm using to write this. The entire universe is in constant motion. Nothing is stationary, and nothing is fixed and immovable or unchangeable. In fact, research in the field of quantum mechanics clearly shows this to be true.

BEINGS OF LIGHT

Almost every one of the world's religions, every shamanic culture, almost every belief system the world over, uses descriptions such as "we are beings of light," "we come from the light," "we go back to the light," "lead us to the light," "divine light" that is within everyone, "enlightenment," "to find the light," "let

there be light," "festival of light," "Buddhas of light," "inner light," "light of divine consciousness," "illumination on the path," "cross of pure light," and "light of the human soul."

Quantum physics confirms that we are indeed physically made of light and our ancestors were completely correct, if somewhat flowery in their prose; we are beings of light. Now, this area of research also shows us that a photon of light, one of the tiniest particles in the universe, can behave as a particle, a physical object, or it can act as a moving wave of energy that suggests where it might be if it were a particle and still having a physical effect. One of the many confusing things is that it can also be both! But not at the same time. It can alternate, or change randomly and unexpectedly from one to the other, but once the photon is identified and measured as a particle or wave, it becomes fixed in that state and can no longer swap. Everything is made of this confusing matter we call light.

Quartz crystals focus light! You don't have to be a physicist to know this; you can see it for yourself (see box, overleaf).

QUARTZ FOCUSING LIGHT

In a brightly lit room or outside on a sunny day, hold a natural quartz crystal about 1–2 inches (2–5 cm) above the open palm of your hand, with the termination (point) pointing toward your palm. Move the crystal slowly in a clockwise circle above your hand. Look at your palm and you will see a point (or line, or area) of light moving on your palm as the crystal circles your hand. The light may be directly under the crystal or offset to the side, and varies in brightness from one crystal to another. Sometimes the light is clear to see, sometimes you need to observe closely. This varies from one crystal to another, depending on the angle of the crystal lattice and the crystal's termination. The crystal is picking up the light in the room and focusing it on your palm. Everything is made of light, so it is hardly surprising that if a crystal can focus more photons of light on an area where it is needed in the body, then this might aid physical repair and healing. Don't be surprised if you also begin to notice a feeling in your hand, such as a tingling, warmth, or coolness, as the light moves around your palm.

DARK MATTER

So, everything is made of this confusing matter we call light. Except dark matter …

The existence of dark matter has been postulated for some time by scientists. Simply, there is not enough matter in the universe; the cosmologists' sums don't add up! So, to fill the void, these very clever scientists invented the idea of dark matter and dark energy; that is, matter and energy not made of light, so we cannot see it, sense it, or measure it in any way. Does this sound familiar? To me, it's sounding very much like the energy we call chi. Dark matter in this instance is not a reference to something that is bad, evil, negative, or anything else, but simply to something "hidden." We cannot see it.

In the depths of outer space, millions of light years away from our planet Earth, the x-rays emitted from dark matter have recently been observed.[1] In fact, astronomers watched in awe as a cloud of this dark matter appeared to go through a cloud of light matter and … nothing whatsoever happened to either! They both emerged as they had been before the interaction. This suggests that not only does dark matter actually exist, but it can be all around us all the time without anyone being aware of it. There are essentially two universes existing right here together at the same time and in the same space, mostly invisible to one another. Quantum physicists suggest that dark matter might make up 60 to 95 percent of our universe. Might it make up 95 percent of you? Maybe it is the bit we call the soul, or spirit; the part of us that lives on after our mortal body stops functioning.

If the energy we call chi, or ki, or prana, or universal life force, or Tao, or hundreds of other names, is indeed the dark energy of contemporary quantum physics,[2] then the existence of dark matter could start to explain everything from spirits walking through walls—dark and light matter passing through each other without apparent change to either—to extraordinary healing where changes occur to subtle (dark) energy. If some people, under certain conditions, can tune in to the wavelengths of dark matter, either deliberately with training as a healer or psychic, or with the aid of a crystal, or accidentally because this sometimes just happens naturally, then we also have a possible explanation for sensing a presence, seeing a fleeting wisp of something that disappears as soon as we notice it, sensing spirits and energy with any and all of our senses. In fact, dark energy is everywhere in the universe (universal energy), not just in space but also in time (past-life recall, knowing of past events, ghosts, seeing into the future). Perhaps our "sixth sense" is simply our ability to sense dark energy?

If we are partly made up of dark matter—and it is unimportant if that's 60 percent or 95 percent, or whatever number we put on it, just that we are made up in part of enough dark matter—then our whole understanding of how the body works INSTANTLY CHANGES! Suddenly, not only are energy therapies such as crystal healing and Reiki possible, but they are an essential factor in facilitating a long-term "cure." Everything else becomes the proverbial sticking plaster.

FIND THE CAUSE

The thought that stress goes to the weakest part of the body is not new, but understanding the process that causes this observation might shed some light on how crystals work. The acclaimed psychiatrist Bessel van der Kolk explains how emotional and psychological trauma physically manifest in the body.[3] One fascinating discovery is that the same, or similar, traumas can have very, very different apparent manifestations in the body. For example, where one person's blood pressure increases as a result of discussing their experience, another develops a migraine. Some may not feel a change, but in a laboratory their stress hormones are shown to have increased. Each person is reacting physiologically in exactly the same way, but displaying vastly differing symptoms.

And it doesn't have to be anything as big as "trauma"—ongoing stress is quite enough to create physical symptoms. I have observed stressed clients manifesting with headaches and migraines; aches in joints, backs, and muscles; high blood pressure and skin conditions such as eczema, psoriasis, and unexplained rashes; stomach and bowel disorders—for example IBS, colitis, and Crohn's disease; frozen shoulders; hearing loss (especially on one side); anxiety and panic attacks; strange tastes in the mouth; hair loss; breathing problems; susceptibility to colds and winter bugs; behavior changes, some minor, a little annoying and apparently insignificant, others major including developing bipolar disorder, OCD, aggressive behavior, and self harming. In fact, looking back over 26 years of treating clients with crystals, the one common factor is that *all* of them were stressed.

If each person who has a traumatic experience displays unique symptoms, why shouldn't anyone who is stressed do the same? Trauma is extreme stress. We tend to overuse the word "trauma." A traumatic event is one that overwhelms a person's ability to cope. There are no clear, medically accepted boundaries between stress and trauma. In fact, about the only thing that is clear is that whereas one person may cope in a certain situation, another may falter.

So, let's assume for one minute that the medical profession is actually agreeing with an alternative view of how the body works here. The explanation of the process of disease does not actually help in discovering its cause *or effective treatment*. Yes, I agree that medically there are many things that can be prescribed to alleviate symptoms. However, these treatments are rarely if ever successful in "curing" the disease.

Here's a simple example I offer my students in Crystal Healing Level 1 training. A person is taken into Accident & Emergency (Emergency Room) with a broken leg from a road traffic accident. It turns out that she walked out in front of a bus. The medical staff at the hospital are very capable in administering analgesics, resetting the bone, and making a suitable cast for the leg, and in most cases, this will alleviate the immediate symptoms of the broken leg and associated pain, and in extreme cases can be life-saving. However, this completely fails to address the cause of the broken leg, which has absolutely nothing whatsoever to do with the impact of the bus! That was just another symptom. The question the medical staff should ask is, "Why is this patient so stressed and distracted that she didn't even see a great big bus and walked out in front of it?"—because until that stress is treated, the person will keep walking out in front of the proverbial bus.

This is another way that stress can affect us. It is so all encompassing that we stop living in the real world. We stop existing in the present moment and start believing and acting in different ways that can be very unhealthy, like walking in front of buses.

LET'S RECAP:

✶ There is no certain relationship between any single symptom and its actual cause.
✶ All symptoms typically have stress as their cause.
✶ Stress affects everyone differently.
✶ Treating symptoms may give relief but does not facilitate a cure.
✶ To aid the healing of a disease, you must also treat the stress that has caused it.

In my experience, every person who undergoes a full series of crystal-healing treatments experiences a profound level of improvement to their health, often facilitating major, transformative life changes.

SO HOW DO CRYSTALS WORK?

In *The Crystal Healer*, I explained the historic beliefs and scientific evidence ranging from the use of crystals in modern technology (they run our twenty-first-century lifestyle!) through rocket science to the placebo effect, ending with the thought that the "New scientific studies into dark matter and dark energy, along with quantum mechanics, will contribute to our understanding of how crystals work." Over the past decade there have been leaps and bounds in our understanding, leading us to the brink of a new paradigm.

CRYSTALS AND CHRONIC PAIN

Of course, sometimes none of this actually matters at all, such as with chronic pain, which is a long-standing problem of epidemic proportions around the world. For example, in America 100 million people are living with chronic pain that affects their daily activities.[4] This is the type of long-term pain that takes the joy out of life. Something hurts all the time. It is debilitating and draining physically, emotionally, and mentally. It challenges your bodymind (the body's energy system, which links body, mind, and spirit) totally.

There is a simple, magical answer for many people ... and it's called chevron amethyst, also known as banded amethyst, a simple tumble-polished stone costing from as little as about $1.35 (£1). Pop one in your pocket or bra, keep it with you

24/7, and hold it to your most painful area for 20 minutes daily. Don't be concerned if one area seems to improve while another zone hurts more; just follow the pain and hold the crystal to the most painful area. At night, place your chevron amethyst crystal under your pillow or on a bedside table. You will find that quite quickly it will take the edge off your pain, and your pain will ease. Don't expect your discomfort to disappear completely and instantly, but you will notice that it is easier for you to complete everyday tasks that may have become too painful to contemplate. Anyone who suffers from chronic pain will tell you that it stops them doing many things they'd like to do and often prevents them from doing what most people consider to be easy tasks. By taking the edge off the pain, so many things become possible, and the pain bearable, that it is like having discovered a life-changing elixir!

How does this work? I don't honestly know! But here's a theory …

Our nervous system carries pain signals along nerve cells, called neurons. The electrical signal passes very quickly across these highly specialized cells and then, it is believed, dedicated chemicals, known as neurotransmitters, carry the signal across the synapse, the gap between neurons. This has never been proved to happen. In fact, no one knows exactly what happens in the synapse, only that the pain signal magically appears in the next neuron.

What if these nerve signals are transmitted in part as electrical signals, which we know crystals can affect, and part as dark energy, which affects the dark matter that we're now pretty sure makes up a significant part of us? It would give a simple, almost obvious, pathway to healing that would explain why chevron amethyst is so life-changing for so many people. In a recent unpublished *ad hoc* trial at a London hospital's pain clinic, 20 out of 22 people given a chevron amethyst reported that their pain level dropped noticeably to varying degrees over a period of one week, some a little and some greatly.

Now, if we assume that crystals influence dark matter, we have a new way of understanding how they might work. They treat the invisible cause of the problem, which we can call stress, and not the presented symptoms that might seem to disappear visibly with treatment. Perhaps this can also explain the observation that sometimes symptoms appear to get worse before they improve, as our body might be reacting to energy shifts within.

Chevron amethyst can
ease chronic pain.

CRYSTAL COMMUNICATION

Do you talk to your crystals? And if you do, do you sometimes think you're a little crazy? Maybe those around you—husbands, wives, partners, relatives, friends—see you as a little (or even a lot!) odd? Well, come on! If you're talking to an inanimate "rock," you've got to be mad … but are you? Is your rock lifeless? Or is your crystal a living, eating, growing, reproducing being? If it is, you wouldn't be quite as crazy as others might think.

ARE CRYSTALS LIVING BEINGS?

An argument among biologists has been going on for a very long time. It was being discussed before I started studying biology at London University in the 1970s, and the very same dispute continues today within the ivory towers of academia—namely, where is the borderline of life? What is living and what is not?

What is life? One definition is: "The state of a material complex or individual characterized by the capacity to perform certain functional activities, including metabolism, growth, and reproduction." So that's simple—if it can eat, grow, and have little ones, it's living. Other definitions go further and suggest seven criteria for matter to be described as living—see below.

WHAT DEFINES A LIVING THING?

1. **Homeostasis:** It maintains a balanced inner structure.

2. **Organization:** Its structure is highly organized.

3. **Metabolism:** It eats.

4. **Growth:** It changes over time, getting larger.

5. **Adaptation:** It recognizes and changes with its environment over time.

6. **Responsiveness:** It responds to environment (as opposed to over time).

7. **Reproduction:** It can reproduce itself.

OK, so in the 1970s and nowadays the argument over the borderline of life is the same *and* the answer hasn't changed. You see, all biologists agree that bacteria are living beings. However, most biologists also call viruses living, although others do not. Let me explain …

Intuitively, you know a virus is living when you catch it. You catch a cold, fight the cold, kill the virus that's attacking you. Without any doubt a virus is a living being. But viruses reproduce by a different method from all other animals and plants, including bacteria. They reproduce by "binary fission," which requires a specific host cell. They must be in a very specific growing environment to reproduce. Viruses are also very picky eaters and need this same specific growing environment to eat, and viruses probably don't grow at all. In fact, of the seven criteria listed on page 19, viruses do 1, 5, and 6, don't do 2 and 4, and might do 3 and 7 in specific environments. And yet we are happy to call viruses living.

Life cannot simply be defined in the way of many other scientific terms. Life on planet Earth arose naturally from inanimate matter billions of years ago. When was it first living? We don't know. There is no boldly drawn borderline between living and non-living matter, just a hazy, gray mist out of which life evolves.

CRYSTALS AND THE CRITERIA

Now, back to crystals. If a virus can be considered as living, as we have seen it is, a crystal MUST also be described as such, for a crystal fulfills the criteria:

✳ **Homeostasis:** It maintains a balanced inner structure.

✳ **Organization:** It has a highly organized crystalline structure.

✳ **Metabolism:** Yes, crystals "eat" their environment, by absorbing the elements they need to grow from their very specific growing environment and organizing them into their crystalline structure.

✳ **Growth:** You know that you can find small crystals and big crystals; the big crystals have grown from small ones.

✳ **Adaptation:** Crystals such as phantom crystals adapt their growth over time.

✳ **Responding to its environment:** This is questionable, but within a crystal's millions of years of lifetime growth, interference crystals could be counted here. (Growth interference crystals literally have their growth changed by a physical block in their environment. Essentially the crystal grows around the block.)

Green quartz contains phantoms, which adapt their growth over time.

✳ **Reproduction:** Crystals reproduce in two ways—as seed crystals and by adapting to damage or separation in their growing environment.

However, crystals, in exactly the same way as viruses, MUST be in a very specific growing environment to do these things. Put simply, if a virus is considered to be living, a crystal must be thought of in the same way. So, next time you find yourself talking to your crystals, remember you're not as crazy as you might have thought.

LISTEN TO YOUR CRYSTALS

Crystals talk with us all the time they're around us, and sometimes from great distances, too. Occasionally you simply notice this, such as when you become aware of a crystal that you've had for a long time as if it's waving at you, trying to catch your attention, or one seems to jump off a shelf. At other moments, they speak softly and subtly, such as when you hold a crystal and feel an emotion, or place some in an unconscious pattern, forming a crystal grid.

Communicating with crystals can be easy. It's just like learning a foreign language. If you go to a class once a week or once a month, and don't practice each day in between, it can be a long and difficult journey. On the other hand, if you go to live for a while in a foreign country, you absorb the language; it's like osmosis, easy and natural. So it is with the language of crystals. Surround yourself with crystal energy. Carry them with you 24/7, hold them, play with them, talk to them, and very quickly you will begin to hear their messages.

People have been working with crystals for millennia. It is only natural that we can speak their language if we take the time to learn it. The more you listen to your crystals, the easier it is for them to help you. Let yourself to be guided by their ancient wisdom. Most have been living for millions of years! Allow yourself just to be with your crystals and become aware of them. You can enhance your crystal awareness in many ways, such as with a crystal pendulum, meditation, or diet.

A crystal pendulum can help you to listen to your crystals—find out how on page 22.

USING A PENDULUM

One of the simplest ways to listen to your crystals is by working with a crystal pendulum. Work with it to support your intuition. A wonderful time to start is when you feel a crystal is trying to speak to you. Just ask your pendulum if it is, yes or no.

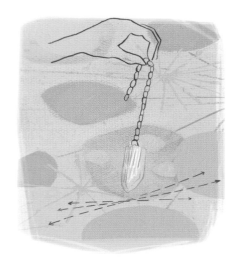

To start working with a crystal pendulum, hold the pendulum's chain in your dominant hand and ask two straightforward questions that have an absolute answer, such as: "Am I a woman?" and "Am I a man?" or "Is the Earth round?" and "Is the Earth flat?". The pendulum will move in two different directions, usually swinging back and forth away from you and toward you, or left and right, or in a circle clockwise and counterclockwise. In this case, these movements mean only "yes" or "no." Once you have identified your yes and no responses like this, you are ready to let your crystal pendulum help you. With experience, you can work with almost anything for a pendulum, but, because crystals have their own innate energy and communication abilities, crystal pendulums are the easiest to start with.

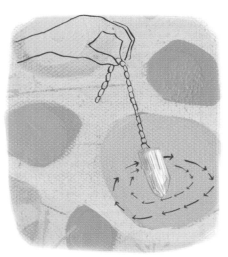

Now the next time you think a crystal is waving at you, simply ask your pendulum if the crystal is trying to speak to you.

MEDITATING WITH CRYSTALS

When you feel a crystal is trying to talk to you, a simple meditation can help. You can try this with any crystal, but a quartz crystal is a good one to start with because it connects to any part of the energy spectrum.

Sit quietly with your chosen crystal where and when you won't be disturbed. Hold the crystal, look at it, explore it. Notice its shape, color, plays of light. Smell it and be aware of any aroma. And with crystals that are safe to do so, you can also taste it with your tongue and try to recognize the flavor. Hold the crystal to your ear and listen to its sound; most people can hear its vibration and often describe it as "like holding a seashell to your ear, but different." With a seashell, the sound you hear is made by the environment resonating inside the shell, but there is no cavity in a crystal for this to happen. What you are hearing in this scenario is the physical vibration of the crystal. Close your eyes and explore the crystal with your fingers, notice the texture, sharpness, smoothness, roughness. Keep your eyes closed, sit quietly, breathe, and see if you can sense the crystal in any area of your body other than your hands. What are you aware of within yourself? When you feel you've explored enough, open your eyes and gently become aware of your surroundings. You could also set a gentle alarm if you have a limited time. If you feel spacey or floaty, hold some hematite to ground yourself.

This meditation exploration demonstrates deeper dimensions of possible meanings and messages from the crystal. You can continue this meditative process for each of your crystals as and when you have time available over the next weeks, months, and years. This will greatly broaden your personal knowledge of crystals and help you to listen to, and hear, their messages.

GOING MEAT-FREE

A Peruvian shaman I knew used to visit the US to run workshops for one month each year. For the other eleven months, he lived in a small village in the Andes mountains in Peru. He was a vegetarian because he believed that eating meat hinders our awareness but he found it very difficult to cope with the excessive energies of the American cities he visited, and his unusual remedy was to eat red meat at every meal for a month before he went to the States. This reduced his awareness of energy and helped him cope while he was there. As soon as he returned to his mountains, he restored his vegetarian diet to raise his awareness to the full.

To increase your awareness, you can try opting for a vegetarian diet for one month, and see if, after 30 days, you notice that you are more aware of the energies around you.

CHOOSING CRYSTALS

As you discover crystals further, you become more aware of their impact and that minute details in a crystal can sometimes have unexpected and most welcome effects. Some of the more obvious influences, such as color and shape, are explained here and, along with The Crystal Finder in Chapter 3, will help you understand why you are drawn to a particular crystal at any specific time. You will also find color and shape helpful guides if you're exploring your own healing techniques.

A crystal's color and conformation can affect the focus and intensity of energy it is channeling for healing. For example, a pointed crystal will direct energy both through the point and in a narrow field, whereas a sphere will radiate energy more or less equally in all directions. Neither is intrinsically more powerful, just different; a crystal point may be more beneficial in directing healing to a specific area of the body, a sphere if you want the energy to fill a room. A green variety is more likely to focus on emotions, red on practical matters.

THE COLOR OF CRYSTALS

Colors affect the wavelength of light, and this in turn affects healing and can also have a deep psychological consequence. So even crystals of the same variety can show different properties, depending on their color. For example, blue tourmaline aids communication, green tourmaline digestion, pink tourmaline the heart center, and black tourmaline is grounding. All these varieties are protective, support new challenges, aid mental health, and help to bring balance between yin and yang, female and male energies, within us all.

These are all tourmaline crystals, but each one will have a particular energy influence depending on its color and shape.

CRYSTAL COLOR	ENERGY INFLUENCE
Red	Base chakra, survival instinct, awareness of danger, passion
Orange	Sacral chakra, creativity, energy
Yellow	Solar plexus chakra, fun, intellect, ability to direct energy like a power cable or socket
Green	Heart chakra, healing, emotion, success
Pink	Heart chakra, love, romance, friendship, openness
Rainbow colored	All chakras, possibilities, opportunities, rebirth
Multicolored	Ability to see different angles or sides, helps you to deal with confrontation
Blue	Throat and brow chakras, calmness, intuition, awareness
Violet	Crown chakra, spirituality, imagination, creativity
White	Crown chakra, purity, personal cleansing
Clear	All chakras, amplification, healing, intuition, connection
Black	Base chakra, protective, grounding, change—dealing with it and encouraging it
Gray	Helps you deal with sadness and feel safe, promotes intelligence
Brown	Base and sacral chakras, earthiness, friendship

CRYSTAL SHAPES AND THEIR MEANING

Natural crystal formations, such as points and geodes (a geode is a rock with a hollow center), and crystals carved into pyramids, cubes, merkaba (a star tetrahedron, made of two tetrahedrons), other geometric shapes, and animals all direct the crystal's energy differently, and therefore they have different effects. For those carved by hand, the sculptor puts his intent and energy into creating the shape, and this essentially programs the crystal and refocuses its energy. It doesn't change the basic properties of a crystal, just its focus. For example, a green aventurine helps muscles throughout the body and has a relaxing and calming influence; when shaped as a heart, it focuses this on the heart chakra, and is particularly good for soothing emotions and relaxing the heart muscles.

The following charts give the most common shapes and colors, although the possibilities, for both shades of color and variety of shape, are almost endless.

SENSING CRYSTAL ENERGY

Try sensing the different energy patterns created by various shaped crystals. To start with, stand a crystal, point upward, alone on a table or flat surface. Hold your hand about 1 inch (2–3 cm) from the right side for a minute or so and try to sense the energy, then the left side, and finally above the point. Can you sense the difference?

If you are uncertain whether you are sensing the crystal's energy, try shaking your hands vigorously for two minutes before repeating the exercise. This makes your hands physically more sensitive to energy.

If you have difficulty sensing the energy with your hands, you can do this exercise with your pendulum (see page 22). Hold your pendulum to the right of the crystal and ask it to show you the intensity of the energy by the size of its movement. Then repeat this on the left and finally above the crystal. The pendulum should clearly show a different intensity at the top of the crystal. It's much more powerful at the top!

Now try the same exercise working with a sphere. You can sense that the distribution of energy is more even around the whole crystal.

CRYSTAL SHAPE	ENERGY INFLUENCES AND EFFECT	
Animals	Connection to pet, totem, or spirit animal; movement or flow of energy brings the qualities of the specific animal to the energy (see pages 28–30)	
Cluster	Families, teamwork, groups; buzzes, re-energizes, and cleanses the energy of any room	
Cube	Solid, reliable support; energy is equally distributed on the sides, but can be more focused in the corners; building blocks which can support any project or type of healing	
Egg	Birth, creation, new beginning, or start of a project; creates an energy field ovoid in shape, more powerful at the bottom and sides than at the top	
Geode	Rooms, meditation; creates a focus within the hollow space of the rock, which amplifies as it travels out into the room	
Heart	Love, relationships, emotions; brings a loving energy to the crystal's natural effects	
Merkaba	Visions, connections to higher realms; creates an energy field as if there were eight cells, one around each of its points; this is connected to the moment of compaction in embryonic development, which is when the embryo has grown to 8 cells, and is perhaps the time when the soul enters the body or is born	

CRYSTAL SHAPE	ENERGY INFLUENCES AND EFFECT
Obelisk	Connection between the physical and spiritual worlds; directs energy toward the sky
Point	Focus and direction, toward the point (termination); brings positivity to any crystal work
Pyramid	Energy fields, healing, meditation; enhances the size of energy fields, and focuses energy at each of its five points, especially the top
Sphere	Wholeness, completion, the world; unfocused but powerful equal spread of energy all around; space filling

CRYSTAL ANIMALS

Crystal animal carvings bring the essence of the animal to you. Whether a pet, totem, or spirit, the carving represents not just the shape but also the qualities of the animal. This is a small selection of myriad possible animal shapes. If the animal exists, or even if it has been imagined, such as a dragon or unicorn, it has probably been carved by someone in crystal, wood, clay, Fimo, or solidified hippopotamus dung. Occasionally, you might even find a crystal or stone whose natural shape resembles an animal, and you might be surprised to discover that its energy feels like that animal, also. Such unusual crystals can add another dimension to your healing.

There are often differences, sometimes subtle ones, between adult and infant animals of the same kind. For example, whereas a dog might imply loyalty, knowledge, teaching, and protection, a puppy could suggest playfulness, adventure, and learning.

ANIMAL CARVING	ENERGY INFLUENCES
Bat	Change, attention to detail, communication, sociability, dreams
Bear	Healing, strength, protection, wisdom, tranquility
Bird	Freedom, lack of restriction, perspective, message carrying, bridge between the spirit and physical worlds
Boar (wild pig)	Lust, overindulgence
Butterfly	Change, transformation, hope, life, renaissance, reincarnation
Cat	Magic, guardianship of the underworld, rebirth, resurrection, darkness, fear, hidden things
Crab	Cycles, emotion, protection, trust
Crocodile/Alligator	Stealth, power, protection, fertility, judgment
Deer	Gentleness, sacrifice, intuition, inner child
Dog	Loyalty, faithfulness, vigilance, guardianship, guidance, teaching, protection
Dolphin	Friendship, playfulness, courage through troubled waters, confidence
Dove	Peace, love, message carrying
Dragon	Power, ancientness, strength, good luck for those who deserve it, water, fire, inspiration
Dragonfly	Dreams, prosperity, luck
Eagle	Opportunity, skill, power, leadership
Elephant	Memory, wisdom, stamina, cooperation, longevity, contemplation
Fish	Subconscious, emotion, therapy, overcoming obstacles
Fox	Cunning, playfulness, quick thinking, message carrying, abundance
Frog	Adaptation, balance, sudden change, cleansing, metamorphosis, opportunity
Hippopotamus	Fertility, motherhood, reliability, relaxation
Horse	Freedom, elegance, attractiveness, strength, journey

ANIMAL CARVING	ENERGY INFLUENCES
Hummingbird	Joy, vivacity, playfulness, healing
Lion	Strength, courage, leadership
Monkey	Intelligence, wisdom, mischief
Mouse	Survival, innocence, dark magic
Panther	Strength, overcoming fears, adventure, partnership, truth
Peacock	Beauty, morality, awakening
Pig	Fertility, gluttony, laziness
Rabbit	Stillness, sex, vulnerability, abundance, growth, new beginnings
Rat	Recycling, adaptability, relentlessness
Scorpion	Death, change, sex, control, shielding
Sea horse	Patience, generosity, contentment, serenity
Sheep	Innocence, child-like attitude, groups, community, spiritual living, following others
Snake	Cycles, rebirth, renewal, healing, transformation
Spider	Fate, death, resourcefulness
Squirrel	Fun, intelligence, practicality
Swan	Loyalty, grace, love, enlightenment, endeavor
Tiger	Wealth, power
Tortoise	Patience, longevity, protection, stability
Turtle	Mother Earth, good luck, long life
Unicorn	Possibilities, transformation, magic, success
Whale	Wisdom, nature, emotion, family
Wolf	Teaching, pathfinding, guardianship, loyalty, ritual

CHAPTER 2

ADVANCED CRYSTAL HEALING TECHNIQUES

Traditionally, crystal healing is focused on the chakras and visible symptoms. I've already shown in chapter 1 why we need not concentrate on presented symptoms. Naturally, you can help to relieve symptoms by working with crystals, but you must be looking further into the body's energy system to effect any possible long-term fix. So, now is a perfect opportunity to explore what happens not only within the chakras (I've covered this extensively in *The Complete Guide to Crystal Chakra Healing*), but what happens in between the chakras and how chakras can be related to, and can affect, each other.

TREAT THE UNDERLYING CAUSE

As we have seen in chapter 1, physical symptoms are not the primary cause of any condition; all of them will have an energetic cause or source rooted in one or more chakras, and usually it is because the chakra(s) is (are) blocked, so we need to release the energy. But there can also be blocks in other regions of the energy system. We can help to release this energy by creating an amethyst trail (see below).

AMETHYST TRAILS

Small amethyst tumble stones, or natural crystals, placed as close together as possible in a line, ideally touching, help to link physical symptoms to their underlying causes and release energy through a specifically selected crystal and the major chakra(s) associated with the cause.

This crystal healing technique can only be performed on someone else. First, choose an appropriate time when you won't be disturbed in a space where you can both relax, and your friend or client can lie down.

Amethyst tumble stones can form an amethyst trail to release blocked energy.

1 Place your crystal chakra set (see page 9) on her correlating chakras. You might also like to place hematite crystals by her feet for grounding and rose quartz crystals in her hands for emotional support, as this treatment can have dramatic effects.

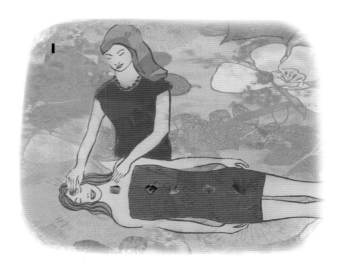

2 Then you will need to find the energetic block that is causing dis-ease. This may be an apparently obvious area corresponding to a physical symptom that is being displayed, or not. So, let's keep an open mind and embrace all possibilities. Select a crystal to represent this block; as we are working with the seven chakra crystals, we can call this the "eighth crystal." You can do this intuitively, employ your pendulum, or simply work with a clear quartz crystal.

3 Imagine a grid of parallel lines running up the body and a similar set of lines running horizontally, like a big transparent sheet of graph paper. Pass your pendulum up the center line of the body asking, "Is this where this crystal needs to go?" When you receive the first positive indication from your pendulum, stop.

4 Next, run your pendulum along the corresponding horizontal line until you have another affirmative reply. This marks the area where treatment is required; place the eighth crystal here.

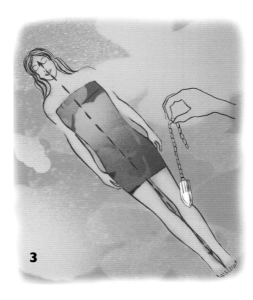

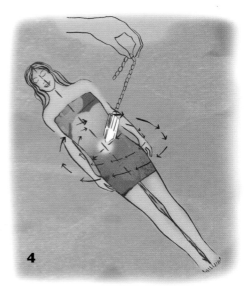

5 With your pendulum, dowse the seven major chakras one at a time, asking, "Is the eighth crystal linked to this chakra?" If you find it is linked to one or more chakras, create an amethyst trail from the eighth crystal to each chakra involved. It is important to avoid any chakras not involved in this, because their energy might become unbalanced. If the eighth crystal is on one side of the body, that is where the trails should be. If the eighth crystal is central, twin or mirror trails can be employed. The crystals in the trail should be kept as close together as possible— touching is best. However, this won't always be practical and will depend on the person's shape and areas that need linking. Also remember that crystals will work over a distance of 2–3 feet (60–90 cm). You can place amethyst crystals on or around the body or a combination of both.

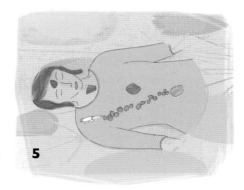

6 Once all the crystals have been laid on the body, you will need to activate them with a quartz master crystal. To do this, hold your quartz master crystal about 1–2 inches (2–5 cm) above each crystal in turn and move it in a clockwise direction for approximately two minutes, or until you notice an energy change and you feel ready to transfer your attention to the next crystal. Start from the base chakra and activate clockwise for the chakra

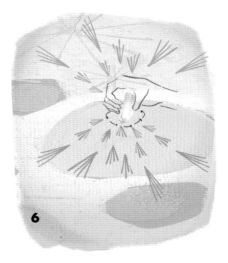

crystals and eighth crystal, and then counterclockwise on the amethyst trail. Moving the quartz master crystal in a clockwise direction focuses energy to a point; counterclockwise spreads it out.

7 Once the activation is completed, it is lovely to leave the crystals in place, so the person receiving treatment can soak in a bath of crystal energy. After ten minutes or so, remove all the crystals one at a time, starting from the crown and working all the way down the body. This process may release deep-seated "old stuff" leading to major life changes; treat your friend gently, especially when placing and removing these crystals. We always work with amethyst in this treatment to facilitate a gentle release of this long-term trapped energy.

In the rare case that you find the eighth crystal is not linked to ANY of the chakras, there is no need to work with an amethyst trail. Just work with your quartz master crystal to activate the crystals you have placed on the body.

8 To end the treatment, comb and seal the aura (see pages 37–38).

BLOCKS BETWEEN THE CHAKRAS

Chakras can be blocked, a condition in which, for various reasons, energy is not flowing as best it could through a chakra. This is the common target for traditional crystal healing—release the energy blocks, then energy flows, the body rebalances, and healing occurs on all levels.

However, blocks can occur in between the chakras as well as within them. Also, an unhealthy chakra can pull or push the adjacent healthy one out of balance. The healthy chakra will naturally rebalance, but if this continues, the healthy chakra will learn to "unbalance" itself so that the unhealthy chakra "appears" in balance. Over time this creates an unhealthy pattern, which can result not just in physical symptoms, but also in behavior changes. Such created behavior patterns might be useful when they start. An example is a child who, having been rejected each time he or she approaches a parent for a hug and love, stops asking and pulls away from physical contact to avoid the learned and expected hurt. This has the short-term benefit of stopping the rejection; the child has naturally learned to avoid creating the situation that results in pain. But in adult life that person may become non-physical and find relationships difficult, or react oppositely and give him or herself to partners in the desperate attempt to find the child's missing hug and love. We cannot see this, and even if you dowse each chakra with your pendulum, the two affected chakras will indicate they are balanced! Both the chakras are indeed keeping each other in this weird state of superficial balance. The problem lies in the space in between.

Most people will have small energy jams in many places through their bodies. This is the result of living life. When these jams grow and start to affect our lives, it becomes an issue, and one of the problems is that because we get a benefit, such as not experiencing rejection, we don't see a problem. Releasing a blockage of energy in between two chakras can have dramatic, life-changing effects.

DOUBLE-TERMINATED CRYSTALS

Naturally, double-terminated crystals (DTs) channel energy in both directions and, when placed between two chakras, will help to release the energy of this block and rebalance both chakras to a healthy state.

Create a comfortable space where you can lie down and won't be disturbed. Perhaps dim the lights or light a candle and play some relaxing music. You can also practice on other people.

A double-terminated quartz crystal; you can find out more about its properties on page 103.

1 First, identify for yourself which pair of adjacent chakras might have an energy jam between them. If you're uncertain about this, you can easily ask your pendulum with a series of straightforward questions, such as, "Is there an energy jam between my base and sacral chakras?" Then, "Is there an energy jam between my sacral and solar plexus chakras?" Continue asking for each pair of chakras up the body (see Steps 3 and 4, page 32). Make a note of the responses you receive.

2 Next, place a crystal chakra set (see page 9) on the appropriate chakras. (Helpful tip: It's easiest if you place crystals on your own chakras from the base up to the crown.)

3 Check the responses you noted from step 1 and add your DTs where they are needed between chakras. When you have placed all the crystals, close your eyes and relax for at least ten minutes and up to one hour. Try to be aware of any sensations.

4 If you are treating someone else, once you've placed all the crystals, activate them with your quartz master crystal (see Step 6, page 33).

5 In either scenario, when you're finished, remove the crystals (and don't forget to cleanse them—see pages 10–11).

6 To end the treatment, comb and seal the aura (see pages 37–38).

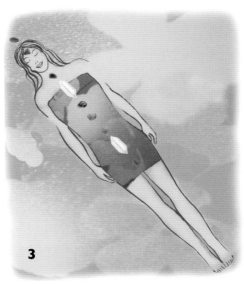

LEMNISCATE HEALING

A lemniscate, more commonly known as the infinity symbol, is a curve with a characteristic shape, consisting of two loops that meet at a central point. A lemniscate has no beginning and no ending—like the infinite healing journey of the soul …

The idea is to link adjacent chakras so that they can work effectively on the same issue. As with all energy blocks, a jam between the chakras can have two possible

The lemniscate symbol is also called the infinity symbol.

causes—not enough energy or too much energy being present. Both have the same effect, and look exactly the same to the skilled observer, or pendulum dowser. Imagine you have a water pipe between your chakras. If there's only a tiny trickle of water dripping through, it appears that there's a "block" as not a lot of water is coming out. Conversely, if too much water is trying to get through, it all spills out and still not much water gets through, and so it also appears as a "block."

With the DTs, we released an excess of energy that had built up over years and had changed a natural, healthy behavior into an unnatural but safe experience. The DTs help to release such energy jams. The lemniscate helps to fill the pipe with energy.

This is a technique to use on other people; try it out on friends. Start the same way as you start the amethyst trail (see page 31)—choose a suitable time and setting, crystal chakra set to hand.

1 Once all the crystals have been placed along the body, activate them with your quartz master crystal (see Step 6, page 33) and then ask your pendulum if any pair of adjacent chakras need lemniscate healing.

2 Where you get a positive answer, move your quartz master crystal in a figure 8 around the two chakras, so that one is in each part of the 8, until you feel a change in the crystal. Continue for a little while longer until it changes again. If you don't feel a change, keep doing this for a few minutes. With practice, you will feel more sensations. (Helpful tip: Shaking your hands vigorously for a couple of minutes before you start will make them more sensitive.)

3 You may find that several consecutive chakras need to be linked together and this can be achieved with continuing multiple figures of 8 joined together.

4 This technique works with any layout or combination of techniques and can work very effectively with double-terminated crystals between the chakras. Either perform the DT crystal healing method, then the lemniscate method, or combine them: place the DT crystals and leave them in place while performing the lemniscate healing.

5 To end the treatment, comb and seal the aura (see pages 37–38).

ENDING TREATMENTS

I like to end all treatments by combing and sealing the aura, the subtle energy field around the body, with a selenite aura wand; however, you could work with any selenite crystal. You see, what happens during any healing treatment is that energy passes through the chakras and is released through the aura. Some of it can be quite sticky and become trapped in the aura as it tries to escape. It is not uncommon after a treatment for these energies, or for any emotions and thoughts, to be still bubbling away. Combing the aura after a treatment has the effect of settling any wayward energy and removing the emotions and thoughts that are no longer needed.

A selenite aura wand.

COMBING THE AURA

After removing all the crystals, while the person is still lying down, comb through her aura by working with the side of your selenite aura wand as if it were a hair brush. Start above the head and work down the body past the feet, holding your crystal 2–3 inches (5–8 cm) off the body. Treat the aura as if you are brushing long hair. If you find a knot, gently go over it several times until it feels free. The knot might feel sticky or treacly, as a hot or cold spot, or uncomfortable, even slightly painful, as you pass your wand through the aura. Brush through the whole aura from head to toe, and both sides of the body.

Receiving this practice often feels like a very gentle release of something you can't quite identify. It feels pleasant and comforting. After treatment, many of my clients report that they felt the crystal passing through their aura and they now feel lighter. It is also amazing what you, as the person giving the treatment, can feel through the selenite aura wand as you comb through someone's aura.

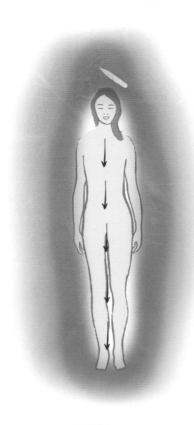

SEALING THE AURA

The final stage is to seal the aura. Again working with the selenite aura wand, this technique locks in the treatment, helping it to last much longer, which results in ongoing and deeper healing even after the recipient has left. Your intention is very important during this part of the process. Pass the crystal once along the center line of the body, from head to toe, about 3 inches (8 cm) above the body with the intent that the crystal is collecting any unhelpful energies that remain. Then, make a very large arc from the feet back to the head, intending to push the aura as high as it can possibly go. Finally, pass the crystal one last time the length of the body and direct the selenite crystal toward a window, as if you are throwing the energy the crystal has collected out of that window. If the room is windowless, you can employ a crystal ball to act as a window: point your selenite aura wand toward the crystal ball, with the intent of throwing the unwanted forces into it—but remember to cleanse it afterward!

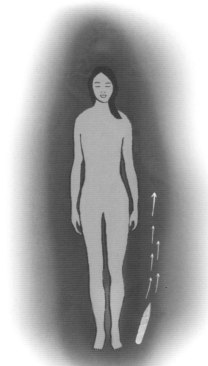

CHAPTER 3

THE CRYSTAL FINDER

The task of revisiting and expanding the Crystal Finder after ten years gives me a wonderful opportunity to share a further 250 crystals with you here, to inspire you to work with these wonderful Stone People and discover their amazing life-enhancing and healing benefits.

HOW TO USE THE CRYSTAL FINDER

To help you identify your own crystals, they are listed by color. Many crystals naturally occur in several colors so they are recorded here in their most common variety, with descriptions, color references, and photographs to aid recognition. (See also the glossary on page 154, which explains some of the terms used to describe the form these crystals take.) When a crystal is highlighted in **bold**, this means that it has a separate entry in this book and those *italicized* have a full entry with further details and descriptions in *The Crystal Healer: Volume 1*.

The common sources are for those stones you are likely to find in your local crystal store. Except where the listing is for the "only source," most minerals have many sources around the world and local sources may vary significantly.

I've used the same format as I did in the first volume, again choosing quartz and amethyst to lead the pack because they are two of the most powerful healing crystals, before introducing the color sections. The healing qualities of each crystal are listed along with astrological and chakra associations and alternative names. (Again, the glossary explains acronyms for conditions and other terms related to healing that you may not be familiar with.)

QUARTZ

Quartz is the most abundant mineral on Earth and comes in a mind-boggling array of varieties and forms. Over 70 percent of the planet's surface is formed from quartz in its many guises.

Quartz crystal is the healing crystal. It can channel any type of energy and will help in all healing situations. If you're stuck or unsure which crystal(s) to work with, then turn to quartz because, although there will often be a different and more beneficial crystal to help a specific condition, quartz will help everything.

Some of the many varieties of quartz and their specific healing qualities are covered within this chapter.

QUARTZ CRYSTAL

Clear or white hexagonal crystals and masses sometimes with inclusions. (See also profiles for specific quartzes.)
Common alternative names: clear quartz, rock crystal
Common sources: worldwide—especially Brazil, China, Colombia, Madagascar, Russia, Republic of South Africa, Tibet, USA (specifically Arkansas)
Astrological associations: all
Chakras: all

HEALING QUALITIES

Quartz crystal is a feel-better stone—it improves your quality of life, makes you feel happier, and re-energizes you in all situations. It channels any energy, so helps any condition.
Physical: helps diabetes, ear infections, hearing and balance, heart health, malaise, MS, CFS/ME, obesity, pain and discomfort, spinal health, tinnitus, and weight loss.
Emotional/spiritual: focuses the mind, aids meditation, and relieves negativity.

AMETHYST

Variety of quartz found as crystals or masses. Its classic purple color is due to manganese and iron inclusions. Also found, almost **black amethyst** (rare), purple/white banded **chevron amethyst**, *prasiolite*, which is green amethyst colored by mineral inclusions, and a combination of amethyst and prasiolite called **amegreen**.
Common sources: worldwide—especially Brazil, India, Madagascar, Republic of South Africa, Uruguay
Astrological associations: Virgo, Capricorn, Aquarius, Pisces
Chakra: crown

HEALING QUALITIES

Amethyst magnifies the energy of other crystals. It is good for overall protection, and physical, emotional, and mental balance. It can be worked with to encourage chastity and relieve homesickness. It helps negotiation skills, decision making, wealth, business success, moving forward in life, coping with responsibility and change, and public speaking. It is beneficial for purification during ceremonies.

Physical: heals the causes of dis-ease (see glossary). Good for hearing, hormone regulation, insomnia, headaches, migraine, acne, asthma, blood clots, bacterial and viral infections, bad posture, cancer, and arthritis (as an elixir). Encourages the health of the immune, circulatory, and sympathetic nervous systems. Good for bones, heart, stomach, skin, teeth, liver, and endocrine glands. Helps with drunkenness and addictions, especially alcoholism. Aids detoxing and blood cleansing.
Emotional/spiritual: helps with OCD, anger, and violent tendencies. Calms passion, nerves, oversensitivity, tension, emotional energy, and grief. Enhances aura, self-esteem, meditation, spirit contact, and spirituality.

RED

BRECCIATED JASPER

Formed as *jasper* is shattered by tectonic activity and the created spaces are filled with more jasper, *chalcedony*, and different varieties of macrocrystalline quartz. The deep red colors are due to *hematite* embedded within the jasper.

Common sources: worldwide—especially Australia, Brazil, Canada, Egypt, India, Madagascar, Russia, Republic of South Africa, USA, Uruguay

Astrological associations: Aries, Taurus

Chakra: base

HEALING QUALITIES

Brecciated jasper offers protection and brings grounding.

Physical: helps with alcoholism, stomach cramps, problems with the womb, ovaries, fallopian tubes, fibroids, and fertility.

Emotional/spiritual: pulls different areas of the mind into concentrated focus so that diverse possibilities and points of view become clear.

HARLEQUIN QUARTZ

Quartz crystal with inclusions, which may include one or more of **lepidocrocite**, *hematite*, *goethite*, and titanium.

Common alternative names: hematoid quartz, haematoid quartz, ferruginous quartz

Common sources: worldwide—especially China, Madagascar

Astrological association: Gemini

Chakra: base

HEALING QUALITIES

Physical: gives energy and vitality, and helps with concentration, communication, and

ADHD. Good for grounding, legs, knees, ankles, feet, and lower back.

Emotional/spiritual: brings clarity to emotions and encourages expression of them, so helps understanding between lovers. Can relieve anxiety and panic attacks. Promotes connection between people, and to the spirit world. Larger crystal clusters can help to remove negativity from rooms, creating a space for loving and healing energy to flow.

STRAWBERRY AVENTURINE

Quartz variety, with inclusions of *hematite* or *goethite* giving a speckled or sparkly effect.

Common alternative name: red aventurine

Common sources: Brazil, Canada, China, India, Italy, Madagascar, Nepal, Russia, Republic of South Africa

Astrological associations: Aries, Virgo, Libra

Chakra: base

HEALING QUALITIES

Strawberry aventurine rejuvenates, stimulates, revitalizes, and generates a zest for life. Brings enthusiasm to most things, but is also grounding. Improves fertility and creativity.

Physical: boosts stamina, blood circulation, red-blood-cell production, and metabolism, and may help to reduce cholesterol levels. Skin conditions such as eczema and psoriasis may benefit from a strawberry aventurine elixir.

Emotional/spiritual: helps with challenges, bringing inner strength and confidence. Restores your sense of humor and helps you to laugh at yourself and reconnect with your soul. Keeps your feet on the ground and brings a connection to reality. A grid of strawberry aventurine placed around your house can encourage family harmony and heal domestic rifts.

REALGAR

Bright red, translucent-to-transparent prismatic striated crystals and rocks.

Common alternative names: ruby sulfur, ruby of arsenic

Common sources: Australia, China, Germany, Hungary, Romania, Switzerland, Turkey, USA

Astrological associations: Gemini, Libra

Chakra: base

HEALING QUALITIES

Realgar brings good luck and abundance. It soothes emotions, emotional pain, and discomfort; it calms anger, rage, and violent behavior.

Physical: aids fertility and sexual problems. Promotes a fire in your heart, boosting desire and sex drive, improving relationships, and enhancing love.

Emotional/spiritual: cleansing, illuminating past lives, and enhancing memory. Brings thoughts to the surface and helps to release past trauma. Boosts energy on all levels, compassion, and acceptance. Helps to clear your mind so you can think clearly, especially under stress, and keep your focus on the goal.

No elixir. Wash hands after handling. Do not smell, sniff, or lick. Never ingest. Avoid prolonged exposure to bright light. Store in a dry, dark place.

PIEMONTITE

Translucent-to-opaque prismatic, bladed, or acicular crystals, lustrous, deep magenta-red, red-violet to red-brown in color. Manganese-rich *epidote*. Specimens are often mixed with quartz.

Common alternative name: red epidote

Common sources: worldwide—especially Australia, Canada, China, Europe (especially Italy), India, Japan, Morocco, Russia, Scandinavia, Republic of South Africa, USA

Astrological association: Aries

Chakra: heart

HEALING QUALITIES

Helps detox on all levels, physical, emotional, mental, and spiritual.

Physical: good for healthy heart and circulation.

Emotional/spiritual: good for healing emotional wounds, dispels negative emotions, and brings joy. Promotes courage and strength to have fun and try new adventures. Encourages you to understand your inner self and walk your talk. Can help with grief and depression.

LEPIDOCROCITE

Red to red-brown scaly or fibrous crystals, often found as inclusion with other crystals.

Common sources: worldwide—especially Brazil, Europe, India, USA

Astrological association: Sagittarius

Chakras: heart, brow, crown

HEALING QUALITIES

Physical: good for eyes and eyesight, balances hormones, and improves fertility. Its calming effect can help ADHD and ease breathing, aiding the lungs and heart.

Emotional/spiritual: grounding from the crown chakra down through the body. Boosts awareness so you can see the signposts on your spiritual path, helping with decisions and life choices. Calms emotions, helping you regain control. Eases the release of irrational fears and anxiety and can be beneficial in the treatment of bipolar conditions. Brings love and harmony. It can help bring up matters from the past, leading to forgiveness. Good for protection and connection to angels and spirit guides.

ALASKAN GARNET

Almandine *garnet* from Alaska.
Common alternative names: cherry red Alaskan garnet
Only source: Alaska
Astrological associations: Virgo, Scorpio
Chakras: base, heart

HEALING QUALITIES

This garnet brings energy, warmth, and comfort. It helps you to see hidden things, as well as both sides of an argument, discussion, or debate.
Physical: good for heart, liver, pancreas, wounds, and post-operative healing, and for anemia and other blood disorders.
Emotional/spiritual: eases inner turmoil and emotional trauma. Helps you to deal with change, death, and the dying process. Enhances self-awareness, meditation, and understanding of your dark side.

CATLINITE

Brick-red variety of argillite occurring in matrix of Sioux quartzite. Fine grained, easily worked, and prized by Native American and First Nation peoples as a sacred stone for making bowls for ceremonial pipes. Color ranges from light pink to dark brick-red; may exhibit lighter spots on surface, known as "stars."
Common alternative names: sacred pipe stone, pipestone, pipe clay
Only sources: Pipestone (Minnesota, USA) and Pipestone River (Manitoba, Canada)
Astrological associations: all
Chakras: all

HEALING QUALITIES

Brings sacredness into everyday life. Helps you to find your own spiritual path and walk your walk.
Enhances care, compassion, and kindness. Brings connection to ancestors, past lives, spirit world. Native American and First Nation peoples believe catlinite

connects you to The Great Spirit, so will keep you safe and help with any healing.
Physical: primarily helps breathing, lungs, and respiratory disorders such as asthma and emphysema. Boosts energy, so good for athletes, manual workers, and anyone who is physically active.
Emotional/spiritual: gives emotional support and inner guidance. Aids dowsing and amplifies your inner pendulum. Promotes the desire for freedom, justice, equality, connection, and sharing, giving a sense that we are all one.

TANZANIAN AVENTURINE

Quartz variety, with inclusions of *lepidolite* giving a speckled or sparkly effect. Pinkish-red to purply red.
Common alternative names: cherry tanzurine, cherry quartz—but beware. Many items called "cherry quartz" are on the market—ALL the others are man-made and mostly glass.
Common source: Tanzania
Astrological associations: Aries, Libra
Chakra: heart

HEALING QUALITIES

Physical: eases breathing, relieving asthma and other chest conditions as well as minor illnesses and infections, such as colds and flu.
Emotional/spiritual: calming. Helps to release anger, tension, and anxiety. Can bring focus and concentration to any task.

ORANGE

TANGERINE QUARTZ

Quartz crystal colored orange to red-orange by *hematite* surface coating.

Common sources: Brazil, Madagascar
Astrological associations: Leo, Libra
Chakras: base, sacral, solar plexus

HEALING QUALITIES

A sexy crystal that can help relationships, boosting passion and emotional connection, eliminating inhibitions, releasing the desire for physical contact.

Physical: helps with weight loss, AIDS, the reproductive system, intestines, absorption of vitamins and iron, blood, red blood cells, energy, fertility, sexual dysfunction, and associated lower abdominal pain. Balances acidity, so will help with all cancerous growths/tumors and eliminates free radicals.

Emotional/spiritual: promotes change, self-awareness, self-understanding, self-healing, growth, inner strength, forgiveness, courage to move forward. Helps you overcome inner turmoil and trauma, and get rid of self-defeating, self-sabotaging, self-limiting, and self-judgmental beliefs. Gives a sense of worth or self-value, allowing you to let things go. Boosts intentions, especially those directed at love, relationships, and creativity. Releases your inner child, promoting playfulness and creativity, aids manifestation of dreams and goals, encourages grounding ideas. Helps emotional stress and releases tension. Aids psychic protection, bringing a sense of spiritual security, calmness, and comfort.

BUMBLE BEE JASPER

Trade name for colorful fibrous *calcite* with distinct yellow, orange, and black banding. Colors come from inclusions of **realgar** and *pyrite* and possibly *anhydrite*, *hematite*, **orpiment**, *sulfur*, *angelite*, and arsenic. "Jasper" is a misnomer, as all true *jaspers* contain quartz and this has none.

Common alternative names: bumble bee agate, eclipse stone, fumarolic jasper
Only source: Mount Papandayan (West Java, Indonesia), although often mistakenly identified as coming from Australia
Astrological association: Cancer
Chakras: sacral, solar plexus

HEALING QUALITIES

Brings za za to your mojo! Promotes teamwork.

Physical: boosts energy. Helps yin/yang balance, allergies, dexterity, small and large bowel, digestion, nerves, heart, blood, and circulation. Protects from EMF.

Emotional/spiritual: promotes change, helping you to make choices without emotion; gives drive, passion, busyness. It removes blocks, allowing your creativity and desires to manifest and be expressed freely, enabling you to discover new opportunities, take charge of situations, make decisions, and move forward, all with positivity. Helps lift depression, negativity, and self-limiting beliefs, letting your creativity and confidence flow. Aids intellect. Removes distracting thoughts and emotions, allowing you to focus, and helps you to see clearly through the fog in your mind.

No elixir. Wash hands after handling. Do not smell, sniff, or lick. Never ingest.

PEACH AVENTURINE

Mica and *pyrite* inclusions give sparkle and color.
Common source: India
Astrological associations: Virgo, Libra
Chakra: sacral

HEALING QUALITIES

Peach aventurine is the crystal for optimism and confidence.
Physical: good for muscles, bowel function, lungs, urogenital system, thymus, and blood pressure. Relieves physical stress, headaches, migraines, inflammation (especially skin), and allergies. Balances cholesterol and improves sleep patterns. Improves yin/yang balance.
Emotional/spiritual: brings good luck, success. Promotes boldness and confidence. Reduces shyness, stress, and worry. Calms emotions. Good for mental clarity. Helps decision-making, toleration, leadership, and creativity. Brings harmony in the home and a zest for life. Centers and stills the mind at the start of meditation.

ORANGE MIST AURA QUARTZ

Created by atomic bonding of natural iron and *gold* with quartz.
Common alternative names: melon aura quartz, imperial gold aura quartz, tangerine sun aura quartz
Common sources: China, USA
Astrological associations: Leo, Libra
Chakra: sacral

HEALING QUALITIES

Like the sun rising at dawn, it takes away the darkness. At those moments of dread when you can't go on, it reveals the light at the end of the tunnel.
Physical: boosts energy and strengthens the aura.
Emotional/spiritual: helps you surmount life's challenges and obstacles put in your path. Eases mood swings, depression, bipolar disorder, and nervous exhaustion. Heals emotional trauma and emotional wounds. Enhances sexuality and psychological strength. Expands consciousness, creativity, and inspiration. Relieves writer's block and other creative blockages.

ORANGE MOONSTONE

Pearly or opalescent variety of **microcline**, displaying adularescence (like chatoyancy) due to light diffraction between layers of the mineral.
Common sources: India, Madagascar
Astrological associations: Cancer, Libra
Chakra: sacral

HEALING QUALITIES

This is a feminine stone, supporting mystery and intuition.
Physical: good for the libido and combating sexual dysfunction. Helps with menstruation issues and PMS. Good for the female reproductive system.
Emotional/spiritual: brings balance to any situation, including work/life balance and with family and friends. Brings good luck and abundance. Promotes self-esteem, emotional healing, selflessness, honesty, nurturing, and connection to ancient knowledge. Relieves anxiety and depression. Supports psychic development, clairvoyance, and awareness.

GOLDEN FELDSPAR

Prismatic crystals in aggregate groups, often displaying chatoyancy.

Common sources: worldwide—especially Republic of South Africa

Astrological associations: Libra, Sagittarius

Chakras: sacral, brow

HEALING QUALITIES

Brings emotional strength, courage, and inner confidence.
Physical: helps to heal wounds and reduce scar tissue. Helps with thyroid, hormonal, and fertility issues, and boosts the immune system.
Emotional/spiritual: supports meditation, changes behavior patterns, and soothes loss, grief, and guilt. Promotes self-esteem, confidence, willpower, femininity, and sexuality.

ANKERITE

Pearly rhombohedral crystals, orange-brown, white to gray, yellowish-brown, tan, fawn, greenish.

Common alternative name: often confused with iron-bearing dolomite

Common sources: worldwide—especially USA

Astrological associations: Aries, Capricorn

Chakra: solar plexus

HEALING QUALITIES

This stone connects with and clears the past, dealing with past lives, the Akashic records, and past trauma.
Physical: helps detox process, kidneys, lymphatic system, liver, and blood.
Emotional/spiritual: helps to break unhealthy behavior patterns created from emotional trauma or karmic events, facilitating an emotional release.

ORANGE SELENITE

Occurs as the satin spar crystalline variety of *selenite*, orange to pale peach in color. Often displays chatoyancy, with a distinct **cat's-eye** effect when polished.

Common alternative names: peach selenite, orange gypsum

Common sources: worldwide—especially Morocco, UK, USA

Astrological association: Taurus

Chakras: sacral, crown

HEALING QUALITIES

This stone connects to the new moon, bringing new beginnings and positive change.
Physical: reduces nausea, sickness, and fluid retention. Good for joints, menstrual cycle, ovaries, osteoporosis, memory, and Alzheimer's disease.
Emotional/spiritual: good for relationships, letting go, release of emotions, and centering. Promotes sexual connection between partners; releases sexual frustration and tension. Gives confidence and self-esteem. Lifts the spirit, giving a positive outlook, and protects from unwanted external influences.

ORANGE MOSS AGATE

Massive, translucent-to-transparent variety of *agate* with orange and brown moss-like patterns.

Common source: India
Astrological association: Gemini
Chakra: sacral

HEALING QUALITIES

This agate brings the energy of the sun to people working with the Earth, physically and enviromentally, or with grounded Earth energy and plants, such as gardeners.

Physical: supports breath, breathing, and lungs, storing energy for future use. Good for athletes, swimmers, and other sports people.

Emotional/spiritual: brings relief from anxiety. Calming, helping you to overcome challenges, obstacles, and stress. Promotes self-confidence and self-expression, allowing you to walk your walk.

ORPIMENT

Orange-yellow to lemon-yellow reniform or botryoidal mineral, found in foliated (repetitive layering) columnar form or as fibrous aggregates, granular powders, and, rarely, as prismatic crystals.

Common sources: worldwide—especially Australia, Canada, China, Czech Republic, Hungary, Italy, Japan, Mexico, Peru, Russia, USA
Astrological association: Leo
Chakra: solar plexus

HEALING QUALITIES

Orpiment stimulates intellect and understanding of self and others. This is a protective stone.

Physical: speeds recovery from injury.

Emotional/spiritual: promotes innocence, purity, intimacy, investigations, growth and development of ideas, dreams, and dream recall. Eases change and the impact of death and the dying process.

No elixir. Wash hands after handling. Do not smell, sniff, or lick. Never ingest.

VORTEX HEALING CRYSTAL

Quartz crystal, with surface *hematite* deposits creating an orange or red color.

Common alternative names: Sedona healing crystal, Sedona vortex crystal
Only source: Sedona (Arizona, USA)
Astrological associations: Aries, Leo
Chakras: sacral, brow

HEALING QUALITIES

A crystal for creativity, connection, and expression.

Physical: supports all self-healing. Helps wounds, pain relief, arthritis, cardiovascular disease, heart, arteries, veins, blood pressure, memory, nerves, insomnia, headaches, and stomach upsets.

Emotional/spiritual: good for releasing anger, post-divorce sadness and guilt, grief, loss, sadness, mood swings, depression, anxiety, panic attacks, and worry. Supports communication, especially of deeper issues that might be hard to express. Promotes contact with spirit guides, spirituality, and finding your own path.

YELLOW

STELLA BEAM CALCITE

Golden, yellow, or white scalenohedral crystals, typically double terminated with distinct, long terminations. It has a smooth, soapy feel, like many *calcite* crystals, and may have *pyrite* inclusions.

Common alternative name: dogtooth calcite
Common sources: Brazil, USA
Astrological association: Cancer
Chakras: solar plexus, brow, crown

HEALING QUALITIES

Acts as a signpost on your spiritual path, and boosts connection to all around you, in both environment and spirit.
Physical: good for brain, head, neck, eyes, ears, nose, mouth, nerves connecting to senses, and skull.
Emotional/spiritual: calms the mind, allowing for expansion of thought and ideas. Good for dreams, intuition, meditation, and magic. Brings inner peace. Helps to direct distant healing to its target. Boosts spiritual energy, easing gentle change. Relieves stress, insomnia, and oversensitivity. Releases trapped energy from past trauma and past lives. A library card to the Akashic records. Can be worked with to remove negative energy from the aura.

GOLDEN SELENITE

Bright gold "fishtail" crystals and crystal clusters.
Common alternative names: golden fishtail selenite, golden butterfly selenite
Common sources: Canada, Peru
Astrological association: Taurus
Chakras: solar plexus, crown

HEALING QUALITIES

Adds the power of the sun to cleanse mind, body, spirit, and spaces we inhabit.
Physical: helps to detox. Aids all physical healing, menstruation, and sexuality, and helps to prevent hair loss.
Emotional/spiritual: detox for the soul, clearing out stuck emotions and helping your spirit to flow. Helps you to see the other side of an argument and is excellent for healers, as it enhances your ability to listen without becoming judgmental or emotionally involved. Aids manifestation of creative ideas and plans. A happy stone, helping to lift depression, ease mood swings, and relieve SAD, tiredness, and stress. Raises spiritual awareness. Aids communication with spirit guides and angels especially, helping you to hear what they say. All varieties of selenite connect with the energies of the moon, helping with cycles and behavior patterns.

LEMON CHRYSOPRASE

Lemon-yellow to lemon-green variety of *chalcedony*.
Common source: Australia
Astrological association: Libra
Chakra: heart

HEALING QUALITIES

Helps you to see through the mist of your emotions.
Physical: good for heart, spleen, dexterity, and fertility, and helps to prevent scurvy.
Emotional/spiritual: expels anxiety, depression, fear, inferiority and superiority complexes, arrogance, and judgmental attitude. Good for general mental health and healing, schizophrenia, neurotic patterns, and stress. Heals a broken heart. Good for meditation. Brings balance, as well as acceptance of others, yourself, and your own sexuality. A feel-better stone that helps you to find and accept the root cause of your emotional stress.

TIBETAN CITRINE

This is a natural *citrine* crystal.
Only source: Tibetan plateau
Astrological associations: Aries, Gemini, Leo, Libra
Chakra: solar plexus

HEALING QUALITIES

Tibetan citrine makes everything easier in every way, as long as it has a spiritual benefit for you or others.

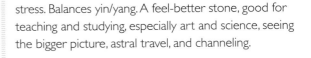

Physical: good for all of the digestive system, from mouth to anus, and all related disorders. Also good for heart, jaundice, kidneys, liver, nausea and sickness/vomiting, tissue repair, toxins/detox, anemia, eyesight/vision, thyroid, and thymus.

Emotional/spiritual: crystals from Tibet help you to get to the point quickly and effectively, and enhance your spiritual connection. Especially helpful in keeping the balance between your spirituality and your business or work and how you make your living. Promotes abundance and wealth; known as a money stone. Helps choice, decisions, relationships, and yin/yang balance. Boosts aura, self-esteem, awareness, and energy. Calms anger and emotional toxins. A feel-better stone that's good for teaching and studying (learning), problem solving, new beginnings, and selling houses!

YELLOW CALCITE

Calcite forms masses, stalactites, scalenohedral, and rhombohedral crystals.
Common sources: worldwide
Astrological association: Cancer
Chakra: solar plexus

HEALING QUALITIES

Yellow calcite balances emotions.
Physical: good for kidneys, pancreas, and spleen. Helps reduce bone growths and calcium deficiency.
Emotional/spiritual: calms emotions, overenthusiasm, and fear, and eases stress. Balances yin/yang. A feel-better stone, good for teaching and studying, especially art and science, seeing the bigger picture, astral travel, and channeling.

GOLDEN HEALER QUARTZ

Yellow iron coating on or included within quartz crystals.
Common alternative names: golden quartz, **yellow quartz** (this is a misnomer; the entry under this name is a different crystal)
Common sources: see quartz
Astrological associations: all
Chakras: all, especially heart

HEALING QUALITIES

Eases energy shifts and facilitates all emotional healing.
Physical: helps energy flow through meridians supporting all physical healing and the immune system. Helps to repair skin damage, including burns, sunburn, cuts, and abrasions.
Emotional/spiritual: good for self-healing, strengthening the aura, removing unhealthy blocks to lifestyle changes and behavior patterns. Releases you from fear, past hurts, and self-judgmental thoughts, and is particularly good if you feel that things "aren't for the likes of you." Attracts abundance and prosperity, and is good for relationships, cutting ties with the past, cutting cords, bringing emotional balance, and restoring your self-esteem after disappointment. Cleanses, clears, re-boots; a stone of re-birth. It's a happy crystal that will help you to walk your walk through life. Heals rooms holding traumatic energy. Balances yin/yang.

LIBYAN GOLD TEKTITE

A variety of *tektite*, which is meteoritic glass created from the immense heat of a meteorite impact with the Earth. The heat is so intense that both the meteorite and the Earth's surface melt, and tektite is formed as this mixture of space material and Earth cool together. Libyan gold tektite is rare, the only yellow variety; more common are *black*, brown, and the also rare green *moldavite*.

Common alternative names: Libyan desert glass, Libyan glass
Only source: Sahara desert (Libya)
Astrological associations: Aries, Cancer
Chakra: crown

HEALING QUALITIES

Brings connection with distant friends and family.
Physical: good for circulation, fever, fertility/ovulation, dehydration, and exposure.
Emotional/spiritual: good for yin/yang balance, creativity leading to artistic abundance, reasoning, telepathy and ESP, psychic surgery (a type of psychic healing—see glossary), meditation (reaching and maintaining peak experience), distant healing, and contact with other worlds.

HONEY CALCITE

Masses and rhombohedral crystals.
Common source: Mexico
Astrological association: Cancer
Chakras: base, sacral

HEALING QUALITIES

Slows everything down a little so you can have more time to pursue the important things in life.
Physical: good for fertility, female and male reproductive systems, bone growths, and calcium deficiency.
Emotional/spiritual: brings stability, balance. Curbs overenthusiasm, fear, and stress. Good for yin/yang

balance. Calms emotions that might be preventing pregnancy or success in any subject or venture. Good for astral travel and grounding.

KUNDALINI CITRINE

Yellow, deep golden, yellow-brown, or lemon variety of quartz. Color is due to heat from volcanic and other Earth activity. Often found in clusters with "baby" crystals attached at the base.

Common alternative name: kundalini quartz
Only source: Democratic Republic of Congo
Astrological associations: Aries, Gemini, Cancer, Leo, Libra
Chakras: all

HEALING QUALITIES

Activates kundalini energy. An uplifting crystal, helping you to develop in both everyday life and on your spiritual path.
Physical: alleviates stress-related digestive problems. Helps to move energy through the body and aura to reach the areas where it is most needed. Good for post-operative healing and detox.
Emotional/spiritual: brings abundance, success, and awareness. Raises consciousness, enhances clarity of mind and thought, and brings dreams into reality. Good for creativity, problem solving, and teaching, and is excellent as a focus stone in crystal grids. Boosts relationships, sexuality, sex drive, and tantric energy. Good for teamwork and willpower.

URANOPHANE

Uranophane comes in various shades of yellow, from light lemon to deep honey and green-yellow. Transparent to translucent, these wedge-shaped crystals are waxy or dull when massive. This mineral contains uranium, is radioactive, and should be worked with in limited and focused time.

Common alternative name: uranotile
Common source: Brazil
Astrological association: Aquarius
Chakra: solar plexus

HEALING QUALITIES

Uranophane supports complementary therapies.

Physical: supports chemotherapy and radiotherapy treatment of tumors; may counter radiation damage.

Emotional/spiritual: speeds karma, brings dramatic change, can help release hidden talents.

No elixir. Wash hands after handling. Do not smell, sniff, or lick. Never ingest. Do not hold or have contact with for extended periods of time.

YELLOW PREHNITE

Yellow to yellow-green massive botryoidal and globular structure with layered "plates"; tabular and prismatic crystals. Also found in *green*, white, and brown.

Common sources: Australia, India, Mali, Republic of South Africa, USA
Astrological association: Libra
Chakras: solar plexus, heart, brow

HEALING QUALITIES

Clears the fog in your mind so you can see your own true spiritual path through life.

Physical: good for kidneys, bladder, heart, blood, blood cleansing, lymphatic system, RBC, anemia, connective tissue, and gout.

Emotional/spiritual: brings calmness, eases agitation, and facilitates letting go. Promotes clairvoyance, divination, visualization, meditation, dreams, and dream recall. Inspires flow in all aspects of your life.

GOLDEN LEMURIAN QUARTZ CRYSTAL

Hexagonal quartz crystal with horizontal "bar code" lines on all six sides. Colored pale yellow to golden. Unlike *citrine*, **kundalini citrine**, **smoky citrine**, and **Tibetan citrine**, the color in this crystal is due to iron inclusions.

Common alternative names: golden healer Lemurian crystal, warm golden healer Lemurian seed crystal, golden healer Lemurian seed crystal
Common source: Brazil
Astrological associations: all
Chakras: all

HEALING QUALITIES

Promotes self-healing, looking within.

Physical: can assist all physical healing; particularly helpful for physical symptoms of stress-related conditions. Good for heart, immune system, pain, burns, and vertigo. General tonic helping to keep you well.

Emotional/spiritual: removes blocks you put in your own way, finds positivity, and rejects negativity; good for the soul. Improves meditation, insight, leadership, inner strength, confidence, courage, and inner wisdom. Helps you to connect to ancient wisdom and ancient civilizations, such as Lemuria and Atlantis, past lives, and Akashic records. Helps memory. Good for ceremony, bringing in sacredness to any group. Promotes awareness. Helps you to listen to the universe. Helps spiritual development. Good for ego, intuition, intellect, universal love, connection, and dreams. Heals a broken heart. Balances emotions. Alleviates stress and tension. A happy stone, bringing joy into your life. Helps to connect to spirit guides.

CELESTITE WITH SULFUR

Forms as masses, nodules, pyramidal, and tabular crystals.
Common alternative names: sulfur crystal with celestite, *sulfur*, sulphur
Common sources: France, Italy (specifically Sicily)
Astrological association: Leo
Chakra: solar plexus

HEALING QUALITIES

Insects and pests really don't like this crystal combination.
Physical: good for insect bites and can act as fumigant. Helps to fight infection, increase energy, reduce fibrous tissue growths and swelling, and relieve the discomfort of arthritis and painful joints.
Emotional/spiritual: reduces willfulness, restores mental balance, and promotes reasoning, inspiration, determination to succeed, visualization, dreams, and inner power. Releases deep-seated feelings.

MIMETITE

Forms druse, crusts, botryoidal, reniform, globular and granular masses, tabular and acicular crystals. Colors include white, shades of yellow, orange, and brown.
Common alternative name: it's very similar to and often confused with *pyromorphite*
Common sources: Mexico, Namibia, USA
Astrological association: Capricorn
Chakra: throat

HEALING QUALITIES

Brings renewal and confidence.
Physical: Aids weight loss. Good for skeletal system (bones and joints) and mobility. Good for acid indigestion, reflux, and throat.
Emotional/spiritual: helps you to break free from trapped patterns and relationships, bringing a sense of

independence and adventure. Helps you to recognize what you are responsible for and what you are not, and to stop worrying too much about what others think of you. Helps expression and brings balance. On the psychic level, boosts clairvoyance and protects.

SUNSET AURA QUARTZ

Quartz crystal bonded with titanium and silicon. Most sunset aura quartz crystals exhibit deep yellow, gold, orange, rust, pink, and red colors.
Common alternative name: sunrise aura quartz
Common source: USA
Astrological associations: all
Chakra: solar plexus

HEALING QUALITIES

Encourages motivation, bringing creativity without stress.
Physical: enhances energy, including sexual energy, and vitality. Good for digestion, stomach and small-intestine health, IBS, and Crohn's disease.
Emotional/spiritual: brings motivation to change, releasing past trauma and behavior patterns, allowing you to leave the past behind and move forward in your life. Boosts creativity, inspiration, manifestation, self-confidence, self-worth, self-love, passion, libido, and general happiness. Good for new projects, dreams, and dreamwork. Promotes relaxation, relieving stress, writer's block, and other creative barriers.

SMOKY CITRINE

Citrine and *smoky quartz* combined within the same crystal. Golden brown variety of quartz colored by natural heating activity and radiation within the Earth.
Common sources: Brazil, China, Democratic Republic of Congo, Madagascar, Tibet
Astrological association: Gemini
Chakras: base, solar plexus, crown

HEALING QUALITIES

Grounds inspiration, bringing
ideas to fruition and dreams
into reality.
Physical: combats addictions.
Good for detox, cleansing,
lymphatic system, kidneys, and liver.
Emotional/spiritual: helps practical application of ideas,
getting on with it, creativity, confidence, making things
happen, new beginnings, letting go, and leaving the past
behind. Offers protection during spiritual endeavors.
Helps relieve SAD, bipolar disorder, depression. Brings
abundance, wealth, and past-life recall.

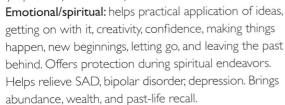

GOLDEN LABRADORITE

Just like the more common gray variety of *labradorite*
with its display of colors, this golden crystal is also a form
of feldspar.
Common alternative names: sunstone, American
sunstone
Common source: USA
Astrological associations: Leo, Scorpio, Sagittarius
Chakras: solar plexus, crown

HEALING QUALITIES

Helps you discover a happier life, as
if capturing golden hues of
sunshine.
Physical: good for right/left
brain balance (magic and
science, intuition and intellect).
Emotional/spiritual: promotes self-confidence. Gives an
elevating feeling, bringing lightness and a positive sense of
purpose to you and everything and everyone around
you. Good for creativity, inspiration, originality, and new
beginnings.

GOLDEN CALCITE

Bright, golden-colored rhombohedral crystals.
Common source: China
Astrological associations: Cancer, Leo
Chakra: solar plexus

HEALING QUALITIES

Encourages positivity.
Physical: good for kidneys, liver, and
hormones. Helps fight infection.
Emotional/spiritual: enhances feelings of security and
safety. Helps you to set aside self-limiting beliefs. Good
for past-life recall, calm communication, creativity, and
inspiration. Calms nerves.

CHAMPAGNE AURA QUARTZ

Quartz crystal bonded with *gold* and iron oxide.
Common alternative name: majestic champagne aura
quartz
Common source: USA
Astrological association: Aries
Chakras: base, crown

HEALING QUALITIES

Gives the ability to link the spiritual and physical worlds,
creating a bridge between the two and helping you to
achieve balance in physical, emotional, mental, and
spiritual dimensions of your life. It really acts to
interweave all the pathways in your life into one
directional flow.
Physical: beneficial for restless leg syndrome, leg cramps
and muscle spasms, headaches, and itches and irritations.
Emotional/spiritual: a very liberating crystal, freeing your
mind while grounding you and holding you down at the
same time. Deals with mental yearnings and emotional
irascibilities. Good for meditation and clearing the mind.
It dispels negative thoughts and protects against negative
influences.

GOLDEN ROD CALCITE

Rare *calcite* rod crystal formation.
Common source: Germany
Astrological associations: Cancer, Leo
Chakra: solar plexus

HEALING QUALITIES

Brings happiness.
Physical: good for vitality, nerves, endocrine glands, detox, kidneys, and spleen.
Emotional/spiritual: a feel-better stone, enhancing confidence and feelings of security, inner strength, independence, and self-reliance. Good for meditation, mental energy, stamina, overcoming self-limiting beliefs, emotional stability, and creativity. Calming, especially for spaces/rooms. Helps you to see the bigger picture and alleviates mental stress and fear.

YELLOW AVENTURINE

Quartz variety with inclusions of mica, giving a speckled or sparkly effect.
Common source: India
Astrological association: Aries
Chakra: solar plexus

HEALING QUALITIES

Brings inspiration and drive.
Physical: good for muscles—especially core muscles and diaphragm—stomach, spleen, and kidneys.
Emotional/spiritual: enhances inner strength, creativity, motivation, and yin/yang balance. Gives support and structure. Helps decision making and gives protection from "energy vampires."

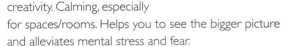

YELLOW DANBURITE

Prismatic striated crystals. Other colors include *clear/ white*, **pink**, and lilac.
Common alternative name: agni-gold danburite
Common sources: Madagascar, Myanmar, Republic of South Africa, Vietnam
Astrological association: Leo
Chakras: solar plexus, crown

HEALING QUALITIES

Helps you to see the signposts on your life's path.
Physical: good for stomach, digestion.
Emotional/spiritual: brings happiness and the ability to see all sides of an argument or discussion. Alleviates depression. Helps you to get back into the world after an absence due to a breakdown, hospitalization, or any other reason.

LION SKIN STONE

A natural fusing of *tiger's eye* and quartz.
Common alternative name: lion skin jasper (misidentified—it is not a *jasper*)
Common sources: Namibia, Republic of South Africa
Astrological association: Leo
Chakra: solar plexus

HEALING QUALITIES

A stone for inner strength.
Physical: alleviates the effects of radiation and EMF. Protects from positive ions emanating from computer screens. Good for stamina.
Emotional/spiritual: reduces fear, anxiety, depression, and negativity. Good for courage, confidence, all psychic abilities, yin/yang balance, abundance, memory, concentration, and meditation. Gives protection, calms emotions, and guards against laziness and procrastination.

YELLOW QUARTZ

Opaque, yellow, milky quartz.
Common alternative names: *citrine* is often called yellow quartz—it is NOT.
Common source: Republic of South Africa
Astrological association: Gemini
Chakras: solar plexus, brow

HEALING QUALITIES

Reboots your system.
Physical: helps digestion and stomach and small-intestine health. Helps relieve food allergies, coeliac disease, and CFS/ME; aids recovery from exhaustion, tiredness, and fatigue.
Emotional/spiritual: good for people who tend to overwork, helping work/life balance and relieving burnout, panic, and nervous exhaustion. Combats SAD, ADHD, and excessive self-criticism. Boosts self-confidence, but deflates the ego, bringing balance. Focuses the mind, promoting meditation, memory, and learning from experience, and bringing fun and humor into your life—there is a funny side to everything.

COPAL

Copal is fossilized resin from prehistoric trees and may have inclusions of animal and/or plant material. It can be golden, yellow, or orange.
Common alternative name: *amber* (usually refers to Baltic amber)
Common source: Columbia
Astrological association: Leo
Chakra: solar plexus

HEALING QUALITIES

Associated with fulfillment of dreams, goals, or ideals.
Physical: has antiseptic and disinfectant properties (topical elixir). Combats acne, bacterial infection, and constipation (elixir). Good for babies teething (chew), heart, hormones, post-operative healing, chest, breathing, asthma, emphysema, detox, throat, kidneys, and bladder.

Emotional/spiritual: helps to remove emotional blockages. Good for memory, absent-mindedness, yin/yang balance, schizophrenia, calming, intellect, choice, and neutralizing abuse and negativity. Brings good luck and protection to warriors. Symbolizes renewal of marriage vows (like an eternity ring). Purifies body, mind, and spirit. Can be burnt as an incense to cleanse the air.

YELLOW SAPPHIRE

Tabular prismatic crystals with hexagonal double pyramid structure. A tiny amount of iron within the *sapphire* is the cause of the coloration.
Common alternative name: oriental topaz
Common sources: Sri Lanka (main source), Australia, Madagascar, Tanzania, Thailand
Astrological associations: Aries, Taurus, Cancer, Leo, Libra
Chakra: solar plexus

HEALING QUALITIES

Encourages practical application of your creativity.
Physical: combats flatulence and indigestion. Good for spleen, gall bladder, liver, jaundice, pancreas, throat, lungs, coughs, colds, as a cleansing detox (elixir), skin conditions (topical elixir), vitality, and tumors. Reduces excessive bleeding.
Emotional/spiritual: connected to the Hindu god Ganesh, bringing prosperity to the home, wealth, wisdom, protection, good luck, and creativity. Encourages new beginnings, new projects, and success. Enhances ambition, intellect, agreeable demeanor, and the ability to see the bigger picture. Focuses the mind, removing unwanted thoughts and tension. Helps you to see the beauty in everything. Promotes interest in the world around you. Good for depression, hope, and enthusiasm.

TOURMALINATED CITRINE

Hexagonal terminated citrine crystals with tourmaline growing through. The tourmaline might be black *schorl*, blue *indicolite*, or green *elbaite*.

Common alternative name: tourmaline in citrine

Common source: Brazil

Astrological association: Libra

Chakras: solar plexus, brow, crown

HEALING QUALITIES

Helps you to see different possibilities and find unexpected answers.

Physical: good for digestion, intestines, and all digestive problems, from mild stomach ache to severe conditions such as Crohn's disease. Acts as a preventative by protecting the gut and boosting the microbiota.

Emotional/spiritual: gives inner strength and confidence to help you on your path. Good for new beginnings. Eases endings by helping you to let go of the past and move forward. Aids digesting ideas and concepts and turning dreams into reality. Brings abundance in all areas. Benefits all psychic abilities. Good for protection, mindfulness, and all forms of meditation. Helps mental health, depression, bipolar disorder, and all healing of the mind.

SCHEELITE

Pseudo-octahedral, massive, columnar, granular; comes in many colors, including white, golden yellow, brownish green to dark brown, pinkish to reddish gray, and colorless.

Common sources: Australia, Brazil, Canada, China, Finland, France, Italy, Korea, Pakistan, Sri Lanka, Switzerland, UK, USA

Astrological association: Libra

Chakra: sacral

HEALING QUALITIES

Encourages time management, punctuality.

Physical: alleviates lower backache. Good for vitality, virility, male reproductive system, and hormones. Improves blood flow to hips, legs, and feet.

Emotional/spiritual: supports creativity, drive, determination, and stamina. Dispels a tendency toward lateness, making you more reliable. Helps you to recognize linked thoughts and spiritual signposts directing you on your path. Good for developing psychic abilities, remote viewing, and shamanic journeying. Helps to focus the mind in meditation.

LIMONITE

Generic term for iron oxides and hydroxides occurring as masses, stalactites, cubes, and botryoidal formations. Colors are brown, yellow, orange, and red, depending on iron content.

Common sources: worldwide—especially Brazil, Namibia

Astrological association: Virgo

Chakra: base

HEALING QUALITIES

Promotes male qualities, such as strength, physical energy, endurance, and single-mindedness.

Physical: good for virility, male reproductive system, and hormones.

Emotional/spiritual: grounding crystal. Enhances male sexuality. Encourages you to reach for goals. Provides uplifting energy that can raise you out of depression. Stabilizes mood swings. Good for bipolar disorder and other similar conditions.

GREEN

OLIVINE ON BASALT

Crystal druses on surface of basalt, formed as olivine/ *peridot* masses, are carried to the surface by basaltic magma and gases and ejected into the atmosphere during a volcanic eruption (hence the alternative name, "bomb"). Color ranges from light yellow-green to brown-green. The vibrant lime greens are the best quality. Peridot is a gem-quality olivine. Olivine is one of the oldest crystals; some formed when the Earth, planets, and stars were being shaped four billion years ago.

Common alternative names: peridot on lava, peridot on basalt, peridot bomb, olivine bomb
Common sources: Arizona (USA), Tenerife
Astrological associations: Leo, Virgo, Scorpio, Sagittarius
Chakra: heart

HEALING QUALITIES

Assists manifestation of dreams, desires, and goals.
Physical: gives an extra boost of physical energy. Good for combating pain, headaches, migraine, sinus issues, nausea.
Emotional/spiritual: alleviates stress. Good for spiritual adventure, expression of your natural talents, and confidence. Boosts chi, positivity (can-do attitude), and youthfulness. Reduces signs of aging. Protects the home from psychic attack (the malicious sending of negative energy). Elevates the oppressed and helps to declutter. Helps deal with death and the dying process, rebirth and reincarnation. The basalt helps to bring creative ideas into your mind for clarity and empowerment. Promotes contact with spirit guides, strengthening your personal spiritual connection. Connects you to your deepest, innermost thoughts.

INCA JADE

Nephrite jade from Peru, with inclusions of *pyrite* making it very dark green. A sacred stone of the Inca.
Common alternative names: Lemurian jade (misnomer; see listing under black), Peruvian nephrite
Common source: Peru
Astrological association: Libra
Chakra: heart

HEALING QUALITIES

Physical: aids heart, immune system.
Emotional/spiritual: good for long life. Offers both psychic and physical protection, especially for the accident prone and in dreams. Reduces effects of abuse and problematic childhood, enhancing courage. Good for environmental issues, relationships, and travel. Supports shamanic journeying, ceremony and ritual, and connection to spirit guides and totem animals.

INFINITE

A mixture of *serpentine* and chrysotile with patterns but indistinct banding. Color range is yellow, green, gray.
Common source: Republic of South Africa
Astrological association: Gemini
Chakra: heart

HEALING QUALITIES

Gives endurance.
Physical: good for muscles, joints, and connective tissue. Combats pain, including muscle cramps, backaches, and headaches. Helps to fight fatigue and EMF.
Emotional/spiritual: heals the aura, bringing comfort and soothing worry, grief, and loss. Brings a positive outlook on life. Increases the potency of other healing modalities, such as Reiki and African tribal medicine. Boosts awareness and connection to angels. Helps you deal with energy vampires. Boosts ambition and endurance to help you surpass challenges and reach your life dreams.
No elixir. Wash hands after handling. Do not smell, sniff, or lick. Never ingest.

DRAGONSTONE

A mixture of green *epidote* and red **piemontite** forming a translucent-to-opaque rock.

Common alternative name: dragon jasper (NB **septarian** nodules are also sometimes called "dragonstone," but are not related)

Only source: Limpopo province, Republic of South Africa

Astrological association: Gemini

Chakras: all

HEALING QUALITIES

A very positive and optimistic stone that promotes inner wisdom and happiness, and gives the strength and courage needed to change.

Physical: boosts the immune system and physical regeneration. Good for detox, the central nervous system, thyroid function, smooth skin, and healthy hair and nails. Negates effects of dehydration.

Emotional/spiritual: relieves grief and loss and helps you to see the beautiful things in life again. Dispels self-pity, helps you to develop patience and learn from your mistakes. Benefits matters of finance, science, and research in any field.

No elixir.

GREEN SELENITE

Fragile, small, slender *selenite* crystals, colored green from copper inclusion. Looks like artificial turf.

Common alternative name: green Pernatty selenite

Only source: Australia

Astrological association: Gemini

Chakra: heart

HEALING QUALITIES

A nurturing crystal—home is where the heart is.

Physical: good for the heart, immune system, arthritis, detox, avoiding water retention, youthful skin.

Emotional/spiritual: helps with ceremony and travel, and alleviates homesickness. Good for emotions, Earth healing, environmental issues, decisions, change, friendship, harmony, and understanding. Heals rifts between people and families, helps deal with jealousy and envy, and is good for positivity. Merchant stone, said to bring wealth and success. Helps identify the underlying cause of disease and understand the steps needed for healing. Water soluble.

No elixir.

GREEN JASPER

Green variety of cryptocrystalline quartz.

Common alternative names: plasma bloodstone (note that this green jasper is not helioptrope *bloodstone*, which has red inclusions)

Common source: India

Astrological associations: Aries, Libra, Pisces

Chakras: base, heart

HEALING QUALITIES

A cleansing crystal.

Physical: combats acidity, acid indigestion, and cancer. Good for detox, blood, kidneys, bladder, intestines, and liver.

Emotional/spiritual: brings courage and strength. Good for dealing with change, distress, and anxiety. Encourages renewal of relationships and friendships. Helps connection with diverse groups of people, promoting harmony.

GREEN QUARTZ

Quartz crystal with *epidote* inclusions, surface druse and phantoms giving the crystal a green hue or turning the crystal green.

Common alternative name: be careful of confusion with another "green quartz" that comes from Brazil, colored by chromium and chlorite and that has a more

even coloring throughout the crystal than this one
Common sources: Brazil, India, Madagascar
Astrological associations: Libra, Pisces
Chakra: heart

HEALING QUALITIES

Green quartz brings transformation and supports shamanic healing.

Physical: good for the endocrine system, glands, hormones.

Emotional/spiritual: calms the nerves, anxiety, and stress. Aids intuition, love, creativity, success, abundance, ritual, connection with totem animals, shamanic ceremonies, and Earth healing.

AEGERINE

Dark green, red-green, and black prismatic to acicular crystals.

Common sources: Brazil, India, Madagascar
Astrological association: Pisces
Chakra: heart

HEALING QUALITIES

A crystal for self-discovery.

Physical: supports tissue repair and the immune system.

Emotional/spiritual: good for self-esteem, breaking the need for conformity. Encourages self-acceptance, self-confidence, growth, spiritual development, and positive emotions. Gives protection and is empowering, especially when you feel there is nothing you can do about a situation.

DIOPSIDE

Diopside has several varieties. The one here is chrome diopside, the chromium-rich gem variety. Diopside forms prismatic crystals, often with rhomboid terminations. It can also be found as crystalline inclusions and massive form.

Common source: Afghanistan
Astrological association: Virgo
Chakras: brow, crown

HEALING QUALITIES

Diopside is an all-round healer and calming crystal that brings a sense of well-being and contentment.

Physical: good for heart, lungs, blood pressure, ulcers, and upset stomach.

Emotional/spiritual: balances emotions; releases trapped emotions and tears. Clears the mind, bringing peace and tranquility. Good for meditation. Strengthens intellect, and learning. Gives a competitive edge, enhances psychic abilities, generates wealth, and brings prosperity. Helps yin/yang balance and to raise consciousness, advancing your spiritual development. Helps Earth healing and to dissipate a victim mentality. Diopside is also calming for distressed animals.

CHRYSOTILE SERPENTINE

Green and white bands of *serpentine* and chrysotile.

Common alternative names: green zebra jasper (it's not *jasper*), dragon's scale stone
Common sources: Canada, Poland
Astrological association: Gemini
Chakras: heart, crown

HEALING QUALITIES

A crystal to help you learn from the past.

Physical: good for blood vessels, and eyesight.

Emotional/spiritual: releases past hurts, helping you to let go of old, unhelpful behavior patterns from past lives or childhood. Connects to the Reiki healing ray.

No elixir. Wash hands after handling. Do not smell, sniff, or lick. Never ingest.

ATLANTISITE

Green *serpentine* with purple **stichtite**.
Common alternative names: Atlantis stone, stichtite-serpentine, tasmanite
Common sources: Quebec, Tasmania, Republic of South Africa
Astrological associations: Virgo, Libra
Chakras: heart, brow

HEALING QUALITIES

Connects to ancient wisdom.
Physical: general tonic helps to keep you well. Relieves stomach complaints, acid indigestion, acid reflux, and menstrual pains and cramps. Good for diabetes, hypoglycemia, skin elasticity, muscles, muscle spasms, and hernia. Boosts stamina.
Emotional/spiritual: mood balancer; helps bipolar disorder and depression. Helps you to connect to past lives and ancient civilizations, such as Atlantis and Lemuria. Promotes love, spiritual awareness, intuition, understanding the cause of dis-ease. Elevates kundalini energy, fire in the loins, and passion. Encourages business success, drive, transformation, change.

PREHNITE WITH EPIDOTE

Apple green *prehnite* with very dark green needles of *epidote* growing through it.
Common alternative name: epidote in prehnite
Common source: Mali
Astrological associations: Gemini, Virgo, Libra
Chakra: heart

HEALING QUALITIES

A stone to heal the healer within.
Physical: good for detox, immune system, physical strength and stamina, and recovery from major illness or surgery.
Emotional/spiritual: promotes trust, happiness, lucid dreaming, and protection. Relaxes tension and stress. Brings calm, inner peace, and awareness of the higher self. Aids intuition and psychic abilities, enhancing powers of divination, such as with tarot, runes, and crystal ball. Encourages learning, memory, meditation, and clarity of thought—helps you to see through the fog in your mind.

KIMBERLITE

A conglomerate of several minerals in various proportions raised from the Earth's mantle. It occurs in vertical structures on the surface, known as kimberlite pipes. The world's most important source of *diamonds*. Some specimens may actually contain small diamonds.
Common sources: Russia, Republic of South Africa, USA
Astrological associations: Cancer, Sagittarius
Chakras: solar plexus, throat, crown

HEALING QUALITIES

A crystal to help you reach your true potential.
Physical: good for the intestines. Aids digestion, absorption, energy, stamina, and mobility. Good for athletes and sports people. Reduces fever. Restores hormone balance. Helpful in childbirth.
Emotional/spiritual: promotes the emergence and digesting of ideas, helping you to reach the heights you deserve. Encourages living in the moment, walking your walk, putting the mojo back in your life, reaching meditation peak experience, magic. It helps you to create your own possibilities, enhancing spiritual awareness and development, protection, out-of-body experiences, and dowsing. Helps you to avoid burnout and mental overload, and to achieve work/life balance, desires. Brings safety and beauty to ceremonies. Good for bipolar disorder, depression, self-assessment, and positivity.

MALACHOLLA

Combination of *malachite* and *chrysocolla* in one stone.
Common alternative name: malachite and chrysocolla
Common source: Democratic Republic of Congo
Astrological associations: Taurus, Gemini, Virgo, Scorpio, Capricorn
Chakra: heart

HEALING QUALITIES

"What to the caterpillar is the end of the world, to the master is a butterfly." (Chuang Tzu)

Physical: aids tissue repair, detox (especially from pollutants), and cleansing. Protects from EMF.

Emotional/spiritual: good for rebirth, new beginnings, and new projects. Encourages awareness of inner truth. Promotes feelings of self-worth, confidence, and compassion. Releases old thoughts and ideas that are trapped within you and holding you back. Helps with getting in touch with your female side, femininity, mystery. Helps mood swings, emotions, communication from the heart, individualism, expression, and discovering your life path. Provides protection.

OLIVE SERPENTINE

Olive variety of *serpentine* that usually forms masses.
Common alternative name: olive jade (it's not *jade*)
Common source: Peru
Astrological association: Gemini
Chakras: sacral, heart

HEALING QUALITIES

A stone to help you let go.

Physical: good for detox, menstrual pain, and cramps. Acts against parasites.

Emotional/spiritual: raises kundalini energy, releasing fears in the process, enabling you to let go of anything holding you back. Permits you to take a leap of faith, allowing change to happen. Gives protection, enhancing fearlessness and innocence. Helps you to contact angels and guides, and find inspiration. Helpful when exploring past lives.

GREEN CHALCEDONY

Green cryptocrystalline variety of quartz.
Common alternative name: green onyx
Common source: USA
Astrological associations: Cancer, Virgo, Sagittarius, Aquarius
Chakra: heart

HEALING QUALITIES

A nurturing stone.

Physical: good for eyes, circulatory system, heart, blood vessels, blood, lungs, breathing, asthma, and detox.

Emotional/spiritual: boosts maternal and nurturing instincts. Alleviates stress and helps deal with childhood issues. Helpful in ceremony and ritual to connect groups and contact the divine. Promotes kindness, openness, and insight. Decreases irritability and melancholy. Good for group bonding. Brings mental stability, defending against mental decline, senility, and dementia. Supports natural talent and skill in any field.

OLIVE OPAL

Massive olive-green color; rarely, displays fire.
Common source: Madagascar
Astrological associations: Aries, Sagittarius
Chakras: heart, throat

HEALING QUALITIES

A cleansing stone.

Physical: good for blood, lymph system/glands, kidneys, liver, detox, diabetes, and immune system. Alleviates ailments such as colds, fever, and flu. Helps stamina, PMS, childbirth, and dieting. Promotes a youthful appearance for skin (topical elixir), reducing effects of exposure and hypothermia.

Emotional/spiritual: gives the emotional energy to overcome breakup. Good for love, relationships, faithfulness, self-esteem, meditation, dream recall, and problem solving in dreams. Relaxes pre-conceived ideas. Encourages you to think before you speak. Promotes a youthful outlook on life.

KAMBAMBA STONE

A sedimentary stone made up of fossilized algae (**stromatolite**) creating black circular patterns with green centers in mottled green groundmass (the finer-grained mass of material wherein larger grains, crystals, or clasts are embedded). Both black and green areas are mostly quartz and feldspar, with cristobalite in black regions and **amphibole** in green.

Common alternative names: Kambamba jasper (it is not a *jasper*), Kumbaba stone, Khambab stone, Khumbaba stone (sometimes mistaken for *Nebula stone*), crocodile rock, crocodile jasper, green stromatolite jasper
Common sources: Madagascar, Republic of South Africa
Astrological associations: Libra, Pisces
Chakra: brow

HEALING QUALITIES

This is a crystal of invention.
Physical: good for endurance. Affects body fluids; helps with dehydration and water retention. Good for pregnancy.
Emotional/spiritual: good for art, painting, music, sculpture, creativity, design, ergonomic understanding, and visualization of concepts, grounding them and bringing them into reality—almost as if you can see your invention working in the future. Promotes environmental issues, plants, agriculture, crops, crop yields, gardening, and farming. Good for the mind, learning (especially languages), observation, detective and police work, examining the past, patience, and stamina. Enhances meditation and stillness in motion. Encourages connection to dispersed family members and the land your ancestors originally came from. Gives courage and self-confidence, and helps relieve anxiety.

ROSASITE

Spherical structures, botryoidal and sometimes drusy crusts with tiny crystals. Colors include blue-green, green, and sky blue.
Common sources: Mexico, USA
Astrological association: Virgo
Chakras: heart, brow

HEALING QUALITIES

Rosasite provides quietness.
Physical: good for hernia, rupture, muscle tears, chickenpox, measles, and skin disorders (elixir).
Emotional/spiritual: calms emotions, stills the mind, and brings a peaceful feeling. Good for meditation (especially with a mantra), sleep, dreams, and dream recall.

CHROME TREMOLITE

Green variety of tremolite, forming prismatic bladed crystals, fibrous, granular, or columnar aggregates.
Common sources: Canada, USA
Astrological associations: Gemini, Libra, Scorpio, Pisces
Chakras: brow, crown

HEALING QUALITIES

Brings inner peace.
Physical: good for heart, heart conditions, immune system, ME, chronic fatigue syndrome, AIDS, and brain.
Emotional/spiritual: brings joy, happiness, inner strength and confidence, contentment, harmony, and access to Akashic records.
No elixir. Wash hands after handling. Do not smell, sniff, or lick. Never ingest.

BUDDSTONE

Mottled green stone similar to verdite.
Common alternative names: African jade (it's not *jade*), budd stone, jade of Africa
Common source: Republic of South Africa
Astrological association: Virgo
Chakra: heart

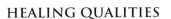

HEALING QUALITIES

Promotes action and intuition.
Physical: good for hearing, vertigo, diabetes, and your feet. Frees movement. Eases pain, including headache, migraine, and period pains.
Emotional/spiritual: promotes courage, insight and change, spiritual growth, and development of new skills. Helpful for making successful business decisions. Releases blocked energy, taking away drains and giving you more stamina, patience, and authenticity. Good for carers, dreams, dream recall, dementia, and Alzheimer's disease.

LIBETHENITE

Dark green druzy crusts, masses, and orthorhombic crystals that are short prismatic or slightly elongated with wedge-shaped terminations.
Common sources: Slovakia, USA, Zambia
Astrological association: Virgo
Chakra: base

HEALING QUALITIES

This crystal cultivates a sense of adventure.
Physical: combats incontinence and promotes muscle control.
Emotional/spiritual: releases self-imposed restrictions and rules. Supports an adventurous spirit and conquers fear of the unknown. Encourages you not to worry too much about what others think. Promotes expression through actions and speech, dispelling procrastination, leading to speedy change. Enhances work/life balance, sense of direction,

and will to live. Overcomes disability. Boosts libido. Grounding, centering, and stills the mind; consequently, good for meditation.

CONICHALCITE

Crusts, reniform masses, and prismatic crystals. Colors from yellow to emerald green.
Common sources: Chile, Mexico, USA
Astrological association: Pisces
Chakras: heart, brow

HEALING QUALITIES

Brings the heart and mind into balance.
Physical: good for kidneys, bladder, detox.
Emotional/spiritual: encourages the expression of love, communication, and free-flowing energy, allowing you to make changes in your life where they are needed. Enhances courage and inner fortitude. Enables you to pause and reconsider before being judgmental in any situation. Gives you the inner strength to make the toughest decisions. Protects you from your worldly worries when meditating, making it easier to focus your mind and get into the zone. Promotes intuition, independence, imagination, and flexibility. Helps to shed the baggage of past relationships. Good for mental disorders, helping you to tell the real from the imagined in your mind.
No elixir. Wash hands after handling. Do not smell, sniff, or lick. Never ingest.

GREEN ZOISITE

Variety of zoisite, forming masses and striated crystals.
Common alternative name: green thulite (*thulite*, by definition, is pink zoisite)
Common sources: Kenya, Tanzania, USA
Astrological associations: Taurus, Gemini
Chakra: heart

HEALING QUALITIES

Don't let them get you down.
Physical: good for the bowel, combating flatulence, and wind pains. Good for heart, lungs, spleen, pancreas, and vitality.
Emotional/spiritual: helps you to find your true inner self. Dispels negativity, lethargy, and sluggish inclinations, giving a get-up-and-go attitude to sort out problems, issues, and people blocking your path.

ACTINOLITE IN QUARTZ

Clear quartz crystals with green, needle-like *actinolite* crystals growing through.
Common alternative name: dream quartz (**epidote in quartz** and **scenic quartz** are also called dream quartz)
Common source: Brazil
Astrological association: Leo
Chakra: heart

HEALING QUALITIES

A crystal to promote respect.
Physical: aids the immune system. Fights infection. Good for adrenal glands, throat infections, laryngitis, and pharyngitis.
Emotional/spiritual: helps you to change behavior patterns and develop self-esteem. Dispels sarcasm and derision. Gives you an agreeable attitude, making you a nice person to be with. Encourages the sharing of love and kindness. Helps you to make new friends and sparks new relationships. Enhances premonition in making

decisions, clairvoyance, dreams, and dream recall. Good for architects, builders, and interior designers, helping them to see possibilities in their creations. Mitigates against stress. Encourages expression from the heart. Good for plants, plant health, and plant healing.

CHALCOSIDERITE

Crusts and prismatic crystals, dark green to apple green.
Common alternative names: white turquoise, green turquoise (it's not *turquoise*, but chemically very similar. Most "green" turquoise on the market is probably chalcosiderite or faustite)
Common sources: France, Germany, UK, USA
Astrological association: Scorpio
Chakras: heart, throat

HEALING QUALITIES

Helps you to let go; especially good for healers who suffer from empathic pains or worry too much about the people they are trying to help.
Physical: general all-purpose fix. Helps most physical healing and is particularly good for joints, arthritis, neuralgia, colds and flu, and allergies such as hay fever.
Emotional/spiritual:

encourages communication, particularly from the heart. Inspires you to talk your talk and express emotions. Good for public speaking and creative expression. Teachers, politicians, and business leaders can all benefit. Protects travelers. Eases travel sickness. Helps divination, such as psychic and tarot-card readings.

GREEN KYANITE

Blade-type crystals, fibers, and masses. Other colors include black, *blue*, gray, white, yellow, and pink.
Common source: Brazil
Astrological associations: Aries, Taurus, Libra
Chakras: heart, throat

HEALING QUALITIES

Talk your talk—express yourself from your heart.
Physical: good for throat, chest, heart, lungs, and connective tissue. Helps those with asthma and epilepsy.
Emotional/spiritual: connects the heart and throat chakras, allowing you to express your emotions and feel your thoughts. Brings calm and helps balance all chakras. Promotes psychic development and protection, grounding spiritual knowledge and wisdom into your everyday life, spiritual attunements, dreams. Helps you to connect to plants and nature spirits; good for gardeners.

GREEN SMITHSONITE

Green druses, masses, botryoidal structures, scalenohedral and rhombohedral crystals.
Common source: Namibia
Astrological association: Pisces
Chakra: heart

HEALING QUALITIES

This is the nicest stone in the world.
Physical: improves vitality, immune system, acne, osteoporosis, sinus issues, digestion, and veins. Helps combat alcoholism.

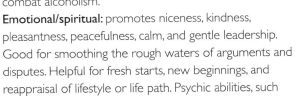

Emotional/spiritual: promotes niceness, kindness, pleasantness, peacefulness, calm, and gentle leadership. Good for smoothing the rough waters of arguments and disputes. Helpful for fresh starts, new beginnings, and reappraisal of lifestyle or life path. Psychic abilities, such as clairsentience and clairaudience, can be improved.

LIZARD SKIN AGATE

Pale green patterns on white rock resemble lizard skin.
Common source: Asia
Astrological association: Scorpio
Chakra: heart

HEALING QUALITIES

A stone for inner conflicts.
Physical: good for heart, blood pressure.
Emotional/spiritual: reduces fear, nightmares. Encourages adaptability. Alleviates anxiety, panic attacks, and stress, encouraging calmness.

ATACAMITE

A secondary copper formed through oxidation, especially in arid, saline conditions. Transparent-to-translucent slender, prismatic, striated crystals, ranging from bright green through dark emerald green to blackish green. Also, fibrous, sandy granular to compact, and massive.
Common sources: Chile, Mexico, USA
Astrological association: Sagittarius
Chakras: heart, crown

HEALING QUALITIES

Always look on the bright side of life (and death).
Physical: alleviates arthritis, rheumatism, painful joints, muscle problems, eye issues, and convulsions.
Emotional/spiritual: brings confidence and enthusiasm to achieve, promoting optimism and a can-do attitude. Dispels self-defeating, self-judgmental thoughts and replaces them with coolness, dreams, and visions of success. Promotes charity, altruism, kindness, and contentment. Emotionally cleansing, allowing you to let go of the past. Good for meditation, crystal-ball readings, psychic diagnosis of disease, premonitions, and receiving psychic warnings when they're needed.

PINK

PINK TOURMALINE AND LEPIDOLITE IN QUARTZ

Pale pink to violet leaf-like *lepidolite*, with pink rods of rubellite *tourmaline* growing through or on quartz matrix.

Common alternative names: lepidolite with pink tourmaline on/and quartz

Common sources: Brazil, Madagascar, Namibia

Astrological associations: Libra, Scorpio, Sagittarius

Chakra: heart

HEALING QUALITIES

A stone for problem solving and transition.

Physical: good for balance. Helps combat physical addictions, allergies, and Alzheimer's disease. Protects from EMF. Eases menopause.

Emotional/spiritual: gives inner strength to overcome adversity, emotional addictions, and unhealthy behavior patterns. Helps to bring and ease change, reduces stress, and brings intuitive thoughts to the surface. Good for ADHD, eating disorders such as anorexia and bulimia, insomnia, nightmares, night terrors, fear, anxiety, panic attacks, depression, bipolar disorder, mood swings, irritability, and PTSD. Helps reduce excessive aggression.

PINK TOURMALINE IN LEPIDOLITE

Pale pink to violet leaf-like *lepidolite*, with pink rods of rubellite *tourmaline* growing through.

Common alternative name: lepidolite with pink tourmaline

Common sources: Brazil, Madagascar

Astrological associations: Libra, Scorpio

Chakra: heart

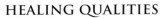

HEALING QUALITIES

Soothes the mind.

Physical: good for heart and lungs.

Emotional/spiritual: brings love from your heart center into your mind to create peace and tranquility, and calm anxiety, panic attacks, and stress. Helps your self-awareness, mental health and healing, depression, bipolar disorder, and insomnia. This inner love lifts a heavy heart. Provides protection and encourages happiness, joy, and abundance.

TUGTUPITE

White, rose-red to crimson, forming masses, granular material, and rare pseudo cubic crystals. Exhibits tenebrescence—that is, the ability of minerals to change color when exposed to sunlight, like photochromic sunglasses lenses. This transformation can repeat forever, but is destroyed by heating.

Only source: Greenland

Astrological association: Leo

Chakra: heart

HEALING QUALITIES

Opens the heart to love.

Physical: good for agility, muscles, joints, ligaments, and tendons. Helps to reduce swelling, pain of sports injuries, and travel sickness, including airplane, car, and sea sickness.

Emotional/spiritual: Helps in finding new love or rekindling love after breakup or divorce. Enables you to let go of past events that hold you back from expressing your true love through voice or action. Brings the cause of dis-ease into consciousness, allowing you to make lifestyle adjustments accordingly. Good for compassion, family coherence, and harmony with other beings that live with you, including pets and pot plants. Relieves stress. Inuit people believe that the stone glows "fire" with lover's passion and that the depth of color displays the intensity of love.

BUBBLE GUM TOURMALINE

Shocking-pink, vertically striated, prismatic crystals. Color "pops" and looks artificial, but it is natural.

Common alternative names: bright pink *tourmaline*, but there are many variants, including *elbaite*, rubellite, **liddicoatite**

Common sources: USA (especially California); similar material is occasionally found in other tourmaline locations such as Brazil or Pakistan

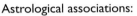

Astrological associations: Scorpio, Sagittarius

Chakra: heart

HEALING QUALITIES

Sharpens the intellect.

Physical: good for digestion, small and large bowel, heart, blood vessels, reproductive system, fertility, and hormone balance.

Emotional/spiritual: promotes digestion of ideas, invention, and creativity. Gives protection, confidence, and emotional balance. Enhances attractiveness, compassion, love, romance, and the appeal of new beginnings and new challenges. Combats self-defeating behavior patterns and is calming, encouraging empathy. Good for therapists, allowing an empathic approach without taking on the issues, pains, and distress of others.

PINK DANBURITE

Pink, prismatic striated crystals. Other colors include *white/clear*, **yellow**, and lilac, each with their own subtle healing focus.

Common sources: Mexico, USA

Astrological association: Leo

Chakras: heart, crown

HEALING QUALITIES

Enables the spreading of love.

Physical: good for muscle stiffness, gall bladder, liver, detox, and healthy weight gain.

Emotional/spiritual: promotes sharing love, helping others through altruism, and socialization. Helps you to get back into the world after absence (due to breakdown, drugs, hospitalization, unemployment, grief, prison, or whatever the reason may be) and connect to your angels.

ROSE QUARTZ CRYSTALS

Rose quartz normally forms cryptocrystalline masses; actual hexagonal crystals are rare, small, and generally found in clusters.

Common source: Brazil

Astrological associations: Taurus, Cancer, Libra

Chakra: heart

HEALING QUALITIES

This crystal is for love!

Physical: good for fertility, female reproductive system, menstrual cycle, asthma, heart, blood, circulation, kidneys, general aches and pains, spleen, varicose veins, detox, vertigo, adrenal glands, coughs, colds, and flu.

Emotional/spiritual: some say this configuration is the most powerful love crystal there is, bringing love as a life force. Supports relationships, romance, and female energy and qualities. Balances sex drive and sexual frustration. A perfect crystal to bring comfort in a crisis. Releases anger, stress, tension, fear, guilt, grief, inadequacy, jealousy, resentment, unhappy childhood experiences, phobias, upset, and emotional wounds (the feeling of being wounded). In fact, it's like a spa day for the emotions. Try a topical elixir to improve complexion, banish wrinkles, and gain a youthful appearance. Promotes creativity, art, music, writing, and imagination.

RHODONITE IN QUARTZ

Pink *rhodonite* in white quartz, possibly with black manganese inclusions.

Common alternative name: rhodo silica
Common source: Madagascar
Astrological association: Taurus
Chakra: heart

HEALING QUALITIES

Brings the feeling of love into your everyday life and everything you do.

Physical: good for ME, emphysema, bones, arthritis, light sensitivity, throat infections, and heart.

Emotional/spiritual: dissolves worry, stress, and anxiety, mitigating against contradictory behaviors and confusion. Brings love, calm, self-esteem, compassion, empathy, and inner knowing.

AGNITITE

Translucent quartz with inclusions of beryllium and iron.

Common alternative name: pink fire azeztulite™ (when Azozeo Super Activated)
Common sources: Brazil, Madagascar
Astrological associations: all
Chakras: heart

HEALING QUALITIES

Brings passion to everything you do.

Physical: good for heart, auto-immune diseases such as celiac disease, congenital heart block, Crohn's disease, and fibromyalgia.

Emotional/spiritual: enables love, enlightenment, ecstasy, and fire-up passion. Gives energy and excitement. Opens the heart, emotions, and emotional expression, easing the pain of abandonment and unrequited love.

ROSE OPAL

Deep rose pink common *opal*; does not exhibit fire.

Common alternative name: peppermint candy stone (when varying shades of color)
Common source: Peru
Astrological associations: Virgo, Libra, Sagittarius
Chakra: heart

HEALING QUALITIES

Road map of life's journey.

Physical: good for heart, lungs, spleen, and connective tissue. Elixir can help diabetes; applied topically, soothes skin.

Emotional/spiritual: enhances intuition, air of mystery, and womanliness. Allows you to connect to your feminine side. Good for renewal, relationships, letting go of the past, releasing old patterns and inhibitions that hold you back, connection, spiritual awareness, love, and release of ego. Makes a calming elixir.

RAINBOW

The rainbow color section includes those minerals that usually exhibit several colors at once.

PINK TOURMALINE IN QUARTZ

Pink rubellite crystals growing through clear or white quartz.

Common alternative name:
pink *elbaite* in quartz

Common sources:
Australia, Brazil, Namibia, Pakistan, Republic of South Africa

Astrological associations:
Taurus, Libra, Scorpio

Chakra: heart

HEALING QUALITIES

Replenishes love.

Physical: good for heart, lungs, spleen, vitality, digestive system, pancreas, fertility, reproductive system, and blood vessels.

Emotional/spiritual: a reinvigorating crystal, good for love, success, protection, new relationships, repairing emotions and refilling emotional energy, getting back your mojo, inner strength, creativity, tactfulness, and survival skills. A good crystal for politicians.

GREEN TOURMALINE IN QUARTZ

Green *elbaite* crystals growing through clear or white quartz.

Common alternative name: Verdelite in quartz

Common sources: Australia, Brazil, Namibia, Pakistan, Republic of South Africa

Astrological association: Capricorn

Chakra: heart

HEALING QUALITIES

Enables you to find another way of looking at the world.

Physical: good for brain, eyes, heart, thymus, immune system, alleviating eating disorders, constipation, diarrhea, and combating weight loss.

Emotional/spiritual: offers a different way of thinking and seeing things in a different light. Promotes ideas, peace of mind, ease of feelings, visualization, and compassion. Helps you deal with abuse. Dispels negativity, offering abundance, creativity, and success.

RAINBOW MOONSTONE

White variety of feldspar that exhibits a schiller effect, adularescence that gives the stone a blue sheen and makes it appear to glow gently inside.

Common sources: India, Sri Lanka

Astrological association: Cancer

Chakras: sacral, crown

HEALING QUALITIES

Associated with the moon, lunar cycles, creation on all levels, birth, death, and rebirth.

Physical: good for fertility, pregnancy, childbirth, and menstrual cycle. Eases menopausal symptoms, PMS, period pains, and excessive menstrual bleeding. Good for hormones, detox, kidneys, bladder, liver, and lymphatic system.

Emotional/spiritual: promotes femininity. Boosts sexuality, passion, confidence, composure, happiness, gentleness, joy, fun, and intuition. For men, promotes getting in touch with your female side. Brings change—endings and beginnings. Encourages optimism. Brings insight, flashes of inspiration (rainbow moments to remember forever), and creativity. Helps break repeated, unhealthy behavior patterns. Connects you to Gaia—Mother Earth. Promotes the cycle of sending healing to the planet in return for the Earth's nurture.

BISMUTH

Elemental bismuth is naturally occurring, but rarely forms crystals. The commonly available rainbow-colored crystals (pictured) are high-quality bismuth, heated to encourage crystallization. The amazing colors are natural, appearing due to a thin oxidized surface layer that causes light to interfere constructively when reflected from the surface, resulting in the observed rainbow colors.
Common sources: Bolivia, Canada, Japan, Mexico, Peru, Russia
Astrological association: Aquarius
Chakras: all

HEALING QUALITIES

Removes blocks we put in our own way.
Physical: good for increasing stamina, reducing fever, and strengthening muscles.
Emotional/spiritual: stone of transformation, positivity. Encourages you to find reasons for doing rather than avoiding. Promotes connectedness, socialization, and groups, rather than isolation and individualism. Good for visualization, dreams, goal setting, shamanic journey, soul retrieval, past-life work, and astral travel.

LIDDICOATITE

Naturally striated hexagonal crystals of *tourmaline*, showing distinct and unique banding when sliced and polished.
Common alternative names: *watermelon tourmaline* (but not all watermelon tourmaline is liddicoatite), mathematician's stone
Common source: Brazil
Astrological association: Virgo
Chakras: heart, brow, crown

HEALING QUALITIES

Allows you to see opportunities.
Physical: digestion, brain, frozen shoulder and other unexplained shoulder pains.
Emotional/spiritual: helps both numeric and spatial awareness, meditation. Brings protection, luck, and the ability to know your inner self and recognize the cause of dis-ease, melting blocks in your path. Promotes love in everything you do. Enhances the placebo effect in all healing in all modalities. Encourages thoughts, ideas, creativity, invention, and seeing things differently.

AMEGREEN

A combination of amethyst and *prasiolite*, forming hexagonal crystals.
Common source: Brazil
Astrological associations: Virgo, Scorpio, Capricorn, Aquarius, Pisces
Chakras: crown, heart

HEALING QUALITIES

Amegreen often displays a band of white between the purple and green, representing the veil between worlds.
Physical: good for healing somatic injury, and the heart.
Emotional/spiritual: heals the aura balancing the energy field around you. Promotes compassion and emotional healing. Good for bipolar disorder, depression, grief, trauma, anxiety, past, and letting go of ego. Enhances psychic abilities, such

as clairvoyance and mediumship. A stone of transformation, easing change, choice, decisions, death and dying, and bringing yin/yang balance and creativity. Makes it easier to focus and start the meditation process. Good for healing spiritual disappointments and regaining your inner connection to your higher self.

RUBY AND KYANITE IN FUCHSITE

Blue *kyanite* and red *ruby* growing through green *fuchsite*.
Common source: India
Astrological association: Aquarius
Chakras: heart, throat

HEALING QUALITIES

Emphasizes individual uniqueness.
Physical: good for muscles, RSI, carpal tunnel syndrome, detox, intestines, peristalsis, diarrhea, constipation, counteracting the effects of food poisoning and viral and bacterial infections of the bowel, fever, fertility, reproductive system, urinary function, kidneys, bladder, and liver.
Emotional/spiritual: truth, communication, and balance come from this unique, natural, combination. Helps you to reach a deep meditative state. Aids connection and communication with angels and spirit guides, and people. Enables you to talk your talk. Good for balance and extra-sensory perception. Helps you deal with abuse, insecurity, and nervousness, and speeds up karmic process, a feeling of I am what I am.

RUBY IN FUCHSITE

Fuchsite is a green variety of *muscovite* mica colored by the inclusion of chromium. Rarely, also contains red *ruby* crystals.
Common alternative name: ruby fuchsite
Common sources: Brazil, India, Pakistan, Russia, Zimbabwe
Astrological association: Aquarius
Chakra: heart

HEALING QUALITIES

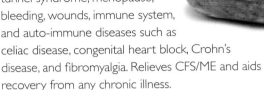

Brings renewal.
Physical: good for heart, blood, circulation, vitality, stamina, carpal tunnel syndrome, menopause, bleeding, wounds, immune system, and auto-immune diseases such as celiac disease, congenital heart block, Crohn's disease, and fibromyalgia. Relieves CFS/ME and aids recovery from any chronic illness.
Emotional/spiritual: helps to cleanse the heart from past hurts and blocks, clearing a space for fresh, new, loving, joyful, happiness. Balances emotions. Supports new relationships, connections, aura, psychic abilities, spirit contact, connection with totem animals, mediumship, and meditation. Breaks the pattern of insomnia.

RUBY IN KYANITE

Red *ruby* crystals growing through long blue column or blade-like *kyanite* crystals. Often tumbled (polished) when this structure is indeterminate, and looks more like a blue stone with red dots or blotches.
Common source: India
Astrological association: Gemini
Chakras: heart, throat

HEALING QUALITIES

Encourages communication, especially regarding matters held dear to your heart.
Physical: good for throat, heart, lungs, shoulders, neck and upper back, mouth, nose, nose bleed, infections, immune system, detox, lymphatic system, kidneys, and bladder.
Emotional/spiritual: enables emotional expression, encouraging yin/yang balance and the balance between female and male. Aids intuition and logic, realization of dark and light. Brings a calm, quiet confidence and inner strength to help you through the darkest times. Good for starting a meditation.

POLYCHROME JASPER

Jasper displaying earthy colors in swirls and sometimes patterns that accidentally appear symbolic.

Common alternative names: royal Savannah jasper, desert jasper

Common sources: Madagascar, USA

Astrological association: Leo

Chakra: base

HEALING QUALITIES

Keeps you on the path.

Physical: elixir makes a good general tonic to help keep you well. Promotes vitality and mobility of joints and limbs, reducing general aches and pains.

Emotional/spiritual: helps you to see the road ahead, spiritual signposts, and stepping stones. Keeps your feet on the ground. Inspires passion, drive, action, and creativity. Dispels lethargy, boredom, inaction, and the feeling of being trapped in your life. Good for change, confidence, self-respect, feeling uplifted, positivity, and direction. Promotes your connection to nature and aids Earth healing.

BLACK SEPTARIAN

Concretion forming nodules containing limestone, *aragonite*, *calcite*, *dolomite*, and *jasper*, sometimes with *barite* and other minerals.

Common alternative name: dragon's egg (not the only crystal called this), dragonstone (but it is not **dragonstone**)

Common source: Madagascar

Astrological association: Taurus

Chakra: base

HEALING QUALITIES

Promotes growing together.

Physical: good for flexibility of joints, muscles and bones (elixir), teeth (elixir as rinse/mouthwash), and melanoma.

Emotional/spiritual: groups, families, and teams can all benefit from this stone. A stone of transformation, bringing change in a safe and secure environment.

Grounding, protection, and psychic abilities are enhanced. Good for public speaking. Boosts sound therapy, art therapy, dance movement therapy, and NLP (neuro-linguistic programming). Promotes patience, endurance, tolerance, awareness of the environment, and emotional adaptability.

EPIDOTE IN QUARTZ

Clear or milky quartz with crystals of green *epidote* growing through.

Common alternative names: dream quartz (**actinolite in quartz** and **scenic quartz** are also called dream quartz), pistacite (in older books)

Common source: Brazil

Astrological association: Gemini

Chakra: brow

HEALING QUALITIES

Affects how we see things.

Physical: good for eyes, eyesight, nervous system, and brain. Helps those with Parkinson's disease, Alzheimer's disease, and thyroid issues.

Emotional/spiritual: encourages awareness, perception, seeing things from a different angle, letting go, good mental health, and healing.

ALMANDINE GARNET IN PYROXENE

Red *garnet* crystals in gray **pyroxene** matrix.

Common source: Alaska

Astrological associations: Virgo, Scorpio

Chakras: base, heart

HEALING QUALITIES

Grounds the emotions

Physical: good for vitality, heart, eyes, liver, pancreas, wounds, post-operative healing, and blood disorders.

Emotional/spiritual: promotes meditation and love, encouraging

emotions and improving intellect. Brings yin/yang balance, change, awareness of death and the dying process, self-confidence, inner belief, inner strength, emotional stability, emotional strength, wisdom, and experience.

SILVER LEAF JASPER

Jasper bearing silver to gray-green, black, and white swirling leaf-like patterns.

Common sources: France, Germany, India, Republic of South Africa, Russia, USA

Astrological associations: Leo, Libra

Chakras: base, crown

HEALING QUALITIES

Promotes independence and free thought.

Physical: general tonic for the body, muscles, flexibility, joints, movement.

Emotional/spiritual: encourages open-mindedness and self-assurance—no need to follow fashion, you can go your own way and carve your own path. Keeps you grounded as you discover new ways of doing things. Brings lifestyle stability regarding home, work, and recreation.

CINNABAR IN QUARTZ

Bright red dots of *cinnabar* growing in white *snow quartz*.

Common alternative names: cinnabrite, dragon's blood

Common source: China

Astrological association: Leo

Chakras: base, crown

HEALING QUALITIES

This is a merchant's stone.

Physical: good for blood, tissue repair, fertility, acne, spots, boils, and bacterial infection.

Emotional/spiritual: good for manifestation, transformation, magic, wealth, and dispelling a poverty mentality. Supports

dieting. Clears anger, fear, and resentment. Beneficial for merchants and teachers.

No elixir.

ABALONE SHELL (WHOLE)

Shell of a marine mollusk containing minerals that give a range of brilliant colors. Usually available as one side of shell, cleaned to show iridescence and beautiful rainbow colors. The whole shell is worked with to hold sage leaves or smudge stick in smudging ceremonies; because it represents water, it adds to the cleansing process of this ritual.

Common alternative names: ear shell, sea ears, and muttonfish or muttonshell in Australia, ormer in UK, perlemoen in Republic of South Africa, and pāua in New Zealand; sea opal (but this should not be confused with opalite, which is also known as sea opal but is man-made).

Common sources: Oceans around most continents, Australia, Japan, Mexico, New Zealand, USA (especially California), Vietnam

Astrological associations: Cancer, Scorpio, Aquarius, Pisces

Chakra: throat

HEALING QUALITIES

Associated with cleansing.

Physical: aids detox process, kidneys, and bladder function. Combats water retention. Reduces physical tension. Good for eyes, cataracts, hemeralopia, female reproductive system, womb, ovaries, fallopian tubes, and fertility.

Emotional/spiritual: good for femininity, and for releasing trauma and emotional toxins. Gives a connection to the past, childhood, past lives, and ancestors. Feeds the soul. Good for travel, sea voyages, protection.

CATACLASITE

A type of rock formed by fracturing and reconstituting during Earth's faulting activity, earthquakes, or meteorite impacts. Characterized by brecciated appearance and may show different colors, depending on the source.

Common alternative names: impact quartz, fault rock
Common sources: worldwide
Astrological associations: all
Chakras: all

HEALING QUALITIES

Something went wrong so let's start again and reset to factory settings.

Physical: brain, pineal gland, broken bones and fractures, and immune system.

Emotional/spiritual: calamities, stress, trauma, tremendous changes—this is a stone that really shakes you out of your comfort zone, bringing inspiration, innovative ideas, and a total make-over for your life. It's like hitting the reset button. Good for big decisions and life changes, releasing the past, and freeing you from your beliefs, thoughts, lifestyle, and things you have previously valued, enabling you to explore your possible futures with an open mind. Brings self-acceptance. Heals feelings left over from abuse in any form (physical, mental, sexual) and encourages you to re-take control of your life. Also good for those times when you find yourself in uncharted waters.

LEOPARD JASPER

A white variety of opaque *chalcedony* with distinct black spots.

Common alternative names: There is much confusion over leopard jasper names. This is NOT the same material as leopardskin jasper/leopard skin jasper, *Dalmatian stone*, poppy jasper, *picture jasper*, or *Picasso marble*. It is a different variety of *jasper*.

Common source: USA (especially Utah)
Astrological associations: Leo, Sagittarius
Chakras: base, crown

HEALING QUALITIES

Helps you to relish being alone.

Physical: a good physical pick-me-up when you're run down. Good for backache, muscle cramps, colds and flu, bladder, kidneys, liver, jaundice, MS, nerves, spleen, stomach, and wind pains.

Emotional/spiritual: helps you to enjoy your own company, dispels loneliness and boredom, and keeps your spirits up. Brings emotional balance, promoting yin/yang and an energetic stabilization to your aura. Good for setting goals, fasting, resolutions, and dowsing.

ANDEAN OPAL

A common *opal* (an opal without iridescence/fire), found only in the Andes mountains. Colors include blue, green, pink, and white.

Common alternative name: Peruvian opal
Only source: Andes mountains (Peru)
Astrological associations: Aries, Taurus, Cancer, Sagittarius
Chakra: heart

HEALING QUALITIES

A stone for problem solving and understanding.

Physical: good for detox, immune system, colds, flu, temperature balance, fever, hypothermia, metabolism, iron balance (deficiency/excess), fatigue, and preventing hair loss.

Emotional/spiritual: good for focusing, grounding, insight, divination, relaxation, meditation, mindfulness, understanding nutrition, resolving issues, and communication. Encourages you to talk your talk. Promotes creativity, connection with family and friends, as well as other people, and with happiness, shamanic journeying, hypnosis, and dreams.

MULTICOLORED

The multicolored section includes stones that come in a range of colors.

SCENIC QUARTZ

Quartz crystal with inclusions, which may include Iodolite (a Brazilian slang term, meaning "muddy"), *chlorite*, feldspar, ferrous minerals (such as *hematite* and **limonite**), *calcite*, *epidote*, *rutile*, illite, *smoky quartz*, phantoms, sand, clay, dirt. Looks like underwater scenes, landscapes, or gardens. Colors include green, mud brown to cream, orange, red.

Common alternative names: shaman dream stone, shamanic dream crystal, shaman stone, dream quartz (**actinolite in quartz** and **epidote in quartz** are also called dream quartz), inclusion quartz, included quartz, lodalite, lodelite, landscape quartz, garden quartz (misnomer—**garden quartz** is altogether different), arenite (misnomer—this is sandstone containing grains of quartz and other materials)

Common sources: Brazil, Madagascar, Uruguay

Astrological association: Pisces

Chakras: all

HEALING QUALITIES

Focuses on dreams, and an elixir is a good general tonic.

Physical: good for immune system, glands, liver, lungs, blood, oxygenation, eyes, eye disorders, eyesight, and mucous membranes. Alleviates inflammation, swelling, painful joints, arthritis, rheumatism, aching bones, headaches, and insomnia.

Emotional/spiritual: promotes dreams, dream recall, daydreaming, lucid dreaming, remote viewing, imagination, inspiration, and creativity. Raises consciousness, helps manifestation of desires and goals, and lifts a sagging personality. Good for meditation, Reiki, psychic abilities, awareness, and dealing with past-life and childhood trauma. Enhances shamanic practices, such as vision quests, journeying, healing, and connection to nature, spirits and totem animals. Removes attachments, attitudes, behaviors, feelings, self-limiting beliefs, and thoughts that cause disease in the bodymind. Opens the heart after relationship breakup or divorce. Good for youthful skin (topical elixir).

CAT'S EYE

Almost any color. This is not a type of crystal but an optical effect, chatoyancy, found in different polished crystals, resulting in a narrow band of light across the stone. Chrysoberyl displays the best effect, which can also appear in quartz, *selenite*, *gypsum*, *tourmaline*, *apatite*, corundum (*rubies* and *sapphires*), *emerald*, *danburite*, and more. Cat's eye should be used with the mineral/gem name for correct identification, such as *chrysoberyl* cat's eye.

Common sources: Brazil, China, India, USA

Astrological associations: Aries, Taurus, Leo, Capricorn

Chakra: sacral

HEALING QUALITIES

Brings good luck.

Physical: good for eyes, night vision, headaches, facial tics, detox, kidneys, bladder, liver, lymphatic system, spleen, and leukemia.

Emotional/spiritual: brings good luck, happiness, and serenity. Enhances intuition, awareness, protection, emotional balance, and self-esteem.

BLUE

BLUE SPINEL

Spinel is found as pebbles, cubes, twinned aggregates, and octahedral crystals in many colors. Blue spinel is commonly found in *white calcite* with *dolomite*, as in this photograph.

Common alternative name: often confused with *sapphire*

Common sources: Myanmar, Pakistan, Sri Lanka, Tanzania, Vietnam

Astrological associations: Gemini, Sagittarius

Chakras: throat, brow

HEALING QUALITIES

Helps you to fight your corner.

Physical: good for vitality and stamina, teeth and gums, eyes, and spine. Supports cancer treatment, dieting, and weight loss.

Emotional/spiritual: energizes any actions or thoughts. Brings abundance. Good for memory. Improves intellect. Good for relieving stress and depression. Enhances emotional backbone, inner strength, and determination to fight for your cause and conquer the challenges life puts in your path. Helps with addictions, such as smoking. Helpful for healing the aura and magnifying clairvoyance, clairsentience, clairaudience, and channeling.

LAZULITE

Masses, grains, pyramidal and tabular crystals in many shades of blue.

Common alternative name: often confused with lazurite—looks similar and comes from the same region

Common source: Afghanistan

Astrological associations: Gemini, Sagittarius

Chakra: brow

HEALING QUALITIES

This is the worry stone.

Physical: relieves photosensitivity (sun allergy). Good for glands, liver, broken and diseased bones, and teeth.

Emotional/spiritual: brings calm, stillness, and clarity. Good for stress, anxiety, panic attacks, and OCD. Enhances psychic abilities. Good for connecting to past life, ancient wisdom, and Akashic records. An excellent crystal to meditate with if you find it difficult to settle.

PAPAGOITE QUARTZ

Papagoite forms as clear sky-blue inclusions in quartz crystals, phantoms, miniature snowball-shaped formations, sheet-like veins, and druse.

Common sources: Republic of South Africa, USA

Astrological association: Sagittarius

Chakras: throat, brow

HEALING QUALITIES

Allows you to go with the flow.

Physical: good for pain relief, throat, brain, eyes, and muscles, and is especially helpful for disorders and diseases of the intestine (small and large, bowel, colon, and rectum).

Emotional/spiritual: brings harmony, a feeling of being at one with the flow of the Universe. A very Taoist crystal that creates a sense of there being no need to try to paddle upstream in life. Clears blocked energy in the throat chakra, allowing you to talk your talk. Transforms negative energy into positive, such as changing sorrow into happiness or anger into peaceful calm, resulting in an optimistic outlook on life. Creates a sense of well-being, promotes compassion for yourself and others, and removes antagonism and the feeling of being put upon or a victim mentality. Boosts psychic abilities, such as intuition and clairvoyance. Meditating with papagoite quartz allows you to see the beauty in everything. Drinking an elixir before meditation can bring a euphoric

sensation. Releases stress, brings joy, and builds relationships. Aids manifestation of goals and dreams.

AFGHANITE

Lath-shaped hexagonal crystals and rounded grains, deep blue to colorless.

Common source: Afghanistan
Astrological association: Scorpio
Chakra: brow

HEALING QUALITIES

Brings freedom from your own restrictions.

Physical: good for pain and fever relief, tissue regeneration, and insomnia.

Emotional/spiritual: releases self-limiting beliefs and thoughts, an attitude changer. Brings positivity, expands consciousness, and promotes clarity of thought, understanding, insight, and problem solving. Defeats a fear of the unknown. Good for control freaks, giving them the ability to let go. Aids psychic abilities and shamanic journeys.

BLUE QUARTZ (BRAZIL)

Coarse-grained, massive, cryptocrystalline form of quartz, not unlike aventurine quartz, colored by inclusions of blue minerals such as *dumortierite*, *indicolite*, and *sodalite*.

Common alternative names: Blue quartz covers a variety of minerals including sodalite and dumortierite as well as blue quartz, which displays what is known as the Rayleigh scattering effect, caused by tiny inclusions of riebeckite or tourmaline. One of my favorites is *blue quartz with indicolite tourmaline*. The variety described here is designated (Brazil) for clarity, although all the others mentioned can also come from that country.

Common sources: Austria, Brazil, Madagascar, USA
Astrological association: Gemini
Chakra: brow

HEALING QUALITIES

Gets the message across.
Physical: good for immune system, eyes, ears, nose, and throat.

Emotional/spiritual: soothes stress, calms fear, and aids relaxation, bringing tranquility. A stone for spiritual understanding, diplomacy, cool communication, and organizational skills. Good for aura, dreams, and psychic readings where you can clearly express the message.

DUMORTIERITE IN QUARTZ

Quartz crystals with vibrant pale blue to deep blue *dumortierite* inclusions.

Common alternative names: some confusion, as dumortierite itself is sometimes called dumortierite quartz, but the crystal referred to here is dumortierite in quartz; blue quartz (see **blue quartz (Brazil)**, below left)

Common source: Brazil
Astrological association: Leo
Chakra: throat

HEALING QUALITIES

Help for a fresh start.

Physical: good for immune system, stamina, chronic illness, digestion, nausea, diarrhea and constipation, IBS, Crohn's disease, and colitis.

Emotional/spiritual: gives confidence for new beginnings and new projects. Focuses the mind, bringing clarity and communication of ideas and thoughts, calming emotions, and encouraging patience. Helps you to take a minute rather than flying off the handle. An empowering crystal, it lifts depression and is good for studying, learning new skills and languages. Opens your mind to spiritual concepts and psychic abilities such as clairvoyance and clairsentience. Helps you to understand the cause of disease. Promotes love and the right relationship, attracting your true soul mate. Helps you to connect to spirit guides, angels, and other helpers.

BLUE BARITE

Tabular crystals forming flower or angel-wing patterns. Feels heavier than expected.

Common alternative names: barytes, baryte, barytine
Common source: Morocco
Astrological association: Aquarius
Chakra: throat

HEALING QUALITIES

Gives you a "go for it!" attitude where everything becomes possible.

Physical: good for eyesight, memory, Alzheimer's disease, dementia, detox, and reducing effects of radiation and EMF.

Emotional/spiritual: promotes friendship, harmony, and love. Gives insight into relationships. Helps catharsis, dispels shyness, and supports recovery from addiction. Works exceptionally well on the throat chakra and encourages communication of ideas and thoughts. Connects to angels and facilitates angelic messages. Gives a spiritual connection or direction and helps you to find your spiritual path in life.

SIEBER AGATE

Not an *agate* at all, this is an *obsidian*-like material from ancient copper works at least 1,400 years old, displaying electric-blue swirling patterns.

Common alternative name: blue slag (glass-like by-product left over after a desired metal has been separated from its raw ore. Slag is usually a mixture of metal oxides and silicon dioxide. However, slags can contain metal sulfides and elemental metals.)
Only source: Germany
Astrological associations: Sagittarius, Aquarius, Pisces
Chakras: throat, base

HEALING QUALITIES

Helps you to reconstitute thoughts and ideas into practical ways of working.

Physical: aids recovery after injury or surgery.

Emotional/spiritual: Helps you to shed tears and let go of the past, abandoning self-defeating behavior patterns and thoughts they have created. Good for dreams and dream recall, memory, and remembering past events and past lives. Encourages self-expression, talking your talk and walking your walk.

BLUE SCHEELITE

This is not a type of **scheelite** at all, but *dolomite* with *calcite* showing dramatic blue and white banding.

Common alternative name: lapis lace onyx (but note there is no *lapis lazuli* or *onyx* in this material)
Common source: Turkey
Astrological association: Sagittarius
Chakra: throat

HEALING QUALITIES

Physical: good for throat, infection, fever, tonsils, tonsillitis, laryngitis, pharyngitis, sinus issues, congestion, detox, menstrual cycle, and PMS.

Emotional/spiritual: calms emotions and soothes emotional pain and anguish. Good for communication, voice, expression, relationships, and yin/yang balance. Connects to the Tao and allows life to flow. Helps balance cycles and patterns. Promotes intent, movement, change through evolution not revolution, going with the flow, taking it easy, and a laid-back feeling. Good for removing writer's block and other creative obstacles, and a source of inspiration for authors, artists, sculptors, and other creators. Facilitates emotional detox—a clear-out and release of self-limiting beliefs and feelings. Eases stress, anxiety, and PTSD. Helps connection to angels.

BLUE APATITE

Forms blue to blue-green opaque to translucent prismatic crystals.

Common sources: Brazil, Madagascar

Astrological association: Gemini

Chakra: throat

HEALING QUALITIES

A crystal for individuality and communication of ideas.

Physical: good for weight loss and weight gain (as needed), throat, eyes, ears, and nose. Enhances taste, smell, hearing, and sight.

Emotional/spiritual: supports dieting. Reduces stress, anxiety, and panic attacks. Encourages change and the replacement of conflicting energies with harmony and peaceful progression. Helps you to find your life's path and have the courage to start taking steps along it. Helps you to overcome loss and disaster, giving you courage and strength to carry on. Improves intellect and the communication of ideas and concepts. Boosts the aura, giving a protective field around you—especially as you present innovative ideas to others. Dispels aggression, anger, judgmental attitudes, bias, jealousy, suspicion, and vengefulness as your energy permeates your audience.

BLUE HALITE

Cubic crystals, columnar structures, and masses displaying an illusion of blueness due to pleochroism—that is, the crystal absorbing different wavelengths of light at different angles in the crystalline structure.

Common alternative names: blue salt, common salt, natural salt, mineral salt, rock salt

Common sources: Austria, Canada, Germany, Poland, USA

Astrological associations: Cancer, Pisces

Chakras: brow, crown

HEALING QUALITIES

Clears away illusion.

Physical: good for glands, kidneys, and iodine absorption.

Emotional/spiritual: helps you to see who you are, your truth, and your inner self, and release old habits that are no longer useful. Helps to resolve childhood issues and other things from your past that hold you back. Promotes psychic abilities, awareness, and intuition. Cleanses and heals the aura. Aids contact and communication with spirit guides.

No elixir—salt dissolves in water.

BLUE CORAL

A species of coral forming massive skeletons made from *aragonite*.

Common sources: Indian Ocean, Pacific Ocean ranging from Australia to Japan

Astrological associations: Aquarius, Sagittarius

Chakra: throat

HEALING QUALITIES

Brings a child-like attitude.

Physical: keeps you healthy by benefiting mucous membranes. Generally good for liver, pituitary gland, pineal gland, and circulation.

Emotional/spiritual: good for children—traditionally, coral is a child's first stone. Allows play and exploration while casting an energy safety net around them. Also good for your own inner child. Dispels fear and insecurity. Brings organization and structure to muddled and time-challenged people. Promotes wealth and abundance in all areas. Boosts psychic awareness and skills, and aids communication of information gained through your psychic abilities.

BLUE ARAGONITE

Opaque acicular crystals and masses, pale blue almost white to turquoise blue.

Common source: China
Astrological association: Capricorn
Chakras: heart, throat, brow

HEALING QUALITIES

Empathy.

Physical: good for throat, heart, heart rate, blood pressure, lungs, and chest. Eases breathing, asthma, and bronchitis.
Emotional/spiritual: promotes understanding and expression of ideas, beliefs, thoughts, and feelings, allowing you to share them.
A great stone for teachers and healers. Encourages compassion, empathy, and sympathy. Eases stress, anxiety, panic attacks, depression, despair, bipolar disorder, and effects of draining responsibility, bringing comfort, calmness, relaxation, patience, and optimism. Boosts intuition and psychic abilities, and connects to guides and angels, so is good for spiritual readers such as tarot readers and mediums. In meditation can help you settle, let go of thoughts, and focus your mind. Promotes environmental issues and Earth healing, and soothes animals in distress.

BENITOITE

Flattened, pyramid-shaped, or tabular crystals, usually blue, but also colorless, pink, purple, and white, and occasionally part colored and part clear.
Common source: USA (especially California)
Astrological association: Virgo
Chakra: brow

HEALING QUALITIES

The crystal to get down and boogie with.
Physical: good for flexibility, movement, joints, muscles, limbs, stamina, bleeding and blood clotting, and recovery from injury.
Emotional/spiritual: promotes joy, happiness, fun, and a recognition of beauty. Alleviates fatigue. Good for dancers, musicians, actors, and other performers. Aids distant healing, telepathy, astral travel, and remote viewing.

TANZINE AURA QUARTZ

Quartz crystals bonded with *gold*, indium, and niobium.
Common alternative names: tanzan aura, indigo aura quartz, indigo aura crystal, titanium cobalt blue aura quartz, tanzanite quartz (but is not related to tanzanite at all!), azure aura quartz, celestial aura
Common source: USA
Astrological associations: all
Chakra: brow

HEALING QUALITIES

Brings a new perspective.
Physical: good for sight and skin. Eases headaches, earache, tinnitus, and inflammation. Good for endocrine system, hormones, metabolism, growth, sexual function, fertility, and insomnia.
Emotional/spiritual: eases shock, trauma, confusion, disorientation, and mood swings. Promotes intuition, inspiration, magic, transformation, imagination, new ideas, and change. Good for dreams and dream recall. Changes perception, giving you a new way to view your world.

DENIM LAPIS

Lapis lazuli is a combination of lazurite, *calcite*, and *pyrite* occurring in masses. The stone from Chile is lighter in color, due to a higher concentration of calcite and little if any pyrite, giving it a "denim" appearance.

Common source: Chile
Astrological associations:
Sagittarius, Pisces
Chakra: brow

HEALING QUALITIES

Promotes gentle awareness.
Physical: good for headaches, backache, back, bones, vitality, immune system, glands, insomnia, vertigo, dizziness, hearing loss, and Eustachian tube.
Emotional/spiritual: brings gentle realization of your personal reality, subtle shifts in awareness, and the ability to see things differently. Good for people who find their spiritual truth uncomfortable or shocking. Boosts creative expression, aids relaxation, and eases depression. Helps disorganized people find structure. Promotes psychic abilities, ideas, mental fortitude, yin/yang balance, and relationships.

BLUE JOHN

Massive, banded blue-purple, yellowish white, and colorless variety of *fluorite*.
Common alternative name: blue john fluorite
Only source: Peak District (Derbyshire, UK)
Astrological association: Scorpio
Chakra: brow

HEALING QUALITIES

Physical: alleviates the effects of EMF. Good for bones, joints, arthritis, rheumatism, teeth, lungs, breathing, asthma, and emphysema.
Emotional/spiritual: good for making plans, change, decisions, fortitude, and inner strength. Promotes imagination, invention, creativity, and the ability to see the future. Recommended for everyone working in tech industries, and those who use technology a lot in their jobs or day-to-day life, because it helps to absorb some of the positive ions emitted that make you feel low and keeps you feeling good and on top of any situation.

BLUE SMITHSONITE

Forms crusts and masses with or without drusy surfaces, botryoidal and reniform structures, and rhombohedral and (rarely) scalenohedral crystals.
Common source: Mexico
Astrological associations: Virgo, Pisces
Chakra: throat

HEALING QUALITIES

It's like having a psychic telephone.
Physical: good for immune system, auto-immune diseases, skin disorders, skin elasticity, spots, and acne.

Emotional/spiritual: promotes psychic communication, such as ESP and telepathy. Good for psychic readings, tarot readers, mediums, rune casters, and others exploring the psychic languages. Can help recovering alcoholics keep to their program.

GEM SILICA

Translucent, jelly-like type of *chrysocolla*.
Common alternative names: gem silica chrysocolla, chrysocolla chalcedony, gemmy chrysocolla
Common sources: Peru, USA (especially Arizona)
Astrological associations: Taurus, Gemini, Virgo
Chakras: throat, crown

HEALING QUALITIES

Speeds all healing
Physical: good for throat, vocal cords/nodes, voice, sore throat, laryngitis, and pharyngitis.
Emotional/spiritual: good for vocal expression, voice, singers, teachers, and chanting. Brings eloquence to public speakers. Good for visions, intuition, and clairvoyance. Combats anger and sarcasm. Brings emotional balance, peace, and tranquillity.

PRESELI BLUESTONE

The original circle at Stonehenge was built from this stone. Preseli bluestones contain spots or clusters or "flowers" of white plagioclase feldspar, as well as augite and possibly mica, giving the mysterious glittery effect seen in sunlight and some artificial light. Although called bluestones, their blue color shows only when wet. If dry, they appear green. The way water displays their color is linked strongly with their traditional healing applications in baths and elixirs. The color is also brought up by polishing.

Common alternative names: dolerite, blue stone, Stonehenge stone
Only source: Preseli mountains (Wales)
Astrological associations: Gemini, Pisces
Chakras: brow, throat

HEALING QUALITIES

An ancient voice calling from the distant past.
Physical: helps all physical healing (when added to bath water or as an elixir).
Emotional/spiritual: promotes change and fulfillment of your dreams, goals, and ideals. Aids divination. Facilitates rebirth and astral travel. Gives courage, and emotional strength that helps you to see the funny side of things. Brings peace of mind and calmness, and relief from phobias, insomnia, anxiety, and panic attacks. It benefits any type of public speaking. Linking to the priests of old (predating Druidism—these people worshiped the Ancestors), it offers "the favor of the ancestors or gods," bringing wealth and happiness and answering your prayers. The roughness you feel as you stroke it brings focus and concentration to the mind in meditation. Speaks of communication, especially of spiritual ideas. Brings feelings of compassion. Helpful in healing emotional wounds from relationship breakup. Promotes gallantry, nobility, magic, and protection, and boosts sexual attraction.

K2 JASPER

White granite containing contrasting small spheres of blue *azurite*. Technically, granite composed of quartz, plagioclase, *muscovite*, and **biotite**, but most commonly called *jasper*. Green markings are inclusions of *malachite*.

Common alternative names: K2 granite, raindrop azurite, azurite in granite
Only source: foothills of K2, the world's second-highest mountain (Skardu District, Pakistan)
Astrological associations: Gemini, Sagittarius
Chakras: base, third eye, crown

HEALING QUALITIES

Keeps your feet on the ground.
Physical: relieves any condition exacerbated by stress, such as skin conditions or asthma.
Emotional/spiritual: a centering, balancing stone for emotional control, empathy, and compassion. Good for decision making and communication, being a part of groups and teams, relating to crystal and indigo children, OCD, memory, childhood issues, and connecting with the past, past lives, and Akashic records. Helps you to stay grounded while exploring your spirituality and expanding your consciousness. Promotes dreams and dream recall while protecting you from nightmares and night terrors as you explore other realms in your dream world.

BLUE MOSS AGATE

Massive transparent or translucent blue, white, and clear moss-like patterned variety of *agate*.

Common source: Republic of South Africa
Astrological association: Virgo
Chakra: throat

HEALING QUALITIES

Releases trapped past emotions.
Physical: good for detox, immune system, dehydration, eyes, colds and flu, and skin disorders (topical elixir).

Emotional/spiritual: good for expression, talking your talk, confidence, and public speaking. Enables you to let go of anxiety, stress, and tension. Promotes wealth. Releases you from the past, childhood issues, and past lives.

BLUE JADE

Blue-colored *jadeite* forming masses.
Common alternative name: dianite (but this is not blue jade; it is an amphibole rock marketed as an imitation jade)
Common sources: Canada, Myanmar, Turkey, USA
Astrological associations: Aries, Taurus, Cancer, Libra
Chakra: throat

HEALING QUALITIES

The dream stone.
Physical: good for high blood pressure, post-operative recovery, swellings, male reproductive system, muscle cramps and restless leg syndrome, chronic pain relief, lungs, asthma, and bronchitis.
Emotional/spiritual: brings calming energy to any situation. Good for groups, mending damaged relationships, and enhancing peace and tranquillity. Promotes dreams, dream recall, and understanding. Good for creativity, friendship, and a long life. Helps you deal with divorce, justice, lawsuits, and feelings of guilt. Releases worry into useful, useable, positive energy, so is an excellent stone for anyone in the caring and healing professions.

ARGENTINIAN BLUE CALCITE

Translucent type of *blue calcite* forming masses.
Common alternative name: Lemurian aquatine calcite™
Common source: Argentina
Astrological association: Cancer
Chakra: throat

HEALING QUALITIES

Facilitates connection to the past.
Physical: good for throat conditions and infections.
Emotional/spiritual: good for optimism, memory, learning, ADHD, communication, and expression. Promotes intuition and dreams. A spiritually calming stone, good for nerves and nervousness. Alleviates anxiety, stress, and fear, and helps to resolve childhood issues. Connects to the past, past lives, ancient wisdom, Lemuria, Atlantis.

QUANTUM QUATTRO STONE

Forms aggregates and alluvial masses. A mixed stone consisting of *chrysocolla*, *shattuckite*, *dioptase*, and *smoky quartz*. Some samples may also contain *malachite*. Colors include various shades of blue, green, and gray.
Common alternative names: millennium stone, quantum quattro silica™
Common source: Namibia
Astrological associations: all
Chakras: all

HEALING QUALITIES

Aids communication from the heart and soul.
Physical: good for digestion, pain relief from blocked trauma (usually in the joints), arthritis, and immune system. Eases physical manifestation of stress-related conditions. Good for throat, side effects of chemotherapy, and detox.
Emotional/spiritual: allows you to release past trauma, grief, fear, judgmental attitudes, and jealousy, leading toward acceptance, forgiveness, kindness, mental clarity, and calmness. Helps with addiction and grounding. Gives protection from unhelpful energies. Supports intuition and problem solving. Focuses the mind on issues of the heart. Supports Earth healing and dreams, and speeds karma.

VIOLET

SIRIUS AMETHYST

Phantom amethyst crystals, some with inclusions of *goethite* and/or **lepidocrocite**; deep purple to almost colorless.

Common source: Kenya
Astrological associations: all
Chakras: brow, crown

HEALING QUALITIES

Helps you to understand your inner self.

Physical: weight loss, weight gain, immune system, infections

Emotional/spiritual: good for letting go of past hurts, dealing with addictions, addictive behavior, and eating disorders, and understanding current issues inherited from past lives. Gives courage and inner resolve to make changes and adapt to reach a place of harmony and peace where your inspiration can flourish.

AURALITE-23

Discovered in 2006 and commercially available only from 2011, surprisingly this is not a "new" crystal, but, at 1.5 billion years, one of the oldest on the planet! Primarily amethyst and *citrine* with up to 23 included minerals, including: titanite, cacoxenite, **lepidocrocite**, *ajoite*, *hematite*, *magnetite*, *pyrite*, *goethite*, **pyrolusite**, *gold*, *silver*, platinum, nickel, *copper*, iron, **limonite**, *sphalerite*, *covellite*, *chalcopyrite*, gilalite, *epidote*, *bornite*, and *rutile*.

Common alternative names: auralite, auralite amethyst, Canadian amethyst, kindred spirit stone
Only source: Auralite 23 mine (Thunder Bay, Canada)
Astrological associations: all
Chakras: all

HEALING QUALITIES

Promotes sharing and interacting.

Physical: good for balance. Alleviates headaches, eye strain, muscle aches, cramps, spasms, chronic illness.

Emotional/spiritual: good for groups, families, teams, clumsiness, and poor coordination. Promotes free thinking, breaking off the shackles of self-imposed limitations, beliefs, and unhealthy behavior patterns, enabling you to reach your dreams, ideals, goals, and aspirations. Brings awareness, connection to angels and spirit guides. Improves communication and connection to the past, past lives, ancientness, and karma. Relieves anger, fear, and tension. Helps meditation. Enables you to see arguments and disagreements from different sides.

CHEVRON AMETHYST

Crystals and masses with purple and white banding in chevron pattern. Although included with amethyst in *The Crystal Healer: Volume 1*, this crystal is listed separately here, as we now have more information about its qualities.

Common alternative names: banded amethyst, dogtooth amethyst
Common sources: Brazil, India, Russia, Zambia
Astrological associations: all
Chakras: brow, crown

HEALING QUALITIES

Go-to crystal for all chronic pain relief.

Physical: good for pain relief, resetting neurological pathways, neuropathic pain, nerves, nerve impulses, nervous system, detox, headaches, lungs, intestines, pancreas, liver, thymus, immune system, autoimmune diseases, HIV, AIDS, and eyes.

Emotional/spiritual: helps you explore your relationship with pain and how you feel about it. Good for emotional, mental, and spiritual pain relief, all psychic abilities, relieving tension, shamanic journeying, problem solving, and protection. Enhances spiritual healing.

LAVENDER AMETHYST

Forms lavender-colored crystals and clusters.
Common source: Madagascar
Astrological association: Pisces
Chakras: crown, throat

HEALING QUALITIES

Gives soft, gentle healing.
Physical: good for mild recurring headaches, coordination, muscles, limbs.
Emotional/spiritual: promotes dreams, intuition, coordination, centering, inspiration, free thinking. Can help with relationships and communication. Eases clumsiness, both physical and of thought. Aids gentle release of trapped issues and is excellent for amethyst trails in crystal healing (see page 31).

SUPER SEVEN

A type of included quartz appearing primarily purple in color, comprising seven different minerals: amethyst, cacoxenite, *goethite*, **lepidocrocite**, quartz, *rutile*, and *smoky quartz*. Due to the included minerals it may have areas that look brown, red, white, black, or colorless. Smaller pieces exhibit all the healing qualities, even though all seven different minerals may not be present in the specimen; the original mass gives super seven its wonderful healing potential.
Common alternative names: super 7, Sacred seven, the Melody stone (after the American crystal healer and author Melody)
Only source: Espirito Santo (Brazil)
Astrological associations: all
Chakras: all

HEALING QUALITIES

Brings spiritual connection.
Physical: good for the nervous system.
Emotional/spiritual: boosts the aura and helps you to see auras. Promotes a connection to spirit, psychic awareness, and truth. Encourages the advancement and fulfillment of dreams, goals, and ideals. Connected to karma, reincarnation, past lives, peace, harmony, and love. Good for telepathy, clairaudience, clairvoyance, creativity, and Earth healing.

GRAPE CHALCEDONY

Botryoidal purple *chalcedony*; also gray, green.
Common alternative names: botryoidal purple chalcedony, grape agate (misnomer), Indonesian purple chalcedony, Manakarra grape agate (misnomer)
Common source: Indonesia
Astrological association: Pisces
Chakra: crown

HEALING QUALITIES

A stone for community spirit.
Physical: alleviates the effects of aging and associated diseases, such as dementia and Alzheimer's, arthritis and rheumatism, reduced skin elasticity, and hair loss.
Emotional/spiritual: good for families, groups, teams, and collectives of any type and for any purpose. Brings people together for support in times of need. Good for spiritual development, tranquillity, calmness, and stillness, bringing a sweet taste to life. Alleviates anger, fear, irritability, distrust, melancholy, depression, despair, and bipolar disorder. Balances mind, body, and spirit, and opens heart center. Promotes sharing, self-assurance and confidence, meditation, intuition, and dreams.

PURPLE SCAPOLITE

Masses and prismatic crystals of lavender to purple.

Common sources: Canada, Europe, Madagascar, Pakistan, USA

Astrological association: Taurus

Chakras: brow, crown

HEALING QUALITIES

Good if you feel like you're carrying the world on your shoulders.

Physical: good for eyes (cataracts, glaucoma, iris issues), lessening incontinence, bones, veins, and post-operative care.

Emotional/spiritual: good for problem solving, emotional support, direction, focus, lateral thinking, making a change, achieving goals, and letting go of past issues. Stops you worrying too much about what others think of you and what you do. Helpful for dyslexia.

PURPLE RAY OPAL

White and violet (which can be purple to lilac and blue) *common opal* (no fire).

Common alternative names: violet flame opal, Mexican purple opal

Common source: Mexico

Astrological associations: Aries, Gemini, Cancer, Virgo

Chakra: crown

HEALING QUALITIES

Brings gentle release and transformation.

Physical: good for fertility, digestive system, absorption of nutrients, immune system, temperature control, fever, hypothermia, hair loss, eyes, eyesight, the effects of EMF, pancreas, and diabetes. Improves taste.

Emotional/spiritual: eases changes that could be traumatic. Good for trauma and shock. Helps mediumship and connection to spirit, angels, spirit guides, helpers, and totem animals. Transforms painful emotions and hurts, such as anger and fear, into positive feelings and actions demonstrating love and compassion. Heals

the aura and protects your energy. Acts as a protective shield, allowing you to create effective personal boundaries. Brings awareness, spiritual strength, digestion of new ideas and concepts, visions.

TIFFANY STONE

Masses consisting of *purple fluorite*, quartz, bertrandite, *opal*, *chalcedony*, and manganese oxide in swirls of purple, white, cream, black, and occasionally blue.

Common alternative names: opalized fluorite, ice-cream opal, purple opal, bertrandite (misnomer—there is only a small percentage in Tiffany stone), purple bertrandite (misnomer), ice-cream opalite, opal fluorite, purple passion, beryllium ore, Utah lavender

Only source: Brush Wellman Beryllium Mines (Utah, USA)

Astrological association: Pisces

Chakra: crown

HEALING QUALITIES

Helps you to find your purpose in life.

Physical: good for detox process, kidneys, liver, joints, tendons, ligaments, muscles, arthritis, tennis elbow, and tendonitis.

Emotional/spiritual: promotes dreams, intuition, and intellect. Good for teachers, students, the mind, clarity of thought, and energy cleansing. Breeds optimism and quashes negativity, enabling you to see the beauty in everything. Releases stagnant energy blocks, changing self-limiting behavior patterns, allowing you to enjoy life to the full. Enhances passion and sex drive. Supports major life changes and enables you to see the right direction for you. Good for relationships, including family, career, and business.

No elixir.

PURPLE CHALCEDONY

Lavender to violet variety of *chalcedony*.

Common alternative names: Aztec, royal purple Aztec chalcedony

Common source: USA

Astrological associations: Cancer, Sagittarius

Chakra: crown

HEALING QUALITIES

Promotes connection.

Physical: good for intra-epithelial nerve endings and for refining sensations of heat, cold, pain, touch, and pressure. Helps reduce effects of dementia.

Emotional/spiritual: brings a sense of surroundings and aura. Promotes kindness, generosity, compassion, receptivity, a sense of belonging, resolution of childhood issues, letting go of the past, and spiritual expression. Brings mental stability.

STICHTITE

Rich purple and lilac to rose-pink masses in plate-like layers and occasionally other forms. It is an alteration of chromite containing *serpentine*.

Common source: Tasmania (Australia)

Astrological association: Virgo

Chakra: heart

HEALING QUALITIES

Brings love to the fore.

Physical: Good for heart, blood pressure, muscle tear, hernia, rupture, skin, elasticity of skin, gingivitis, and gum disease. Aids recovery from any illness that has made you run-down. Dissolves stress-related headaches.

Emotional/spiritual: releases emotions trapped in the heart, allowing you to express your love. As love flows, so energy flows and positive changes occur around you. Promotes a give-and-take attitude, sincerity, closeness, and companionship. Good for children's behavior issues and ADHD. Raises the spirit and helps to get you out into the world after a period of confinement. Supports

self-love. Helpful for eating disorders such as anorexia and bulimia.

BRANDBERG AMETHYST

Natural mixture of amethyst, clear quartz, and *smoky quartz* that may have phantoms, enhydros, inclusions (including **lepidocrocite**, *goethite*, and occasionally *epidote*), and **skeletal quartz** crystals, which form prismatic crystals, stubby crystals, druses, and massive forms, all sometimes creating pyramid clusters. Colors vary depending on each crystal's composition and can be purple, clear, brown, or tinted yellow or gray. Translucent to transparent.

Common alternative names: Brandberg quartz, Brandenberg (common misspelling) amethyst, Brandenberg quartz

Only source: the Brandberg, Namibia's highest mountain

Astrological associations: Sagittarius, Pisces

Chakras: all, especially crown, brow, heart

HEALING QUALITIES

Brings divine love.

Physical: good for nervous system (can help to re-pattern nerve impulses), immune system, digestion, and CFS/ME.

Emotional/spiritual: enables deep healing of the heart. Mends a broken heart, releasing the ties that bind and freeing you to find your soul partner. Brings balance and harmony, relieving stress. When stress is unavoidable, helps you to keep cool under pressure. Opens energy pathways, manifesting abundance, creativity, joy, and inner peace. Provides a bridge to spirit guides, angels, and other helpers. In meditation, can help you to find hidden answers. Aids recovery from addictions.

BUSTAMITE WITH SUGILITE

Combination of pale to deep pink, red, brownish red, and red brown bustamite with lavender to purple *sugilite*, usually as masses. May also include blue richterite.

Common source: Republic of South Africa
Astrological associations: Virgo, Libra
Chakras: heart, crown

HEALING QUALITIES

Affects dreams.
Physical: good for adrenal glands, pineal gland, pituitary gland, headaches, and minor aches and pains.
Emotional/spiritual: opens your mind, expands consciousness and mind-body link in disease, and is therefore helpful in the treatment of most illnesses. Gives a sense of security, confidence, courage, and spatial awareness. Good for children, ADHD, crystal children, indigo children, children with learning difficulties, dyslexia, and epilepsy. Encourages playfulness, joy, vitality, sexuality, dreams, creativity, and eccentricity—it helps you be who you are. Releases energy blocks, allowing you to let go of hostility, anger, jealousy, prejudice, and despair.

PHOSPHOSIDERITE

Occurs as purple to peachy pink, brownish yellow, moss green, and colorless botryoidal or reniform masses and crusts with a radial-fibrous structure; tabular or stout prismatic crystals.

Common sources: Argentina, Chile, Germany, Portugal, USA
Astrological association: Virgo
Chakra: heart

HEALING QUALITIES

Brings out your nurturing side.
Physical: reduces insomnia. Good for stomach, adrenal glands, thyroid, combating aging and hair loss, and promoting skin elasticity and youthful appearance. Alleviates colds and flu.

Emotional/spiritual: good for self-love, care for the soul, spiritual love, work-life balance, stress relief, youthful attitude to life, and making you feel younger and bestowing confidence. Gives hope and heals issues from the past, including childhood and past lives. Encourages you to let go of relationships that are holding you back. Good for past-life work and recall. Helps you to focus your heart in meditation. Aids psychic awareness and connection to spirit. Good for partnerships in both business and life path.

AMETHYST ZEBRA STONE

Very distinct bands of deep purple and white within opaque amethyst crystals.

Common alternative names: dark chevron amethyst, deep banded amethyst
Common source: Mali
Astrological associations: Virgo, Aquarius, Capricorn, Pisces
Chakra: crown

HEALING QUALITIES

Encourages action.
Physical: supports all pain relief and is especially good for chronic pain relief. Good for tension headaches, detox, lungs, intestines, pancreas, liver, thymus, immune system, autoimmune diseases, and eyes.
Emotional/spiritual: promotes action and movement as a route to ease and heal stress, tension, anxiety, depression, and bipolar disorder. Helps problem solving. Gives protection. Aids psychic abilities, such as clairvoyance and dowsing, and shamanic journeying, and connects you to spiritual healing.

INDIGO GABBRO

Black, white, gray colors showing a lavender to purple hue in sunlight. Massive coarse-grained form of basalt containing some, or all, of a mixture of feldspar, plagioclase (commonly, *labradorite* or bytownite), clinopyroxene (augite), *chlorite*, *muscovite*, *serpentine*, *magnetite*, and other minerals. Some specimens may be magnetic.

Common alternative names: purple gabbro, mystic merlinite™ (do not confuse with *merlinite*)
Common source: Madagascar
Astrological association: Gemini
Chakras: crown, base

HEALING QUALITIES

Tells you to follow your heart.
Physical: helps with symptoms of menopause, period pains, inflammation, and infection, and generally boosts the immune system. The magnetic gabbro also aids arthritis, rheumatism, and joint pains.
Emotional/spiritual: gentle energy makes this is a real follow-your-heart stone, helping to ground your spirituality into your daily life. Brings up deep-rooted issues that can make you aware of your dark side, encouraging you to let them go and achieve yin/yang balance. Good for releasing energy blockages that create anger, breaking repeated patterns, cycles, and detrimental personality traits. A great stone for underdogs in any situation, bringing strength and courage. Helps you to see the opportunities that surround you. Also helps emotions and tolerance. Promotes psychic abilities, especially communication. Good for dreams and meditation.

KAMMERERITE

Rare red, rose-purple, purple variety of *clinochlore*, exhibiting hexagonal pyramid-type crystals. Recently discovered massive form has rich purple color with white patterns.
Common sources: Norway, Turkey, USA
Astrological associations: Virgo, Pisces
Chakras: brow, crown

HEALING QUALITIES

Reveals inner truth.
Physical: good for sensations, nerve receptors, skin, neuropathic pain, muscular and joint pain, male reproductive system, bacterial infections, and stress-aggravated conditions.

Emotional/spiritual: helps you to see the truth in any situation. Encourages exploration of the inner self and expands consciousness. Surpasses prejudice and narrow-mindedness, so helping decision making. Aids meditation and distant healing and cleanses the aura.

PURPLE THULITE

A pinky lavender variety of *zoisite*.
Common alternative name: purple zoisite
Common source: Norway
Astrological associations: Taurus, Gemini
Chakra: heart

HEALING QUALITIES

Brings calm and gentle energy to ease change.
Physical: good for digestion, stomach, intestines, acid indigestion, reflux, flatulence, and wind pains.
Emotional/spiritual: pride, narcissism, self-importance, and snobbery are replaced by modesty and humility. Promotes eloquence, so is good for actors and performers. Gives focus and direction, helping you to find your path in life, and banishes aimlessness. Makes change easier and more comfortable as you discover your inner self.

PRAIRIE TANZANITE

Purple variety of *zoisite*. A mixture of *tanzanite* and white *jade*.

Common source: USA (especially Wyoming)

Astrological associations: Gemini, Sagittarius, Capricorn

Chakra: crown

HEALING QUALITIES

Provides a stress safety net.

Physical: good for menopause, irregular periods, vaginal dryness, hot flashes, chills, night sweats, slowed metabolism, thinning hair, dry skin, nerves, movement, insomnia, weight loss.

Emotional/spiritual: this is the stone you need when you feel as if your life is heading downward in ever-decreasing circles. Acts as your safety net, calming panic and anxiety and easing stress. A mood balancer, it helps bipolar disorder, and turns confusion and worry into a positive vibe that elevates the spirit and brings you back to the surface. Good for balancing emotions, meditation.

RITZULLITE

I wouldn't normally have included this stone, but I felt particularly drawn to it and how it so rapidly brings emotions and breathing under control. I will update this information on my website as available (see page 160). Massive cryptocrystalline, possibly quartzite, variety with unknown inclusions. I found this at the Tucson Gem and Mineral Show 2018 and cannot find any information or anything similar to compare it to. The name is from the dealer. The information is from the crystal.

Common source: India

Astrological association: Virgo

Chakras: heart, brow, crown

HEALING QUALITIES

Clears emotions.

Physical: good for heart, chest, lungs, diaphragm, muscles, throat, tongue, and breathing.

Emotional/spiritual: connects you to your inner child and inner self. Brings emotional hurts to the surface so they can be released, allowing you to move on, create new relationships, and learn how to smile again. A calming crystal that can help you to remain stable and centered while making challenging choices. Connects you to your higher self.

CACOXENITE IN AMETHYST

Golden radial structures included within amethyst crystal.

Common alternative names: amethyst cacoxenite, cacoxenite

Common source: Brazil

Astrological associations: Sagittarius, Pisces

Chakra: crown

HEALING QUALITIES

A stone for exploring the dark side.

Physical: good for tissue repair, healing injury, post-operative healing.

Emotional/spiritual: the name comes from the Greek meaning "bad guest," referring to the loss of quality of iron its presence in iron ore caused. Helps you to see and explore your dark side. It is part of you, and in your unconscious mind it affects your decisions. Cacoxenite in amethyst brings your dark side into consciousness so you can use the parts that are helpful and consciously accept and let go of those that aren't. Helps you to see the positive side to everything and brings new ideas into a different dimension. Exposes the mind-body-spirit connections in any dis-ease, making effective treatment easier. Helpful for breaking addictions.

VIOLET SAPPHIRE

Violet to purple corundum hexagonal crystals, usually with flat terminations.

Common alternative name: oriental amethyst

Common sources: India, Madagascar, Sri Lanka

Astrological associations: Virgo, Libra, Sagittarius, Capricorn

Chakras: brow, crown

HEALING QUALITIES

Brings the wisdom to lead.

Physical: good for glands, glandular fever, blood disorders, hormones, infection, nausea, stomach, backache, and boils. Can be used as an astringent to tighten and close skin pores.

Emotional/spiritual: encourages fulfillment of ambition, intuition, having dreams and goals, emotional balance, and control of desire, which are all qualities for leadership. Develops connection to the ancient wisdom of the Akashic records. Enhances spiritual connection, meditation, and contact with your spirit guides. Helps you to see the beauty in everything around you. Helps alleviate depression, narrow-mindedness, unhappiness, and aging. Great for worriers, bringing joy and fun into your life.

LEPIDOLITE IN QUARTZ

Pink to purple layered plates of *lepidolite* in and/or on quartz crystal.

Common source: Brazil

Astrological association: Libra

Chakra: heart

HEALING QUALITIES

A stone for mental wellness.

Physical: improves all stress-aggravated conditions, digestion, constipation, tendonitis, muscles, cramps, ligaments, nerves, and erratic heartbeat.

Emotional/spiritual: good for mental health and healing, excessive worry,

nervousness, anxiety, depression, bipolar disorder, schizophrenia, mania, addictions, addictive personalities, addictive behavior, OCD, change, and transition such as death/dying. Promotes trust, calmness, astral travel, rebirth, and a fresh start.

VERA CRUZ AMETHYST

Archetypal quartz hexagonal, transparent-translucent terminated crystals; pale lavender to violet color from iron impurities, typical of amethyst.

Only source: Vera Cruz (Mexico)

Astrological associations: Virgo, Aquarius, Pisces

Chakras: brow, crown

HEALING QUALITIES

Brings tranquil balance.

Physical: good for headaches, hearing, immune system, and endocrine system.

Emotional/spiritual: promotes a calm, peaceful balance to your being. Balances right-brain and left-brain activity, so good for intuition and creativity with intellect and logic. Helps insomnia, bereavement, addictions, and clumsiness. Enhances your internal pendulum, giving you spiritual guidance, improved awareness, protection, and spiritual growth. Focuses the mind in meditation. Connects to angels and encourages humility.

PURPLE MEXICAN FLUORITE

Purple fluorite crystals appear to grow as steps or citadels, often white or clear underneath deep purple.
Only source: Mexico
Astrological associations: Capricorn, Pisces
Chakra: crown

HEALING QUALITIES

Promotes learning new lessons.
Physical: good for bones, bone marrow, teeth, and gums.
Emotional/spiritual: good for study, learning, education, courses, classes, workshops, new skills, abilities, and protection. Reduces the effects of positive ions emitted from computer and TV screens. Seems to help most dis-ease on a deeper spiritual level. Eases communication, psychic abilities, seeing into the future, prophecy, and clairvoyance.

AMETHYST ELESTIAL CRYSTAL

An overgrowth of terminations on a natural crystal structure, colored lavender to deep purple by the inclusion of iron.
Common sources: Brazil, India, Madagascar, Namibia.
Astrological associations: Gemini, Scorpio, Aquarius
Chakra: crown

HEALING QUALITIES

Encourages the unexpected.
Physical: good for fitness, anti-aging, vitality, cysts, and tumors.

Emotional/spiritual: offers spiritual protection to explore, discover things for yourself, learn and remember what it is you have learned, understand the cost of action and reaction, and how decisions may affect not just you but those around you, too. Helps organization and order, banishing chaos and impatience, bringing calm. Excellent for healers, as it seems to amplify the healing intent regardless of the modality. Enhances connection to angels and spirit guides.

LITHIUM QUARTZ

Trade name for pink/purple translucent to opaque variety of quartz, displaying typical hexagonal terminated crystals with lithium, manganese, aluminum, iron, and sometimes kaolinite inclusions.
Common alternative name: lithium included quartz
Common source: Brazil
Astrological association: Aquarius
Chakra: brow

HEALING QUALITIES

Heals the mind.
Physical: picks you up when you're feeling run down with colds, flu, tummy bugs, and infections.
Emotional/spiritual: brings calm and clarity of thought to help mental

health and healing. Alleviates stress, depression, despair, addiction, nervousness, anxiety, unhelpful behavior patterns, damaged personal relationships, anger, compulsive behavior, OCD, bipolar disorder, and other mental illness. When the mind is balanced, it promotes intuition, dreams, and dream interpretation. Can be employed in Earth healing.

WHITE/CLEAR

SPODUMENE

Forms flattened prismatic crystals, vertically striated. Clear or may have yellow tint; other colors include lilac and pink *kunzite*, green *hiddenite*, blue, sometimes bi- or tri-colored crystals.

Common sources: Afghanistan, Pakistan

Astrological association: Scorpio

Chakras: heart, brow, crown

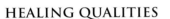

HEALING QUALITIES

Helps to remove energy blocks that cause physical dis-ease.

Physical: good for heart, blood pressure, hormones, menstrual cycle, period pains, effects of pollution, skin, and lungs. Promotes a youthful appearance and helps all stress-related conditions.

Emotional/spiritual: encourages many ways to avoid dis-ease. Good for intellect, intelligence, study, personal spiritual understanding, and emotional control. Helps to temper or satisfy cravings. A comforting stone that dissipates childishness and irresponsibility. Alleviates depression, compulsive behavior, OCD, addictions, and PMS. Boosts confidence, female sexuality, self-worth, expression, and love, and removes obstacles from your path and negativity in your environment. Provides protection. Centering in meditation and spiritual understanding.

MOTHER OF PEARL

The lining of sea shells has a high mineral content. The multicolored blue/green/purple/yellow variety is known as **abalone shell**.

Common sources: worldwide

Astrological association: Aquarius

Chakras: sacral, heart, brow

HEALING QUALITIES

Promotes feminine qualities in everyone.

Physical: like a psychic air purifier, it helps to reduce the effects of irritants, allergens, pollutants. Helps wound healing.

Emotional/spiritual: brings a calm, tranquil energy to ease agitation, tension, and stress. Helps to mend a broken heart. Dispels poverty mentality, allowing wealth to accumulate. Offers the freedom to let go, to release material things and emotional issues from the past. Promotes femininity, intuition, sensitivity, imagination, female sexuality, adaptability, decision making, faith, charity, innocence, and personal integrity. Focuses your attention on detail. Creates a protective energy shield to repel negativity. Provides protection for travelers.

LEMURIAN QUARTZ CRYSTAL

Clear quartz hexagonal crystals with small terminations and "bar code" striations on sides. See also Lemuria in the glossary (page 155).

Common alternative names: Lemurian clear quartz, Lemurian rock crystal, Lemurian crystal

Common sources: Brazil, Columbia, Russia

Astrological associations: all

Chakras: all

HEALING QUALITIES

Regarded by crystal healers as the most powerful of the healing quartzes; allows connection to the wisdom of ancient civilizations.

Physical: channels any energy, so will help with any condition. Specifically, helps all pain and discomfort, diabetes, vitality, ear infections, tinnitus, hearing and balance, general malaise, MS, CFS/ME, issues with the spine, obesity, and weight loss.

Emotional/spiritual: boosts vivacity, focusing the mind, opening the heart, dispelling negativity, and improving the quality of life, making you feel happier and re-energizing your zest for life in all situations. Adds focus in meditation.

SCOLECITE

Variety of *zeolite* forming sprays of acicular, prismatic needle crystals with slanted terminations, striated parallel to the length of the needle, radiating groups, and fibrous masses. Usually white, off-white, or colorless, but can also be pink, salmon, red, and green.

Common source: India
Astrological association: Capricorn
Chakras: brow, crown

HEALING QUALITIES

Brings inner peace.

Physical: good for brain, eyes, spine alignment, getting rid of intestinal parasites such as tape worm and round worm, lungs, atherosclerosis, circulation, dealing with blood clots, bruising, and wounds.

Emotional/spiritual: brings serenity, relaxation, and a sense of tranquil peace. Through the crown chakra, creates a connection for lovers sharing thoughts and ideas as well as love. Promotes team spirit and inspires love, creating united families, groups, organizations, and other functioning units. Helps insomnia, dreams, and dream recall and interpretation. Good for spirit communication, mediums, and shamanic journeying. Brings its peaceful energy to Earth healing rituals.

HIMALAYAN DIAMOND

Small, perfect, clear, bright, stubby, double-terminated quartz crystals.

Common alternative name: pakimer diamond
Only sources: Himalaya mountains, India, Pakistan
Astrological associations: Cancer, Scorpio, Sagittarius
Chakra: crown

HEALING QUALITIES

Allows you to be in the moment.

Physical: good for detox, metabolism, headaches, infectious diseases, aging, longevity.

Emotional/spiritual: aids a relaxing spiritual detox, releasing fear, stress, and tension. Opens the spirit to spontaneity and new possibilities. Boosts memory, psychic abilities, distant healing, and attunements. Good for distant lovers, travelers, friends to keep in touch energetically.

PHILLIPSITE

A rare variety of *zeolite* forming radiating aggregates, spherical-type structures, pseudo-orthorhombic, tetragonal, roughly cubic, and twin crystals that have penetrated themselves, sometimes forming a cross. Can form an encrusting precipitate around hot springs or brittle white crystals filling cavities and fissures in basalt. Colors include bright white, colorless, pink, oranges, reds, and light yellow.

Common sources: Australia, Canada, Germany, Italy, USA
Astrological association: Cancer
Chakra: crown

HEALING QUALITIES

Boosts connection to your inner self. Helps you to find your own answers, your own ways of coping, and your unique path to success.

Physical: good for general aches and pains, chronic pain, neuropathic pain, post-operative pain, tissue repair, injury, post-operative recovery, transplants, plastic surgery, and swelling.

Emotional/spiritual: boosts perception and enhances awareness. Keeps you in touch with the zeitgeist, helping you to make good choices. Promotes love, teaching, and sharing knowledge, and aids communication, allowing you to talk your talk. Balances intuition and intellect, creativity and rationality, and supports common sense. Encourages compassion. Helps psychic abilities, particularly clairaudience, and offers protection.

OPALIZED WHITE AGATE

Massive form of *chalcedony* with patterns or banding, some or all transformed to translucent to transparent *common opal*, without fire.

Common source: Republic of South Africa
Astrological association: Gemini
Chakra: crown

HEALING QUALITIES

Promotes self-love.

Physical: good for stiffness, intestines, gastroenteritis, IBS, wind pains, pancreas, circulation, vitality, lymphatic system, varicose veins, eyes, and eyesight.

Emotional/spiritual: brings love and nurture to create emotional security, balanced energy, and harmony. Stabilizes sexual energy. Brings faithfulness in relationships. Strengthens your aura and acts as a shield, allowing you to build your confidence behind it and develop your natural talents. Brings stillness to any meditation practice and expands awareness, helping with self-diagnosis. Aids channeling.

WHITE MOONSTONE

Variety of feldspar exhibiting chatoyancy.
Common source: India
Astrological associations: Cancer, Libra, Scorpio
Chakra: sacral

HEALING QUALITIES

Calms emotions.

Physical: good for vitality, fertility, pregnancy, childbirth, female hormones, menstrual cycle and menstruation, period pains, menopause, skin (topical elixir), hair (topical elixir), eyes, youthful appearance, and constipation. Reduces water retention, swelling, pain of insect bites, and anaphylactic shock (extreme allergic reaction). Boosts circulation.

Emotional/spiritual: good for the emotions, calming, soothing, gently letting go of blocks, and PMS. Connected to life cycles and the

moon and lunar cycles. Brings compassion, peace of mind, and promotes a caring attitude. Encourages wisdom and insight to see and understand who you truly are, allowing positive changes, new beginnings, and endings of relationships that don't support your ongoing development. Dispels oversensitivity and pessimism. Supports intuition, creativity, confidence building, composure, good luck, and a happy home. Offers protection for travelers. Boosts sexuality and passion.

ELESTIAL QUARTZ

An overgrowth of natural terminations on the body and face of a natural crystal structure.

Common alternative names: jacare crystal (*jacaré* means "alligator" in Portuguese, which is spoken in Brazil), etched crystal
Common sources: Brazil, India, Madagascar, Namibia, USA
Astrological association: Gemini
Chakras: all

HEALING QUALITIES

Brings transformation.

Physical: good for balance, inner ear, vertigo, tinnitus, headaches, Ménière's disease, and sense of taste.

Emotional/spiritual: promotes change, transition from one phase of life to another; just as the alligator goes from land to water, so these crystals help you transform from one emotional mind-set to another. Links emotions and intellect. Helps you to let go of emotional baggage, confusion, judgmental attitudes, and rigidity, and express emotions as well as physical feelings and your needs, so recommended for anyone in hospital or care. Opens the gates to spiritual advancement. Boosts awareness, and psychic abilities. Ties in with an understanding of reincarnation. Aids finding a still and centered place in your mind during meditation and exploring your inner self, your own world in which your soul or spirit resides. Good for contacting ancestors and connecting to past lives and ancient wisdom. Speeds karma (doesn't change it). Good for mental health and healing, recovery from addictions.

OPALIZED JASPER

Conglomerate of *jasper*—some of which is opalized—chert, and *sandstone*.
Common alternative name: wonder stone
Common source: India
Astrological associations: Aries, Leo, Scorpio
Chakra: sacral

HEALING QUALITIES

A nurturing stone.
Physical: general tonic for the body. Boosts immune system and wards off minor ailments such as colds and flu, aches, and general minor pains.

Emotional/spiritual: good for creativity, insight, seeing things how they really are, making the best of things and bringing disparate groups of people together.

SKELETAL QUARTZ

A variety of **elestial quartz** that has short, stubby, **double-terminated quartz** crystals with gaps in their structure due to periods of unstable growth. These usually appear in a triangular "window" form within the crystal structure, characterizing its skeletal appearance.
Common alternative names: fenster quartz, window quartz (*fenster* means "window" in German). Elestial and skeletal quartz are often confused. They are different. Both are elestial, but skeletal has the gaps in its structure, whereas elestial does not.
Common sources: Afghanistan, Brazil, India, Morocco, Namibia, Pakistan, USA
Astrological associations: Scorpio, Sagittarius, Capricorn
Chakra: crown

HEALING QUALITIES

Helps you to look within, as if creating a window to the soul.
Physical: boosts most physical healing and can be applied to any area in a crystal healing treatment.
Emotional/spiritual: encourages you to explore your inner self, seeing yourself as you really are. Good for emotional healing, letting go of the past, and shedding everything that holds you back. Releases addictions to people, behaviors, and substances. Improves clairvoyance and connection to past lives. Helps karmic healing, spiritual learning, and shamanic vision quests.

SILVER AVENTURINE

Quartz variety, with inclusions of mica giving a speckled or sparkly effect.
Common source: India
Astrological association: Aries
Chakras: heart, crown

HEALING QUALITIES

Encourages you to learn from the tortoise and the hare.
Physical: good for muscles, stamina, reactions, lungs, heart, adrenal glands, and urogenital systems.
Emotional/spiritual: brings success at your own pace. Keeps you calm, relaxed, and stress free as you have fun, find happiness in the things you do, and enjoy life. Protects and soothes emotions and supports emotional endurance.

AGRELLITE

Pearly white fibrous masses, sometimes with grayish, brownish, or greenish tint.
Common sources: Canada, Russia, USA
Astrological association: Aquarius
Chakras: throat, brow

HEALING QUALITIES

Encourages altruism.
Physical: boosts immune system. Combats infection and reduces swelling. Helps detox. Counters the side effects of chemotherapy.
Emotional/spiritual: dispels narcissistic tendencies. Digs deep into your being to release long-hidden thoughts and feelings, resolving the need for temper, anger, and

harshness. Opens the door to an altruistic, compassionate, and heart-felt new beginning. Once the deep blocks are removed, anything becomes possible. Good for writer's block and other creative blocks. Aids psychic diagnosis in all cases.

ALBITE

Variety of feldspar forming tabular and plate-like crystals and masses. Usually white, but can be blue, gray, brown, pink, red, or colorless.

Common alternative name: *cleavelandite* is the platy variety (platy refers to the form looking like the pages for a book) of albite

Common sources: worldwide—especially Brazil, USA

Astrological associations: Libra, Aquarius

Chakras: solar plexus, heart, throat, brow

HEALING QUALITIES

Encourages team work.

Physical: good for eyes, blood flow, detox, and arteriosclerosis. Helps identify and ease the underlying causes of stress-related conditions such as asthma, allergies, skin conditions, ulcerative colitis, and heart disease.

Emotional/spiritual: promotes co-operation, relationships, acceptance of others, and interactions. Good for teams, groups, and communication. Dispels fear, uncertainty, and worry. Opens new situations and promotes confidence, adaptability, and transformation. Offers protection for travelers.

AMBLYGONITE

Prismatic crystals and massive. Can be milky white, yellow, beige, salmon pink, pale green, light blue, gray.

Common alternative name: often confused with montebrasite

Common source: USA

Astrological association: Taurus

Chakras: heart, brow

HEALING QUALITIES

Boosts your resolve.

Physical: speeds healing of broken and fractured bones. Helps you to deal with inherited diseases.

Emotional/spiritual: calms the mind, soothes the emotions. Good in classrooms to create a quieter learning environment, and boosts creativity. Helps with resolution of disputes, arguments, and relationship breakdown. Good for mental health and healing. Aids appreciation of music, poetry, and art, and helps meditation.

CATHEDRAL QUARTZ

Hexagonal, terminated quartz crystals with stepped or layered effect on sides, from multiple smaller crystal points growing parallel to the main crystal. Resembles cathedral spires, a pipe organ, or dripping candle. Transparent to opaque, colorless, or white.

Common alternative names: library crystal (transparent), light library

Common sources: worldwide—especially Brazil, India, Madagascar, USA

Astrological associations: all

Chakras: all

HEALING QUALITIES

Boosts meditation, bringing knowledge from ancient civilizations.

Physical: good for pain relief

Emotional/spiritual: allows access to Akashic records and information about any subject through meditation. Helps focus group meditations, group healing, and distant healing. Promotes connection to your inner pendulum for inner guidance, spiritual growth, wisdom, and enlightenment.

CRYOLITE

Crystallizes in white masses, with occasional impurities showing yellow, pink, purple, red, brown, and black. One of the oldest minerals on Earth. Place clear cryolite in water and it disappears; white cryolite will appear more translucent.

Common sources: Canada, Greenland, Russia, USA
Astrological associations: Gemini, Aquarius
Chakras: base, crown

HEALING QUALITIES

Helps you to see things that are not obvious.
Physical: Aids temperature control. Good for chills, fevers, hypothermia, eyesight, and eye infections.
Emotional/spiritual: brings calm in stressful situations. Helps emotional stress affecting speech, public speaking, presentations, and speech impediments such as stuttering and rhotacism (difficulty pronouncing "r"). Can help you to avoid being noticed in a group. Offers inspiration and grounds spiritual energy, enhancing both sensuality and sexuality. Boosts connection to spirit, spirit guides, and angels. Improves all psychic abilities.
No elixir.

GODDESS STONE

Whitish, grayish, brownish mineraloid *opal*, technically known as menilite. Forms natural bulbous shapes resembling prehistoric goddess figures.

Common alternative names: menilite, fairy stone, menalite
Common source: Morocco
Astrological association: Cancer
Chakra: crown

HEALING QUALITIES

Promotes femininity.
Physical: good for fertility and female reproductive system.
Emotional/spiritual: boosts connection to the sacred feminine and the energies of the moon and Gaia (Mother Earth). Conveys love, nurture, comfort, protection, safety, and mystery. Brings out your hidden talents. Gives inner strength and confidence, dispelling fear. Allows femininity and sexuality to come to the fore. Brings manifestation, abundance, and new beginnings. Helps to develop intuition, divination, and other psychic skills.

HIMALAYAN QUARTZ

Quartz crystals from the Himalaya mountains. Mostly completely clear internally, even if the surface is marked.
Only sources: Himalaya mountains, Nepal, Northern India, Pakistan
Astrological associations: all
Chakras: all

HEALING QUALITIES

Spiritual purity.
Physical: quartz crystals help all physical conditions, and these are no exception. Apply these to any pain or discomfort, injury or ailment.
Emotional/spiritual: can help create the energy needed for a personal retreat. Whether you've set aside a few minutes or hours or a few days or weeks for personal exploration, these crystals will open the borders of your mind and guide you to a new spiritual adventure. Brings spiritual knowledge of healing. Good for meditation and consciousness. Amplifies any intention. Protects from negative thoughts and emotions. Cleansing crystals will help you to leave behind anything holding you back on your spiritual journey through this life. Connects you to spirit guides and angels, Hindu and Buddhist teachers, and shamanic totem animals all residing in the Himalayas.

FADEN QUARTZ

Quartz crystal with white hollow line growing through it perpendicular to the direction of growth, edge to edge, appearing threadlike. Usually tabular crystals.

Common sources: worldwide
Astrological association: Scorpio
Chakras: all

HEALING QUALITIES

Brings connection.

Physical: boosts damage repair, so good for cuts and bruises, broken or fractured bones, muscle tears, tendons, and ligaments.

Emotional/spiritual: connects people's energies. Attunes two people to the same energy vibration. Good for healer/client relationship, lovers, and people working on the same creative or intellectual project. Expands consciousness. Heals damaged aura. Gives protection for travelers, especially those going by air. Good for astral travel and Earth healing.

GIRASOL QUARTZ

Quartz containing microscopic water droplets trapped during formation; has milky opalescence.

Common alternative names: milky quartz, white star quartz, Madagascan star quartz, girasol opal (misnomer, that's something different), opalized quartz, quartz aura stone (not to be confused with aura quartzes), blue opal quartz, moon opal, moon quartz, foggy quartz, pearl quartz

Common source: Madagascar
Astrological association: Taurus
Chakras: throat, crown

HEALING QUALITIES

Helps with the big changes in life.

Physical: good for CFS/ME, diabetes, eyesight, reducing hair loss.

Emotional/spiritual: boosts creativity and encourages self-expression. Allows you to talk your talk. Good for group, family, and team situations. Calms anger and discourages fast action. Allows you to take your time and make the correct choice for you, easing momentous changes, such as divorce, house moves, new career, and recovery from illness. Promotes intimacy and brings hope, joy, and happiness. Good for dreams and channeling.

EARTHQUAKE QUARTZ CRYSTAL

These quartz crystals have been damaged by earthquake, tectonic plate movements, and other seismic activity while still in the ground, healed themselves, and continued growing. Often the damage can be seen on the main body of the crystal as well as the termination, rather than just at the termination as is the case with "normal" self-healed crystals.

Common alternative names: tectonic crystal, shift crystal, tectonic quartz, shift quartz, self-healed quartz, self-healed crystal (earthquake quartz is a very specific variety of self-healed crystal)

Common sources: worldwide
Astrological association: Capricorn
Chakras: base, all

HEALING QUALITIES

Boosts self-healing on all levels—physical, emotional, mental, and spiritual.

Physical: aids tissue repair after surgery or injury.

Emotional/spiritual: one of these crystals in your home will take you on a self-healing journey, which you can greatly accelerate by meditating with it daily. Can help you to get yourself together after emotional or mental trauma, breakdown of relationships, or mental breakdown. Releases trauma from the past. Helps you to deal with childhood issues and forgotten events. Boosts survival instincts.

COLEMANITE

Masses and short prismatic crystals; white or milk-white with tints of yellow and gray.
Common source: USA
Astrological association: Aries
Chakras: base, brow

HEALING QUALITIES

Illuminates darkness.
Physical: good for fertility, reproductive system, heart, circulation, lymphatic system, and detox.
Emotional/spiritual: opens your dark side, helping you to see all of your inner self and release the parts that don't support you, replacing them with positive bright-light energy to inspire change. Promotes a relaxed outlook, patience, and open-mindedness. Good for study, especially alternative therapies, healing, and arts. Boosts survival instincts. Guides you through dreams to reach successful outcomes. Helps to gain focus in meditation.
No elixir—water soluble.

HANKSITE

Tabular and hexagonal prismatic crystals and quartzoids (crystals resembling quartz, having two six-sided pyramids, base to base), colorless or white; included clay particles can give shades of yellow-green and black.
Common source: USA
Astrological association: Taurus
Chakra: crown

HEALING QUALITIES

Quietens restlessness.
Physical: good for colds, flu, hair, general well-being, fertility, and female reproductive system.
Emotional/spiritual: smooths transition from life to death, helping you to move on and let go, and cope with grief. Calms impatience and anxiety and lets you see

there's a right time and place for everything. Focuses femininity and intuition. Restores yin/yang balance. Boosts awareness in the physical world of both people and surroundings. A very spiritual crystal, good for Earth healing, distant healing, making connections at distance, and meditation.
No elixir—water soluble.

MICROCLINE

Massive, tabular, or short prismatic crystals, opaque to translucent; colors include colorless, white, cream-yellow, peach-red, green, and blue-green. Some of the largest crystals on Earth are formed of microcline.
Common sources: Russia, USA
Astrological association: Libra
Chakra: brow

HEALING QUALITIES

A comforting crystal.
Physical: good for brain, fingers, toes, hands, feet, and sense of touch.
Emotional/spiritual: soothing, calming, peaceful; promotes stable energy. Creates an internal space, allowing clarity of thought and clear expression of your ideas. Enhances cooperation, so helps family, group, and team bonding. Good for meditation, dreams, and dream recall.

GYROLITE

Variety of *zeolite* forming fibrous radial concretions; white, colorless, yellow, brown, and (rarely) green. Can be transparent to opaque.
Common alternative names: centrallasite, glimmer zeolite, gurolite
Common sources: India, UK
Astrological association: Scorpio
Chakra: sacral

HEALING QUALITIES

Good in a crisis. Helps with yoga, chi kung, tai chi, and other movement therapies.

Physical: good for flexibility, muscles, joints, tendons, ligaments, spinal alignment, and bones. Alleviates arthritis and rheumatism.

Emotional/spiritual: good for the physical layer of the aura and the connection between the aura and the physical body. Stabilizes emotions in an emergency and helps you to hold it together. Boosts connection to ancient civilizations. Brings spatial awareness, so good for designers and architects. Supports and amplifies the healing action of other crystals.

GARDEN QUARTZ

Hexagonal terminated quartz crystals containing more quartz crystals growing internally from one or more sides, so when viewed from above appears as a crystal garden growing within the main crystal.

Common alternative names: (all these names are mis-identification and refer to **scenic quartz**) inclusion quartz, included quartz, lodalite, lodelite, landscape quartz

Common source: Brazil

Astrological association: Virgo

Chakras: base, crown

HEALING QUALITIES

Assists clearing out the old and planting fresh seeds.

Physical: good for back, backache, back pain, and joints.

Emotional/spiritual: connects Earth energies to the crown chakra and channels energy from above down to the base chakra. This brings creative ideas and spiritual concepts into reality and encourages you to look to nature for fresh ideas and concepts. Boosts connection to nature, allowing you to see the beauty in everything. Good for new beginnings, new projects, new careers, new directions, travel, businesses, groups, and associations. Bonds families, friends, relationships, and partnerships.

CLEAR HALITE

Natural mineral form of salt, forming masses, columnar structures, and cubic crystals.

Common alternative name: rock salt

Common sources: worldwide—especially India, USA

Astrological associations: Cancer, Pisces

Chakras: all

HEALING QUALITIES

A cleansing crystal.

Physical: good for detox process, affecting body fluids, bladder, kidneys, liver, colon, and intestines. Reduces water retention.

Emotional/spiritual: boosts energy and emotional cleansing. Lessens mood swings. Aids purification of your environment, clearing energy pathways, removing blocks, and freeing energy to flow so things may happen. Good for psychic abilities, awareness, increased consciousness, and meditation.

No elixir—water soluble.

WHITE TOPAZ

White prismatic crystals and alluvial pebbles.

Common sources: Kenya, USA

Astrological association: Sagittarius

Chakra: crown

HEALING QUALITIES

A stone of true love.

Physical: good for skin, acne, boils, wounds, and bruising (either applying the crystal directly or as a topical elixir).

Emotional/spiritual: replaces sadness with joy, hate and distrust with love. Good for all relationships. Promotes confidence, making you feel better about yourself, self-respect, and sexuality. Adds za za to your mojo! Helps decision making and focusing on details. Promotes the Taoist idea of *wu wei* (literally, "without effort"), doing without action. Allows things to happen around you and for you.

ANGEL WING SELENITE

Clear or white crystallized form of *gypsum* forming angel wing, feathery, fishtail, Christmas tree shapes.
Common alternative name: fishtail selenite
Common source: Mexico
Astrological association: Taurus; also linked with the moon (named after Selene, goddess of the moon)
Chakra: crown

HEALING QUALITIES

Spotlights your best features. Selenite is very feminine and can help balance all cycles in life.
Physical: helps stressful skin conditions such as acne, elasticity issues, eczema, psoriasis, sensitivity, and wrinkles. Gives a youthful appearance. Boosts vitality.
Emotional/spiritual: excellent when it's time to reinvent yourself. Clears out the emotional loft, making space in your heart for a fresh start. Brings your innate talents and abilities to the fore. Connects you to angels and spirit guides just when you need angelic advice in your life. Boosts practical energy and sex drive. Helpful in coping with abuse and other emotional trauma. Said to bring longevity.
No elixir.

WHITE CHALCEDONY

White variety of *chalcedony*, a type of massive quartz.
Common sources: worldwide
Astrological associations: Cancer, Sagittarius
Chakra: crown

HEALING QUALITIES

A stone for creativity and intellect, and balancing the mind.
Physical: good for vitality, blood, circulatory system, spleen, brain, eyes, ears, tongue, and nostrils. Boosts visual, auditory, gustatory, and olfactory senses.
Emotional/spiritual: promotes elasticity of mind to adapt to any situation, keeping you calm under pressure. Good for confidence, public speaking, and learning new languages. Helps balance the right and left sides of the brain and helps with addictions and obsessive behavior patterns, OCD, senility, dementia, gluttony, obesity, and weight loss. By each holding a stone, two people can tune into one another telepathically.

SCEPTER QUARTZ CRYSTAL

This is a naturally formed quartz crystal that has grown over a quartz stem, which now appears to pierce its base.
Common sources: worldwide
Astrological association: Capricorn
Chakra: sacral

HEALING QUALITIES

Focuses energy for healing.
Physical: good for male fertility and male reproductive system. Helps to focus beyond and away from day-to-day issues of chronic illness or long-term disability. Boosts physical strength, endurance.
Emotional/spiritual: employed in ceremony and ritual, it directs a spiritual energy toward the intended purpose. The phallic nature of the crystal implies male attributes, which can sometimes be useful for both sexes. Great when you need a boost of yang energy. Promotes confidence and strength.

DOUBLE TERMINATED QUARTZ CRYSTAL

Quartz crystal with two terminations at opposite ends.

Common alternative name: quartz DTs

Common sources: worldwide

Astrological associations: Gemini, Libra

Chakras: all

HEALING QUALITIES

These crystals can focus or release energy so that it flows in both directions simultaneously, bringing a state of balance.

Physical: helps with most conditions. Relieves nausea when placed on the solar plexus, and headaches when placed on the crown.

Emotional/spiritual: helps to release energy blocks between chakras. Boosts the aura to act as a shield against unhelpful energies. When held, brings balance and stillness in meditation; under the pillow, enhances dreams. Acts as a bridge, so can improve remote viewing/astral projection techniques, as well as linking two people who are separated, such as lovers or old friends. Helps connection for distant healing or Earth healing. Brings patience and persistence to any task.

INTRINSINITE

Massive white translucent quartz (quartzite) with currently unconfirmed mineral inclusions.

Common alternative names: stone of sanctuary, mystery stone, mystry stone

Only source: Ontario (Canada)

Astrological association: Capricorn

Chakra: crown

HEALING QUALITIES

Brings tranquility.

Physical: good for head, neck, and senses. Alleviates headaches, insomnia, colds, flu, throat problems, head, neck and shoulder tension, and frozen shoulder.

Emotional/spiritual: Helps you to keep calm, composed, and cool in stressful situations. Helps combat anxiety, mental blocks, creative blocks, and writer's block. Dispels confusion and lets you see through the fog in your mind. Promotes clarity of thought. Good for exams, tests, and mental challenges. Provides a bridge to spirit guides. Encourages spiritual expression, allowing you to talk your talk.

MANIFESTATION QUARTZ

Quartz crystal that has another crystal of any variety completely enclosed within it. Some people describe crystals growing into a quartz crystal as manifestation crystals.

Common alternative name: creation crystal

Common sources: worldwide, but rare

Astrological associations: all

Chakras: all

HEALING QUALITIES

Brings you what you ask for, which reminds me of the old saying: "Be careful what you ask for because you might get it!"

Physical: manifests health. Can be employed in any healing modality to speed physical healing.

Emotional/spiritual: brings lifestyle changes; can improve or diminish any detail of your life you choose; can benefit the body, emotions, mind, and spirit. Enhances creativity, invention, lateral and intuitive thinking, and discovery. Boosts connection with your inner self, the master within all of us, and can shine a light on your true path in life.

CANDLE QUARTZ

Quartz crystals that are characterized by having many small terminations around their sides and/or base that all point in the same direction as the main termination or point. These often resemble wax running down the side of a candle, hence the name. Each candle quartz crystal is unique; each is a natural work of art. The color can be white or off-white, often with a cloudy appearance. They may have brown, red, pink, or gray markings or inclusions and are often phantom crystals with clearly defined white phantoms within.

Common alternative names: female candle quartz crystal, female quartz crystal, celestial quartz crystal, candle quartz crystal, milky quartz crystal, cathedral crystal, cathedral quartz crystal, female milky quartz crystal, pineapple quartz crystal, white candle quartz crystal, white quartz crystal, seeker transformer crystal

Common source: Madagascar

Astrological associations: Gemini, Pisces

Chakras: all

HEALING QUALITIES

These special quartz crystals are amazing partners for anyone exploring their past lives. The many terminations seem to act as individual time machines, each one taking you back to another life.

Physical: aids recovery from injury.

Emotional/spiritual: nurtures feminine energy, helping to restore both physical and emotional injuries. Good for releasing emotions that are holding you back and may, in the longer term, cause disease. Heals the aura, where all disease manifests before it becomes physically noticeable; can help to prevent diseases manifesting at this early stage. You can brush down or comb the aura with candle quartz crystals after a crystal healing treatment (see page 37), as an alternative to a selenite aura wand. Illuminates our inner workings, emotions, and beliefs, bringing greater understanding of our self. Holding a candle quartz

crystal while you meditate will help you listen to and hear your inner voice and guide. Ideal for therapy and treatment rooms, because it brings healing energy to any space. Place in offices or living rooms or anywhere disagreements or arguments may happen. They are also impressive tools for accessing the Akashic records.

BLUE MIST LEMURIAN QUARTZ CRYSTAL

Clear quartz crystal with internal faulting creating a misty inner appearance, often with yellow-brown limonite near the base. Formed in the mountains of Colombia over 100 million years ago. During their lifetime there was a 20-million-year crisis when they were internally fractured and broken by the earth's tumultuous upheavals. After each one of these catastrophes the crystals healed themselves internally, giving rise to the appearance of the blue mist.

Only source: Colombia

Astrological associations: all

Chakra: solar plexus

HEALING QUALITIES

A stone for self-healing.

Physical: good for lungs, heart, pain relief (especially when pain is aggravated by stress), fertility, sex drive, and balancing hormones.

Emotional/spiritual: makes you feel like a young child and an old wise person both at the same time. Good for spiritual exploration while keeping you grounded, discovering your inner self, releasing trapped emotions and emotional pain, and healing the past. Helps to resolve childhood issues, and the effects of past lives, encouraging self-respect, and confidence. Good for your mind, consciousness. Grounds creative ideas into reality. Calming emotionally and physically and brings a peaceful feeling.

BLACK

CHRYSANTHEMUM STONE

Black rock of *dolomite*, *gypsum*-bearing clay, limestone, or porphyry, with *celestite* or *calcite* growing in unique patterns that resemble flowering chrysanthemums.

Common source: China
Astrological associations: Taurus, Aquarius
Chakras: base, crown

HEALING QUALITIES

Awakens your true purpose in life.
Physical: good for female reproductive system, fibroids, cystitis, and fertility.
Emotional/spiritual: promotes your dreams, goals, and ideals, the dark rock keeping you grounded while you follow your dreams and chase your goals. Helps you to seize opportunities that appear unexpectedly in your path. Brings good luck, and overcomes obstacles to joy, love, and abundance. Brings balance to your physical and spiritual self, helping to keep you in the present moment. Good for change or starting out on a new path, such as a new job, career, or relationship. Meditating with this stone can help you to find answers to some of life's problems when you are feeling stuck.

SHUNGITE

Black, charcoal, or brown non-crystalline mineral; opaque, lustrous, up to 98 percent carbon.

Common alternative names: fullerite, fullerene, buckyballs, Buckminsterfullerene, black ocher (no relationship to red and yellow ocher)
Common sources: top-quality shungite is found only in the Zazhoginskoye deposit near Lake Onega in the Shunga region of Karelia, northwest Russia. Lower-quality shungite is available from Austria, India, Democratic Republic of Congo, and Kazakhstan
Astrological association: Cancer
Chakras: all

HEALING QUALITIES

A cleansing stone.
Physical: good for detox (elixir) and recovery from illness, disease, injury, and surgery. Promotes growth and tissue repair.
Emotional/spiritual: can help stress-related allergies. Cleanses and purifies mind, body, and spirit. Protects against EMF and geopathic stress. Good for balance, emotional and spiritual recovery from illness or stress, and emotional pain relief. Cleanses emotions, helping you to let go of anything holding you back. Purifies water; can be placed in water bottle or jug.

BLACK TOURMALINE WITH MICA

Striated black *tourmaline* crystals with inclusions of mica growing in and/or through the main tourmaline crystal.

Common alternative name: schorl with mica
Common source: Brazil
Astrological association: Capricorn
Chakra: base

HEALING QUALITIES

Offers protection on another level, as it is excellent at sending negative energy back to its source!
Physical: good for arthritis and heart.
Emotional/spiritual: gives emotional support. Allows humiliation and awkwardness to fade away. Removes victim mentality, as it prevents feelings of victimization. Great for discounting internet trolls and bullies! Relieves stress and anxiety, bringing peace of mind and calmness. Good for the mind. Promotes pragmatism. Reconnects you to nature in your environment. Promotes environmental causes.

LAVA STONE

Formed from magma erupted from volcanos.
Common alternative name: volcanic rock
Common sources: volcanos past and present worldwide
Astrological associations: Taurus, Cancer
Chakra: base

HEALING QUALITIES

Effect is like a phoenix rising from the ashes.
Physical: good for feet, toes, sore feet, bunions, corns, verrucas, and in-growing toenails.

Emotional/spiritual: burns away the remnants of a past that holds you back, facilitating new beginnings and starting over. Dispels anger, fear, and negativity, giving a can-do attitude to almost any situation. Grounding, particularly when success beckons. Helps travelers to feel connected to home and relieves homesickness. Good for Earth healing.

LEMURIAN BLACK JADE

A mixture of *jade*, quartz, and *pyrite*. The presence of graphite or iron oxide gives it its color. There is a similar grayish/greenish variety known as shadow Lemurian jade.
Common alternative names: midnight Lemurian jade, black Inca jade
Common source: Peru
Astrological associations: Taurus, Libra
Chakras: base, heart

HEALING QUALITIES

A stone of transformation.
Physical: good for heart, recovery from illness, immune system, female and male reproductive systems.
Emotional/spiritual: gives courage and enhances determination to remove blocks that prevent change and transition. Facilitates endings and new beginnings and truly discovering your inner self. Promotes femininity, nurture, abundance, a work-life balance, appreciation of those around you, and gratitude for what you already have. Augments your connection to nature. Raises

consciousness. Good for intuition and dreams. Provides protection against predatory people and helps recovery from abuse. Supports palliative care and carers.

DOCTOR'S STONE

A form of *black banded agate* forming botryoidal masses.
Common alternative name: botryoidal black banded agate
Only source: Medicine Bow (Wyoming, USA)
Astrological association: Sagittarius
Chakras: base, solar plexus, crown

HEALING QUALITIES

Sends energy to wherever it is needed and seems to help with any condition.
Physical: good for pain relief, especially back pain, sciatica, and throat problems. Predicts illness/disease and acts to prevent it. Alleviates dizziness and vertigo. Good for soles of feet.
Emotional/spiritual: offers protection, dispelling fear of the unknown and bringing joy and happiness. Good for grounding, Earth healing, energizing, wakefulness, and nurturing (like having a best friend or ally helping you out). Gives a positive vibe. Good for new beginnings, a fresh start, and a kick up the backside! Gives off a welcoming energy. Aids communication (especially of difficult ideas), confidence, self-esteem. Helps you to talk your talk and walk your walk. Releases past trauma and facilitates seeing into past lives. A stone of doing and action. Good for mind, thoughts, ideas, and creativity. Eases fear of heights. Takes you on a journey of healing through your chakras.

BLACK ONYX

Black variety of *chalcedony*; takes high polish.

Common sources: India, Republic of South Africa
Astrological association: Capricorn
Chakra: base

HEALING QUALITIES

When the going gets tough, the tough get going.

Physical: good for strength, stamina, endurance, allergies, childbirth, and obesity.

Emotional/spiritual: offers grounding and protection, positivity, and confidence. Provides emotional support when times are tough due to stress, grief, unhappy relationships, or emotional or mental confusion. Permits you to let go of the past and step into the future. Reduces anxiety. Good for dealing with addictions, stopping smoking, and changing behavior patterns. Boosts awareness. Helps you to recognize your achievements.

BLACK RUTILATED QUARTZ

Quartz with black, needle-shaped inclusions of *rutile*, which is usually gold or silver in color. The black variety is rare. Rutile is titanium dioxide with high quantities of iron oxide. When there is little iron oxide, the rutile becomes much darker and sometimes black.

Common source: Brazil
Astrological associations: all
Chakras: brow, crown

HEALING QUALITIES

The light at the end of the tunnel.

Physical: good for vitality, strength, skeletal system, bones, joints, ligaments, immune system, nervous system, neuralgia, and Parkinson's disease.

Emotional/spiritual: intuition and good luck go hand in hand. Brings abundance, awareness of danger, and protection. Good for all mental health and healing, and coping with

breakdown, depression, and despair; when things hit the absolute low, the only way is up. Helps with mood swings, bipolar disorder, addictive behavior patterns, OCD, mania, and schizophrenia.

YIN YANG CRYSTAL

Clear quartz crystals with one side darkened from natural irradiation. There is probably an inclusion, so far unidentified, that is being affected by the natural radiation, changing the color, which is why some of the crystal remains clear and unaffected.

Common alternative names: *smoky quartz*, clear quartz crystal
Only source: Bahia (Brazil)
Astrological association: Gemini
Chakras: base, crown

HEALING QUALITIES

Brings balance to all situations.

Physical: good for fertility, female and male reproductive systems, chronic pain relief, insomnia, joints, flexibility, eyes, and eyesight.

Emotional/spiritual: promotes yin/yang balance. Brings healing energy up from the base and down from the crown, simultaneously coming together in the heart chakra to dissolve trapped emotions and replace them with positivity, giving you a new impetus to change your life and move on. Links the right and left brain (creativity and intellect), so you can see more options and the directions your path may take. Helps with making choices when new possibilities arise. Helps psychic and spiritual development, dreams, visualization, and shamanic vision quests and journeying.

BLACK AMETHYST

Amethyst, by definition, is violet quartz. Black amethyst is a term used to describe naturally darker-than-usual amethyst crystals that appear black or almost black in normal light due to a higher iron content or *hematite* inclusions within the crystal matrix. It is still a dark purple, rather than actually black.

Common alternative names: morion quartz, cairngorm quartz (misnomers as both of these are versions of *smoky quartz* rather than amethyst, since their color is due to natural radiation from the Earth)

Common sources: Brazil, India, Uruguay

Astrological association: Capricorn

Chakra: crown

HEALING QUALITIES

Brings spiritual understanding to everyday events.

Physical: good for headaches, migraine, toothache, ear ache, and eye strain.

Emotional/spiritual: quells emotions to bring calmness in times of change, allowing the necessary changes to be peaceful. Good for divorce and relationship breakdowns. Adds a more spiritual slant to your daily routine. Boosts the aura and offers protection in both physical and psychic domains. Can create a connection to the divine and improves psychic abilities.

GOETHITE ON HEMATITE

Metallic gray/silver to black botryoidal forms with *goethite* growing on and with the *hematite*.

Common source: Morocco

Astrological associations: Aries, Aquarius

Chakras: base, brow

HEALING QUALITIES

Grounds your experiences in life.

Physical: good for blood, blood disorders, anemia, blood clots, menorrhagia, veins, arteries, convulsions, ear, nose, and throat health, digestive system, body building, weight gain, cramps, MS, backache, and broken bones and fractures.

Emotional/spiritual: brings courage and strength to work through the things that are stressing you. Grounds mental processes, turning thought into action and ideas into reality, making life more fun. Relieves air sickness, travel sickness, jet lag, and insomnia. Attracts love. Good for memory, meditation, and grounding psychic abilities into the practicality of everyday life.

HAUSMANNITE

Black granular aggregates or, relatively rarely, pseudo-octahedral crystals.

Common alternative name: black manganese

Common sources: China, Germany, Japan, Mexico, Republic of South Africa, Sweden, USA

Astrological association: Virgo

Chakras: base, sacral

HEALING QUALITIES

A crystal for metamorphosis.

Physical: good for bones, blood vessels, hair, skin.

Emotional/spiritual: a crystal for the sometimes painful but beneficial process of change—new beginnings, fresh starts, leaving the past behind. Releases emotional pain, anxiety, and attachments. Supports the Buddhist concept of non-attachment to possessions, ideas, and people. Guides you along the stepping stones of your spiritual path. Brings love into your meditations. Helps you to learn to trust your inner pendulum, producing self-assuredness and confidence to progress.

BROOKITE

Orthorhombic, tabular, and plate-like crystals, black to red-brown.

Common source: USA
Astrological association: Cancer
Chakras: base, sacral, brow, crown

HEALING QUALITIES

This too will pass.
Physical: promotes
mobility, circulation.
Encourages exercise.
Alleviates the effects
of EMF.

Emotional/spiritual: no matter how bad it seems, it will end and it will get better. Keeps your feet on the ground and clears your mind. Brings optimism and hope for a better time, and helps you to stay in the present moment. Acts as an energy store; when you need a top up, simply hold the crystal to your sacral chakra for a recharge. Banishes lethargy and apathy, avoids worry, and helps you to amend beliefs that are holding you back. Release these and your awareness shifts to another plane.

STEATITE

A massive variety of talc, often intermixed with *serpentine* and *calcite*. Other colors include white, shades of green, gray, and yellow-brown.

Common alternative names: soapstone, black pipestone (Canada)
Common sources: worldwide—especially Canada
Astrological association: Sagittarius
Chakras: base, heart, crown

HEALING QUALITIES

This soft mineral is easily carved by Native American and First Nation plains tribes into black bowls for sacred pipes. The red pipe bowls are made from catlinite.
Physical: good for liver and gall bladder. Promotes healthy microbiota that aid digestion of fatty acids and may have many varied health benefits.
Emotional/spiritual: extends your outlook and stretches your boundaries. Encourages you to try new things and

invent new ways of doing old things. Promotes a *laissez faire* attitude, letting things take their own course and going with the flow. Helps you to open up to new opportunities. Has a very calming effect that can assist your brainpower. Facilitates connection to spirit.

FERBERITE

Black, elongated, flattened, and wedge-shaped crystals and druses.

Common alternative name: confused with wolframite. Part of the group of crystals originally called the hubnerite-ferberite series, wolframite was the intermediate; now renamed as wolframite series. The crystal/mineral trade mostly still uses the original nomenclature.
Common sources: Bolivia, China, Germany, Korea, Russia, UK, USA
Astrological association: Scorpio
Chakra: base

HEALING QUALITIES

There are more ways than one to achieve your goal.
Physical: good for strength, muscles, flexibility, vitality, and action.
Emotional/spiritual: promotes
open-mindedness, adaptability
of thought, inner resolve,
persistence, and a just-do-it
attitude.

COLUMBITE

Black niobium ore crystallizing as short prismatic prisms, thin tabular crystals, pyramids, and masses. Colors range from black to brown.

Common alternative names: niobite, niobite-tantalite, columbate
Common sources: Australia, Brazil
Astrological association: Aquarius
Chakras: base, brow

HEALING QUALITIES

A wonderful anti-worry crystal.
Physical: good for eyesight, fertility, and skin.
Emotional/spiritual: predicts future problems that may arise, giving insight to solutions so you're equipped to deal with any glitches if they come up! Promotes inner strength, resolve, and emotional balance. Gives physical protection

for yourself and possessions, as well as being an effective psychic shield that can deflect any negativity that comes your way. Opens a conduit between the psychic and physical realms. Helps thought processes in decision making. Keeps you focused and helps you to avoid distractions. Good for meditation.

HEMATITE/MAGNETITE

Hematite polymorph of *magnetite* crystals.
Common alternative name: hematite after magnetite
Common source: Argentina
Astrological associations: Aries, Virgo, Capricorn, Aquarius
Chakra: base

HEALING QUALITIES

Gives courage and strength to alter your viewpoint.
Physical: good for blood, anemia, backache, aching bones, MS, hair, and skin.
Emotional/spiritual: grounding and frees the mind to let you see things from a different perspective. Helps you to see positives in everything, including grief, fear, anger,

attachment, and neediness, so you can leave negative feelings behind. Balances yin/yang and attracts love to the new, positive you. Promotes dexterity, and flexibility. Helps you to discover answers in meditation.

HUBNERITE

Tabular, flattened, and prismatic crystals: blades, lamellar, columns, radiating groups, and grains. Colors range from black to brown.

Common alternative name: huebnerite (named after Adolf Hübner. Alternative spellings are attempts at pronunciation)
Common sources: Bolivia, China, Peru, Russia, UK, USA
Astrological associations: Gemini, Libra
Chakra: base

HEALING QUALITIES

Enhances feelings of security.
Physical: promotes the flow of oxygenated blood to major muscle groups, helping movement. Enhances the physical side of the fight-or-flight response. Improves stamina and eyesight. Helpful for anemia, hypoglycemia, flexibility of joints, ligaments, tendons, and muscles.
Emotional/spiritual: boosts awareness and activates your inner pendulum to help you trust your choices and give a feeling of safety. Promotes individuality and uniqueness. Can be held in meditation to find answers to specific questions.

BLACK MOONSTONE

Variety of feldspar exhibiting chatoyancy.
Common sources: India, Madagascar
Astrological association: Cancer
Chakras: base, sacral

HEALING QUALITIES

Divine feminine.
Physical: good for menstrual cycle.
Emotional/spiritual: brings out
your feminine side. Encourages
nurture, nature, intuition, and
psychic development. Gives

protection. Allows you to find a safe space within so you
can explore, especially looking into your heart, seeing the
dark parts, realizing you don't need the trapped energy
that's hiding there, and letting it go. Opens the way for
new beginnings and adventures in your life.

NUUMMITE

The oldest living mineral (almost four billion years old),
massive black to very dark brown in color, with golden
flecks of iridescence due to labradorescence (the display
of an iridescent optical effect caused by an unusual
reflection of the light from submicroscopical planes
orientated in one direction; they reflect and filter light
irregularly, giving the display of color).
Common alternative names: nummite, nuumite (both
common misspellings), sorcerer's stone, magician's stone
Common sources: Greenland. Small quantities of lower
quality available from Canada, Spain, USA
Astrological association: Sagittarius
Chakras: base, crown

HEALING QUALITIES

Connects the crown and base chakras, grounding your
healing experience.
Physical: good for vitality, pain relief, tension, insomnia,
detox, blood, circulation, lymph, kidneys, diabetes, fainting,
throat, speech impediments, eyes, eyesight, ears, tinnitus,
central nervous system, brain and spinal cord, and
Parkinson's disease.
Emotional/spiritual: Relieves stress by removing energy

blocks you put in your own way and
giving you fortitude and willpower to
make positive changes. Provides
protection for both you (when
carried) and your home (when
placed by a door or window).
Improves intellect and memory. Clears and cleanses the
aura before applying spiritual spackling paste/Polyfilla to
the holes. Helps to bridge the veil between the physical
and spiritual worlds. Iridescent flashes act like lightning
bolts of inspiration. Benefits Earth healing.

PYROLUSITE CRYSTAL

Crystallizes in many forms, including prismatic and
equant crystals, druses, botryoidal structures, and
granular masses. Colors range from black to gray-blue.
The following information applies to the crystal and
massive forms, rather than the dendrite form that was
covered in *Volume 1*.
Common sources: Brazil, USA
Astrological association: Leo
Chakra: sacral

HEALING QUALITIES

Helps to join the dots in your picture of life.
Physical: good for metabolism, digestion, and blood.
Speeds healing of injury, wounds, and surgery when
applied as a topical elixir.
Emotional/spiritual: supports making major life changes,
such as moving home, divorce,
ending relationships, making
new connections, and
rebuilding your life with
new friendships,
relationships, colleagues, team
members, classmates, and
coworkers. Enhances connections

between home and work and lifestyle, resulting in a
more fulfilled life. Eases conflicts along the way and
smooths turbulent times. Strengthens the aura, helping
to prevent dis-ease and reducing unwanted attention
from spirit. Helps to digest ideas and brings new ways
of thinking.

GRAY

CRADLE OF HUMANKIND STONE

Agate variety, which comes from caves where the earliest hominid fossils were found, dating back some seven million years. These stones contain the energy of the hominid fossils and DNA. Mostly colored gray, black, off-white banded, sometimes brown.
Common alternative name: cradle of life stone (a similar but different stone comes from nearby in South Africa, trademarked cradle of life stone™ aka healerite®)
Only source: Magaliesberg (Republic of South Africa)
Astrological associations: all
Chakras: all

HEALING QUALITIES

Who are we? Understanding origin.
Physical: good for pain relief, bones, breaks and fractures, and genetic diseases and disorders. Helps healthy physical development in the very young and helps to slow the somatic effects of old age.
Emotional/spiritual: helps us to accept how we and others around us are—each an individual on our own path, but united by a common history and common future. Promotes grounding and patience, at the same time uplifting and energizing. Good for family bonding. Dispels racism, discrimination, and bigotry in any form, reminding us that we all come from the same place. Encourages a connection to family members now in spirit, personal and communal ancestors, past lives, ancient cultures and civilizations such as Atlantis and Lemuria, and communal responsibility for the actions of your forebears. Try meditating with one, together with the question "who am I?"

SILVER MOONSTONE

Variety of feldspar, exhibiting chatoyancy—it appears silver when the light catches it.
Common alternative name: silver-sheen moonstone
Common source: India
Astrological association: Cancer
Chakras: sacral, crown

HEALING QUALITIES

Promotes graceful aging.
Physical: good for skin, youthful appearance, hair, brain, fertility, and female reproductive system.
Emotional/spiritual: Aids memory and combats dementia, senility, and other signs of mental aging. Allows men to get in touch with their feminine side. Encourages emotional openness, Intuition, and psychic skills.

ARSENOPYRITE

Steel gray to silver white, forming acicular, off-square prismatic, stubby, striated crystals and granular and compact masses. Oxidation can tarnish the surface, producing a colorful iridescent layer. Produces a garlic aroma when ground or hammered.
Common sources: worldwide—especially USA
Astrological association: Leo
Chakras: base, heart, brow

HEALING QUALITIES

Acts as a mirror to your soul.
Physical: good for detox, halitosis, teeth, tongue, mouth, jaw (do not put it in your mouth—contains arsenic. Place it on pillow or bedside table).
Emotional/spiritual: brings your dark side to the surface, allowing you to recognize it and the effects it has on your character, and to change it. Keeps it out of disagreements and disputes so they can be resolved more quickly. Releases trapped emotions from the past to make way for fresh, new, bright energy. Aids memory. Good for clairvoyance and scrying.
No elixir—wrap in cloth if applying to the skin.

MICALATED QUARTZ

Any quartz crystals or massive (cryptocrystalline) with the inclusion of any mica.
Common alternative name: mica-included quartz
Common sources: worldwide—especially Brazil
Astrological association: Cancer
Chakra: crown

HEALING QUALITIES

Good for being in the moment and acting on impulse.
Physical: good for skeletal system, and bones.
Emotional/spiritual: helps you to connect to your higher self, allowing you to see all the details and make a conscious choice, at the same time easing the temptation of compulsions, the past, and compulsive behavior patterns. Dispels bias, prejudice, and fixed ideas. Creates flexibility of both thought and deed.

MOLYBDENITE

Blueish silver hexagonal crystals.
Common sources: Australia, China, Germany, Mexico, Norway, USA
Astrological association: Scorpio
Chakra: sacral

HEALING QUALITIES

Brings lubrication for body, mind, and spirit.
Physical: good for joints, synovial fluid and other body fluids, blood, lymph, reducing fluid retention, kidneys, and bladder.
Emotional/spiritual: encourages you to let go of beliefs and thoughts (lubrication for your emotions and actions) that just don't work for you, to stop repeating patterns of behavior, and to try something new. Gives confidence to transcend fear, let go of anxiety, and find a calm, peaceful way to be. Reduces friction in all situations. Good for creativity, art, and writing.

PYROXENE

A group of silicate-based, rock-forming minerals. Here we refer to the massive form, rather than crystalline minerals.
Common sources: worldwide—especially Alaska (USA)
Astrological associations: all
Chakra: base

HEALING QUALITIES

Gives stability.
Physical: good for hips, legs, knees, ankles, feet, and toes.
Emotional/spiritual: grounding. Helps complementary therapists and energy workers to keep you grounded during treatments; helps psychic readers, clairvoyants, and those who use the tarot and crystal balls to avoid becoming involved in their sitter's affairs. Also good for accountants, lawyers, advisors, and anyone who works one to one intimately with clients.

JAMESONITE

Steel gray to dark gray to black, radiating compact and fibrous masses and acicular crystals.
Common alternative names: comuccite, feather ore, and easily confused with boulangerite with which it may be intergrown
Common sources: Bolivia, China, Czech Republic, Mexico, Romania, UK
Astrological association: Leo
Chakras: base, crown

HEALING QUALITIES

Brings thoughts into reality.
Physical: reduces fever, water retention, and swelling. Good for detox, colds, and flu.
Emotional/spiritual: manifests desires and dreams and can help you to find a career path to extend your knowledge and wisdom. Dispels anger, fear, and aggression. Helps diplomacy. Good for the treatment of bipolar disorder, depression, manic behavior, and OCD. Aids diagnosis, psychic development, group healing, distant healing, and meditation.
No elixir.

BROWN

PEANUT WOOD

This has nothing to do with peanuts! The stone is a piece of *petrified wood*, dark brown to black in color, and occasionally lighter shades of cream, with peanut-shaped white to cream patches of *mookaite*. Driftwood from ancient conifer trees floated in the prehistoric sea that covered what is now Western Australia. Clams ate into the wood, creating the peanut-shaped holes, so the wood became waterlogged and sank. Dead radiolarians (plankton with silicon shells) landing on the wood produced a white gunk called radiolarian ooze, which filled the holes as the wood gradually became petrified (turned to stone), leaving the peanut shapes.

Common source: Australia
Astrological association: Scorpio
Chakra: base

HEALING QUALITIES

A stone for death and rebirth.

Physical: good for strength and combating physical stress, mold and fungus (wash down affected areas with elixir and dry thoroughly), and fungal infections of the lungs (take an elixir).

Emotional/spiritual: concerned with life cycles. Promotes constant development, change, transformation, and leaps of faith. Supports dieting, leading to sustained weight loss, and prevents yo-yo dieting. Helps to shed a poverty mentality, leading to the possibility of abundance. Helps relieve stress and promotes attention to detail, living life to the full, sexual energy, attraction, and Earth healing.

NAVAJO JASPER

A misnomer, as this is a variety of *boulder opal* in its common form, showing no fire.

Common source: Australia
Astrological associations: Virgo, Libra, Scorpio
Chakra: base

HEALING QUALITIES

Connects to the old ways.

Physical: general tonic for the body that helps to keep you well. Good for winter bugs, colds, and flu.

Emotional/spiritual: promotes the ideas of herbal medicine, ceremony, sacred lands, and ritual. Strengthens the aura. Offers a feeling of security. Allows a safe place to explore your inner self and expand your consciousness.

ORTHOCLASE

Variety of feldspar forming cryptocrystalline masses—short prismatic and thin tabular crystals. Occurs in many colors, commonly white to cream.

Common sources: worldwide—especially India, USA
Astrological association: Cancer
Chakra: heart

HEALING QUALITIES

Brings youthful gusto and also serenity.

Physical: good for vitality, slowing the aging process, spine, teeth, eyesight, lungs, bronchitis, asthma, TB, pleurisy, pneumonia, and other chest infections.

Emotional/spiritual: calms a raging storm in the mind and helps recovery after trauma or extreme stress. Good for PTSD, changing behavior patterns, and OCD. Aids recovery from addictions, including stopping smoking. Puts you back on the planet and sparks your mojo, giving you a new direction and zest for life. Enhances your intuition.

AMMONITE

Fossilized sea animal that lived 240 to 65 million years ago and became extinct with the dinosaur extinction. Found in every natural color.
Common sources: worldwide
Astrological association: Aquarius
Chakras: base, heart

HEALING QUALITIES

The universal spiral of healing energy.
Physical: good for skeletal system, bones, joints, ligaments, osteoporosis, osteoarthritis, fractures and broken bones, and degenerative diseases.
Emotional/spiritual: everything goes around in cycles: healing the past heals the present, so the past heals the future, solving problems before they arise. Good for connecting with your ancestors and past lives. Gives structure to the present, protection, and enhances your survival instinct. Good for creative careers.

AXINITE

Brown to violet-brown or reddish brown, tabular, wedge-shaped crystals and masses.
Common sources: Australia, France, Mexico, Russia, USA
Astrological association: Aries
Chakra: base

HEALING QUALITIES

Brings energies into alignment so everything flows a little better.
Physical: good for muscles, legs and feet, skeletal system, spine, bones, breaks, fractures, joints, ligaments, and arthritis.
Emotional/spiritual: facilitates a connection to angelic wisdom, spirit guides, and the Akashic records to help you find solutions that do not harm anyone else. Promotes friendship and relationships; also helpful in ending relationships, employment, or business partnerships in a kind way so that everyone feels all right about it.

MOQUI MARBLES

Iron and *sandstone* concretion.
Common alternative names: moqui balls©, shaman stones
Common sources: Utah, Arizona (USA)
Astrological associations: Libra, Aquarius, Aries
Chakra: base

HEALING QUALITIES

Brings balance on all levels—physical, emotional, mental, and spiritual.
Physical: good for inner ear, balance, hearing, blood vessels, bones, immune system, genetic diseases, and tissue regeneration.
Emotional/spiritual: good for balancing yin/yang energies, grounding, shamanic journeying, vision quest, and environmental issues. Brings inspiration. Connects you to ancient wisdom.

LORENZENITE

Forms double terminated orthorhombic colorless, gray, pinkish, or brown crystals.
Common alternative names: ramsayite, ramzaite
Common sources: Canada, Greenland, Norway, Russia
Astrological association: Libra
Chakra: throat

HEALING QUALITIES

Brings balance.
Physical: good for inner ear, balance, mucous membranes, chest, throat, esophagus, nose, and nasal passages.
Emotional/spiritual: helps you to cope with emotional wobbles, regain poise, and get your feet back on the ground. Good for dealing with stress and confusion. Helps you to clear a congested mind and see the answers you need.

BROWN BANDED ARAGONITE

Massive in bands of *chalcedony* and *aragonite* (orthorhombic calcium carbonate).

Common alternative names: Mexican onyx, banded aragonite, cave aragonite
Common source: Peru
Astrological association: Capricorn
Chakra: base

HEALING QUALITIES

Strengthens the weakest parts of the body, which are affected by stress.

Physical: good for bones, joints, teeth, digestion, temperature control, fever, hypothermia, inflammation, CFS/ME, nervous system, fibromyalgia, general aches and pains (elixir), and any stress-aggravated conditions such as asthma, psoriasis, and IBS.

Emotional/spiritual: alleviates stress, burn-out, restlessness, and depression. Helps you to eliminate a judgmental attitude. Turns on your connection with nature, aids Earth healing, stills the mind in meditation, and expands consciousness.

ELESTIAL SMOKY QUARTZ

An overgrowth of terminations on a natural crystal structure, colored brown by natural radioactivity within the Earth.

Common sources: Brazil, Madagascar, Republic of South Africa, USA
Astrological associations: Gemini, Sagittarius, Capricorn
Chakras: base, brow, crown

HEALING QUALITIES

Grounds your psychic and spiritual experiences in your daily life.

Physical: good for knees, legs, ankles, and feet.

Emotional/spiritual: good for study, learning, teaching, expression, and getting your point across. Helps relationships, partnerships (personal and business), and activities involving groups or teams. Encourages you to let go of the past. Alleviates depression, grief, and sadness. Promotes new beginnings. Speeds up karma. Enhances dreams, dream interpretation, awareness, spiritual development, protection, psychic abilities, such as clairvoyance and clairaudience, and connection to angels, spirit guides, nature spirits, and the natural world. Improves appreciation of environmental issues and meditation.

BRYOZOAN SNAKESKIN AGATE

Petrified colonies of microscopic aquatic animals, forming *agate*. Brown and cream patterns resemble snakeskin.

Common alternative names: Petoskey stone (not identical but similarly formed and sometimes confused)
Common sources: worldwide—especially India, USA
Astrological association: Scorpio
Chakras: base, crown

HEALING QUALITIES

Raises kundalini energy from the base of the spine to the crown and allows you to step into the power of your inner goddess.

Physical: enhances flexibility. Good for muscles, joints, ligaments, female reproductive system, and fertility.

Emotional/spiritual: good for inner strength, confidence, self-respect, self-love, femininity, and self-worth. Helps you to resist allowing minor inconveniences to knock you off your path. Connects the past to the present, so you can learn from past mistakes and not repeat them. Supports intuition. Helps memory, mind, Alzheimer's disease, and dementia.

CARAMEL CALCITE

Masses and rhombohedral crystals, red-caramel in color.
Common source: Mexico
Astrological association: Cancer
Chakras: base, sacral

HEALING QUALITIES

Helps changes to stick and healing to be permanent.
Physical: good for vitality, female and male reproductive systems, hips, pelvic girdle, coccyx.
Emotional/spiritual: eases changes and helps them to stay in place. Aids overcoming addictions, stopping smoking, addictive behavior, OCD, and ADHD. Reduces stress and anxiety; relieves panic attacks. Balances emotions and helps to keep you grounded.

SNAKESKIN AGATE

Agate with patterns resembling snake skin.
Common alternative names: there are several varieties of snakeskin agate from around the world, each with different healing qualities
Common sources: Oregon, USA
Astrological association: Scorpio
Chakras: base, crown

HEALING QUALITIES

Helps you to make the best of the world around you.
Physical: rebuilds the body after illness.

Emotional/spiritual: transmutes energies, finding the positive in everything, turning difficult into easy, discomfort into contented, agitated into relaxed. Helps kundalini energy flow, promoting creativity, sexuality, movement, dance, and connection to your higher self. Allows you to enjoy yourself and have fun. Said to be good for investigators, detectives, journalists, and anyone looking into practical matters.

PETRIFIED PALM WOOD

Fossilized palm tree wood. *Chalcedony* has replaced organic material and the original structure and look of palm wood has been retained.
Common alternative names: petrified palm, fossilized palm wood
Common sources: Uruguay, USA
Astrological associations: Taurus, Capricorn
Chakra: base

HEALING QUALITIES

Brings emotional healing into the physical dimension.
Physical: good for knees and heat exhaustion. Also good for the head, including brain, eyes, eyesight, optic nerves, light sensitivity, ears, hearing, inner ear, Eustachian tubes, nose, nasal passages, mucous membranes, mouth, lips, gums, tongue, taste buds, throat, tonsillitis, laryngitis, pharyngitis, and infections of eyes, ears, nose, and mouth.
Emotional/spiritual: helps you to cope with stress by bending with the winds of change rather than trying to stop them. Encourages you to explore your past, childhood, and even past lives, letting go of what you don't need and moving forward. Grounding. Relieves fears and stems aggressive behavior. Good for divination and dowsing.

SNAKESKIN ROCK

Opaque pebbles of *jasper* and quartz, cemented together over time by silica minerals, such as *agate* and *chalcedony*, into a conglomerate, forming patterns resembling snakeskin.

Common alternative name: snakeskin jasper

Common sources: Asia, South America, USA

Astrological association: Scorpio

Chakras: base, crown

HEALING QUALITIES

Transformational energy evocative of the double serpent caduceus, the traditional symbol of healing and medicine, is drawn through this rock.

Physical: Good for all physical healing as a general tonic for the body; especially good for backache, spine, neck, and MS.

Emotional/spiritual: helps you to see problems from different angles, balancing the mind and the right and left hemispheres of the brain (creativity and intellect). Good for yin/yang balance.

CREEDITE

Forms monoclinic prismatic crystals, often occurring as acicular radiating sprays of fine prisms. Colors include brown, lavender (as seen here), orange, yellow, and blue.

Common sources: Bolivia, Kazakhstan, Mexico, USA

Astrological association: Virgo

Chakras: throat, crown

HEALING QUALITIES

Expands awareness.

Physical: Good for broken and fractured bones, torn and pulled muscles, nerve damage, immune system, detox, liver, and heartbeat.

Emotional/spiritual: promotes expression, especially of spiritual ideas that may be difficult to explain. Helps you to talk your talk. Good for discovering blocks in your path and directing remedial action, making you more aware in the process and overcoming seemingly impossible barriers. Helpful for overcoming depression, especially due to an overwhelm of responsibility. Aids meditation and growing consciousness.

STROMATOLITE

Rock-like fossils created by layer upon layer of cyanobacteria, or similar single-celled photosynthesizing bacteria. These are the oldest fossil rocks on the planet, dating back some 3.5 billion years to the first life on Earth. A small tumble stone might have several thousand years of growth within it.

Common sources: worldwide—especially Argentina, Australia, Peru, USA

Astrological associations: Capricorn, Virgo

Chakras: base, heart

HEALING QUALITIES

Emphasizes the spirit of community.

Physical: good for skeletal system, healthy body fluids, and teeth. Combats degenerative bone and joint conditions such as osteoarthritis, reducing swelling and water retention.

Emotional/spiritual: transformation of people, lifestyle, and environment. These crystals are team builders and give you a different, community-centered, view of your world. Good for communities, families, sports teams, all types of teams, work groups, coworkers, partners, and spouses. Promotes inclusivity and sharing, including the stranger in your group or family event. Supports a healthy aura, for you both as an individual and as part of your people. It removes blocks that stop you from organizing your life and helps you to sort the important things from the mundane. Aids past-life recall.

AMPHIBOLE IN QUARTZ

Amphibole is a related group of crystals that form layers, growing as phantoms or inclusions in a quartz crystal. These can include *actinolite*, riebeckite, **limonite**, **tremolite**, *hematite*, caolinite, winchite, hornblende, and richterite in any combination—any one or all may be present in the same amphibole in quartz crystal. They may also have kaolinite and/or lithium present. Colors vary accordingly and may include yellow, brown-gold, lavender, lilac, pinkish gray, deep red to pink, orangey pink, orange, white.

Common alternative names: angel phantom quartz, angel wing quartz, angel quartz, angel wing, guardian angel phantom quartz, red rabbit quartz (in Asia)
Common source: Brazil
Astrological associations: Taurus, Gemini
Chakras: brow, crown

HEALING QUALITIES

Facilitates receiving guidance from angels and spirit guides.
Physical: relieves neuralgia, neuropathic pain, and insomnia.
Emotional/spiritual: boosts your connection to angels and spirit guides, helping you to find answers in unexpected places. Brings love, joy, peace, tranquility, and an ability to see the beauty in everything. Offers empathy for grief or loss. Helps to manifest your desires. Good for receiving answers in meditation, connecting to past lives, past-life recall, intuition, dreams, dream recall, lucid dreaming, and protection.

CUPRITE

Crystallizes as masses, octahedral, dodecahedral, and cubic crystals; dark red to almost black with internal redness.
Common sources: worldwide—especially USA
Astrological associations: Taurus, Virgo, Capricorn
Chakra: base

HEALING QUALITIES

Helps you to cope with concerns that you can have no influence over.
Physical: good for vitality, metabolism, digestion, bladder, kidneys, reducing water retention, problems urinating, female reproductive system, fertility, childbirth, menopause, cystitis, fibroids, blood, stomach cramps, relieving arthritis, vertigo, and altitude sickness.

Emotional/spiritual: provides emotional energy to help you deal with excessive worry, irrational fear, and the stress they cause. Boosts survival instincts. Grounding; helps to reconnect you to the Earth.

STIBICONITE

Forms masses, powder and crystals replacing *stibnite* but retaining its structure, so they have the shape of stibnite.
Common sources: China, Mexico
Astrological association: Capricorn
Chakra: crown

HEALING QUALITIES

Out with the old, in with the new.
Physical: helps to alleviate hypocalcemia. Good for bones, teeth, muscle cramps, and stiffness.
Emotional/spiritual: promotes flexibility of attitude, letting go of old ideas, changing lifestyle, getting rid of outdated thoughts and beliefs, bringing new beginnings and a fresh start to any aspect of your life, such as relationships, careers, or home. It's evolution, not revolution: change must happen, but in a sober way. Like a signpost, it points the way ahead on your path. Helpful in transformational ceremonies, such as a marriage or funeral. Allows spendaholics to think again.
No elixir.

HERTFORDSHIRE PUDDINGSTONE

Conglomerate sedimentary rock composed of rounded flint pebbles cemented together by a matrix of quartz, created by the most southerly advance of a glacier in the last ice age, around 11,700 years ago. Contains *jasper*, chert, quartz. Reputed to be one of the rarest rocks on the planet. I've included it because it is on my doorstep and readily available to collect from local fields.

Only source: Hertfordshire, plus small amounts in the London basin (UK)
Astrological association: Gemini
Chakra: base

HEALING QUALITIES

Helps you to maintain a sense of calm when all around you are losing their heads.
Physical: good for microbiota, blood, tissue repair, and connective tissue.
Emotional/spiritual: good for teamwork, teams, groups, families, workgroups, mending relationships, justice, and putting projects together. Promotes dreams, goals, ideals, dream recall, and confidence. Offers calmness in stressful times.

ANTHOPHYLLITE

Massive, fibrous, lamellar, and orthorhombic crystals. Colors include brown, beige, gray-green.
Common alternative name: compositionally the same and polymorphic with cummingtonite
Common sources: Greenland, USA
Astrological association: Capricorn
Chakras: base, sacral

HEALING QUALITIES

Eases breaking out of self-imposed limitations to create new possibilities.
Physical: good for colon, duodenum, digestion, uptake of nutrients into cells, tissue repair, and recovery from injury or surgery.
Emotional/spiritual: helps you to remove self-imposed blocks. Promotes change. Focuses mind in decision making, research, revision, and study that may be needed to facilitate the new you; in the process, breeds confidence. Improves your dowsing accuracy.
No elixir. Avoid fibrous form entirely—anthophyllite is a form of asbestos which, in its fibrous form, is very bad for lungs. It should not be handled or breathed in. (Other forms are okay to handle, provided they are not consumed.)

TIBETAN SMOKY QUARTZ

Brown *smoky quartz* crystals from the Tibetan plateau, the roof of the world. The color is caused by natural radiation in the ground. The crystals are not radioactive.
Common alternative name: Tibetan smokey quartz
Only source: Tibet
Astrological associations: Capricorn, Sagittarius
Chakras: base, crown

HEALING QUALITIES

Encourages you to move forward and take the next step on your journey.
Physical: good for legs, knees, ankles, feet, and toes.
Emotional/spiritual: a grounding crystal; it also offers strong protection. Good for dreams, ideals, goals, dream recall, and meditation. Helps you to understand that you can't do everything all the time and that you have more ideas than you can possibly follow up in a lifetime. Promotes sharing of ideas, socializing, helping others, compassion, empathy, and letting go of the need to be in control.

LLANITE

A variety of *rhyolite* with inclusions of **microcline** and *blue quartz*, itself colored by inclusions of ilmenite. A little plagioclase, **biotite**, *fluorite*, *apatite*, *magnetite*, and *zircon* are also included.

Common alternative names: que sera stone (very similar but probably different, despite many common attributes), llanoite, llanolite

Common sources: Llano County (Texas, USA) was originally thought to be the only source, but llanite has now been discovered in Brazil, where it is in commercial production (although this might be que sera stone).

Astrological associations: Taurus, Cancer, Capricorn

Chakras: sacral, heart, brow

HEALING QUALITIES

A laid-back stone.

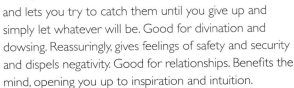

Physical: good for strength and digestion.

Emotional/spiritual: mixes up emotions, jiggles them about, throws them in the air, and lets you try to catch them until you give up and simply let whatever will be. Good for divination and dowsing. Reassuringly, gives feelings of safety and security and dispels negativity. Good for relationships. Benefits the mind, opening you up to inspiration and intuition.

BIOTITE

Variety of mica forming typical "books." Colors dark brown, greenish brown, blackish brown (almost black), yellow to tan, all displaying metallic luster.

Common source: Canada

Astrological association: Scorpio

Chakras: brow, crown

HEALING QUALITIES

All crystal healing is a little like peeling an onion, but biotite is the epitome. Each healing peels a layer and underneath there is another layer, and when you peel that, there's another layer. So life's journey continues each time, feeling a little lighter and happier.

Physical: good for vitality, eyes, reducing tumors and growths, diarrhea, and anemia.

Emotional/spiritual: helps you to strip away layers of pain, feelings, issues from past events, and trauma, and to see your place in relation to everything around you. Supports rationality and helps you to see the big picture. Good for communication skills.

KALAHARI PICTURE STONE

Several *picture jaspers* come from around the world, but the stones from the Kalahari Desert have a unique energy. These are always shades of cream, tan, and brown, showing "pictures" of the Kalahari landscape.

Common alternative names: Kalahari Desert jasper, picture jasper

Only source: Kalahari Desert (Botswana, Namibia, Republic of South Africa)

Astrological association: Leo

Chakra: brow

HEALING QUALITIES

Restores Earth connection.

Physical: good for immune system, connective tissue, skin, bones, kidneys, allergies, and reducing water retention and swelling.

Emotional/spiritual: primarily grounding, keeping your feet firmly on the ground as it helps you to release trapped emotions, particularly to do with grief and loss. Brings hope to dispel fear and the bright light of the desert sun to chase away the darkness. Good for business people, especially those wanting to grow their business. Promotes shamanic healing, natural therapies, awareness of environmental issues, and natural ways of living. Supports Earth healing and aids past-life recall.

CHAPTER 4

CRYSTAL REMEDIES

Within this chapter are more than 350 crystal remedies for common conditions and ailments, referring to the crystals included in the Crystal Finder (chapter 3) in this book. First are physical ailments, followed by emotional issues, with recommended crystal prescriptions for each condition listed. They are presented separately for ease of reference, although many physical symptoms can have an emotional cause. (There is often, perhaps always, an underlying cause of disease. Many illnesses occur because our energy system is in a state of dis-ease. Any stress, whether emotional, mental, or spiritual, may result in the manifestation of physical symptoms of an illness. This is not the same as psychosomatic illnesses, because in this case the illness itself is real. The physical body has been weakened, often by years of stress.)

The last two sections are concerned with spiritual and lifestyle enhancement, where you will find crystals to aid your self-development.

For each remedy, the crystal(s) in **bold** is the one to try first. Feel free to try the others. I have often found different causes can result in the same or similar symptoms—crystals are treating the cause rather than the symptom. Where a + sign appears, the crystals should all be worked with together. The more you work with the same crystal for the same condition, the quicker and more effective it will be. If you have no reaction at all after 30 minutes, try one of the alternatives or look for another description of what it is that ails you.

If in doubt, try bustamite with sugilite, chalcosiderite, double terminated quartz crystal, **Lemurian quartz crystal**, quartz crystal, or skeletal quartz, since these are often helpful for any condition. **Purple Mexican fluorite** helps most dis-ease on a deep, spiritual level, while **rose quartz crystals** can bring love into any healing.

To speed up and/or increase the effects of other crystals, **amethyst** or gyrolite can be carried, worn, held with other crystals, or placed on other crystals or the body.

REMEDIES FOR PHYSICAL AILMENTS

For general pain, hold a **quartz** crystal point a little above the site of the pain and move it slowly in a clockwise direction. Continue until the pain eases. Afghanite, **amethyst zebra stone**, buddstone, bustamite with sugilite, cathedral quartz, **cradle of humankind stone**, **Chevron amethyst**, **doctor's stone**, **golden Lemurian quartz crystal**, infinite, Himalayan diamond, Lemurian quartz crystal, nuummite, olivine on basalt, opalized jasper, papagoite quartz, **phillipsite**, polychrome jasper, **purple chalcedony**, **rose quartz crystal**, and vortex healing crystal can also ease pain by holding or taping to the required area. Hold a blue mist Lemurian quartz crystal to alleviate pain aggravated by stress. Biotite can help strip away layers of pain. Try drinking an elixir made with brown banded aragonite.

To prevent illness, and to maintain your general health when you are ill, carry, wear, and keep around you at home and at work any or all of the following: candle quartz, doctor's stone, pyrolusite crystal, and tourmalinated citrine.

If you think your physical condition (such as asthma, allergies, skin conditions, ulcerative colitis, heart disease, and many others) is related to stress, carry or wear golden Lemurian quartz crystal, kundalini citrine (digestive), peanut wood, quantum quattro stone, shungite (allergies), spodumene, or stichtite (headaches). Albite, **amethyst**, and green selenite can help you to see, realize, understand, and therefore alter the underlying situations giving rise to stress. Handle and play with these crystals often.

ABDOMINAL COLIC Hold any **citrine** crystal (**kundalini, Tibetan,** or **tourmalinated**) or green zoisite, leopard jasper, opalized white agate, or purple thulite to the worst point of pain for 30 minutes. Carry or wear citrine to reduce or prevent further attacks.

ABDOMINAL DISTENSION (bloating) Hold green zoisite to the affected area.

ABSCESS Hold **amethyst** or indigo gabbro to abscess.

ABSORPTION OF FOOD/NUTRIENTS (reduced) Carry or wear any variety of citrine (kundalini, Tibetan, or tourmalinated), purple ray opal, or tangerine quartz.

ACALCULIA Place liddicoatite on your desk or in your workspace.

ACHILLES TENDON Hold faden quartz, gyrolite, hubnerite, or **tugtupite** to the tendon.

ACIDOSIS (acidity excess) Carry or wear green jasper or tangerine quartz.

ACNE Carry or wear any of the following crystals, or keep a larger piece by your bed or anywhere you spend a lot of time: **amethyst**, angel wing selenite, blue smithsonite, cinnabar in quartz, copal, green smithsonite, or white topaz. Hold the crystal to the worst spot each day. Make an elixir from **copal** and apply it topically to the skin.

ADDICTION Carrying or wearing **amethyst**, black onyx, blue spinel, cacoxenite in amethyst, quantum quattro stone, caramel calcite, **lepidolite in quartz**, lithium quartz, **Sirius amethyst**, smoky citrine, or **spodumene** can help. **Pink tourmaline and lepidolite in quartz** is particularly good for mild addictions, as are **Vera Cruz amethyst** and **blue barite**. Brandberg amethyst, elestial quartz, blue barite, and orthoclase can all speed a return to normality after the addiction is broken.

ADRENALINE Carry or wear silver aventurine to assist production.

ACQUIRED IMMUNE DEFICIENCY SYNDROME (AIDS) See Immune system and add specific crystals for individual symptoms of active AIDS-related conditions. Treatment must be daily, if possible, with a trained crystal therapist. Amethyst zebra stone, blue and green smithsonite, **chevron amethyst**, **chrome tremolite**, dumortierite in quartz, golden healer quartz, prehnite with epidote, and ruby in fuchsite can each be helpful.

ALCOHOL (effects of) Carry or wear amethyst when consuming alcohol.

ALLERGIES Carry or wear albite, black onyx, **bumble bee jasper**, **chalcosiderite**, Kalahari picture stone, mother of pearl, pink tourmaline and lepidolite in quartz, or **shungite**. **Peach aventurine** elixir is good for skin allergies. For localized allergies, hold any of these crystals to the affected area. **Yellow quartz** helps alleviate food allergies. Try lazulite for sun allergy (see Photosensitivity). **White moonstone** is helpful in the case of allergic reactions.

ALZHEIMER'S DISEASE Carry or wear blue barite, Bryozoan snakeskin agate, buddstone, epidote in quartz, **grape chalcedony**, orange selenite, or **pink tourmaline and lepidolite in quartz**. Argentinian blue calcite, arsenopyrite, blue spinel, goethite on hematite, golden Lemurian quartz crystal, Himalayan diamond, K2 jasper, **lion skin stone**, nuummite, realgar, sieber agate, **silver moonstone**, vortex healing crystal, and yellow quartz, or an elixir made with copal, are also helpful aids to memory.

ANAPHYLACTIC SHOCK White moonstone speeds recovery after the incident is under control.

ANEMIA Carry or wear **Alaskan garnet**, biotite, **hematite/magnetite**, hubnerite, Tibetan citrine, or yellow prehnite 24/7. Keep goethite on hematite nearby and continue with all this for at least three months after the condition improves to prevent relapse.

ANGINA Carry or wear **Alaskan garnet**, **amethyst**, bumble bee jasper, or **quartz crystal**. Place a large piece of amethyst or goethite on hematite next to your bed or desk, or wherever you spend most of your time. See also Arteries.

ANKLES (swollen or aching) Hold elestial smoky quartz, **harlequin quartz**, pyroxene, or Tibetan smoky quartz to the relevant ankle.

ANOREXIA Carry or wear pink tourmaline and lepidolite in quartz. Meditate with stichtite daily and hold a piece of blue apatite before meals.

ANTISEPTIC When an antiseptic is needed, apply a topical elixir made with copal.

ANUS Discomfort in the nether regions may be caused by hemorrhoids, minor infections, or more serious inflammations, such as Crohn's disease. Place Tibetan citrine beneath a cushion or pillow on your seat.

APPENDICITIS Hold a citrine crystal (kundalini, smoky, Tibetan, or tourmalinated) to your skin at the site of pain.

APPETITE (excessive) Hold blue apatite for two minutes before you eat anything, be it snack or a full meal. After that, eat if you still want to. You'll find that sometimes you don't, and over a couple of weeks or so your appetite will noticeably reduce.

ARTERIES *Arteriosclerosis:* Hold albite to affected areas. *Cardiac:* Carry or wear vortex healing crystal to improve their condition.

ARTHRITIS (osteoarthritis) Hold crystals to the worst affected joint for at least 30 minutes each day. You may find that as one joint improves another will become worse. Each day, hold the crystals to the most painful area: atacamite, axinite, black tourmaline with mica, blue john, **chalcosiderite**, cuprite, grape chalcedony, indigo gabbro, quantum quattro stone, rhodonite in quartz, scenic quartz, Tiffany stone, or vortex healing crystal. Place gyrolite or green selenite on joint gently, as they are fragile. An amethyst elixir may also relieve chronic symptoms.

ASTHMA There appear to be two types of this condition. One is an allergic reaction, usually caused by pollen grains; the other may be genetic and is not made worse by pollen. Carry or wear **chalcosiderite** for the former and **rose quartz crystals** for the latter. Albite, amethyst, blue aragonite, blue jade, blue john, brown banded aragonite, catlinite, copal, green chalcedony, green kyanite, K2 jasper, orthoclase, and Tanzanian aventurine are also helpful in alleviating the symptoms.

ATTENTION DEFICIENT DISORDERS (ADD/ ADHD) Bustamite with sugilite, harlequin quartz, lepidocrocite, pink tourmaline and lepidolite in quartz, stichtite, and yellow quartz can be helpful in treatment. Holding Argentinian blue calcite or caramel calcite can help with immediate symptoms.

AUTISM Carry or wear **Argentinian blue calcite, bustamite with sugilite, pink tourmaline and lepidolite in quartz**, or stichtite. Place under pillow or next to bed at night.

BACKACHE Either lie on your stomach with a piece of **garden quartz** on your spine or put this or goethite on hematite under your mattress at night. Carry hematite/ magnetite, snakeskin rock, or violet sapphire with you. **Leopard jasper** will help if pain is due to muscle damage. For lower backache (lumbago), work with **scheelite**.

BACTERIAL INFECTION Carry, wear, or hold to affected area **amethyst**, cinnabar in quartz, copal, or kammererite; **ruby and kyanite in fuchsite** for infections of the bowel. Additionally, work with specific crystals to relieve symptoms in the area of the body affected.

BALANCE (lack of physical) Amethyst, **auralite-23, elestial quartz, Lemurian quartz crystal**, lorenzenite, moqui marbles, pink tourmaline and lepidolite in quartz, and **quartz crystal** can all help. Hold one of these while sitting quietly for 30 minutes each day until the condition desists.

BELL'S PALSY Hold **moqui marbles** or **petrified palm wood** to the affected area for 5–10 minutes several times a day to help alleviate symptoms. Carry these with you all day and place under your pillow or next to the bed at night.

BITES *Insect:* Hold celestite with sulfur or **white moonstone** to the wound. To repel insects, place celestite with sulfur around your bed at night. *Venomous:* Hold green or white chalcedony to the wound.

BLADDER PROBLEMS Carry or wear cat's eye, clear halite, conichalcite, **copal**, cuprite, green jasper, leopard jasper, molybdenite, rainbow moonstone, yellow prehnite, or yellow sapphire. You can also tape a small piece onto your skin. **Ruby in kyanite** and **ruby and kyanite in fuchsite** are helpful in cases of infection. Keep a whole **abalone shell** next to your bed.

BLOOD Ankerite, cinnabar in quartz, cuprite, goethite on hematite, green chalcedony, hematite/magnetite, Hertfordshire pudding stone, molybdenite, nuummite, olive opal, pyrolusite crystal, rose quartz crystal, ruby in fuchsite, strawberry aventurine, tangerine quartz, white chalcedony, and yellow prehnite can all support the health of the blood. Carry or wear any combinations you are drawn to. *Circulation/flow:* Carry or wear albite, amethyst, blue coral, brookite, **bumble bee jasper**, colemanite, Libyan gold tektite, **nuummite**, opalized white agate, piemontite, **rose quartz crystal**, ruby in fuchsite, scheelite, scolecite, strawberry aventurine, or white moonstone to improve circulation. *Cleansing:* Amethyst, ankerite, and **yellow prehnite** can all help to remove pollutants from the blood and detoxify it after infection. Carry or wear one of these crystals over your heart. *Clotting/bleeding:* Hold benitoite, pyrolusite crystal, or **ruby in fuchsite** to the site of minor wounds. *Clots:* Hold amethyst, **goethite on hematite**, or scolecite to the relevant area. *Disorders:* Almandine garnet in pyroxene, goethite on hematite, and violet sapphire can all support the health of the blood. Carry or wear any combinations you are drawn to or place them by your bed. *Oxygenation:* Carry or wear **Alaskan garnet, hubnerite, scenic quartz**, or **strawberry aventurine**. *Pressure:* Carry or wear diopside or **peach aventurine** for fluctuations in pressure; **stichtite** or vortex healing crystal for low blood pressure; **blue aragonite**, blue jade, and spodumene to help with high blood pressure. *Regeneration:* Carry or wear strawberry aventurine, **tangerine quartz**, or yellow prehnite. *Strength:* Carry or wear green jasper. *Sugar levels:* Carry or wear nuummite. *Vessels:* Hold chrysotile septarian, green chalcedony, hausmannite, moqui marbles, or **pink tourmaline in quartz** to any damaged areas. **Bubble gum tourmaline** can speed the repair of blood vessels around the heart.

BOILS Hold cinnabar in quartz, **violet sapphire**, or white topaz to affected area, or drink elixir made from violet sapphire or white topaz (but not cinnabar in quartz).

BONES *Broken or fractured:* Hold to injury or tape onto adjacent skin amblygonite, ammonite, axinite, **cataclasite**, cradle of humankind stone, or faden quartz. Place creedite or **goethite on hematite** near the injury in bed, on footstool, or wherever is appropriate. *Cancer:* Carry or wear honey calcite or yellow calcite 24/7, and spend some time holding it to any areas of discomfort. *Disease:* Hold **ammonite** to affected areas and carry or wear lazulite. *Disorders:* Carry or wear, and hold to relevant areas, any of the following, and have a larger crystal where you spend a lot of time: amethyst, ammonite, axinite, black rutilated quartz, blue john, brown banded aragonite, cradle of humankind stone, denim lapis, gyrolite, hausmannite, Kalahari picture stone, micalated quartz, mimetite, moqui marbles, purple Mexican fluorite, purple scapolite, rhodonite in quartz, scenic quartz, stibiconite. An elixir made from black septarian can also give relief. *General aches:* Hold amethyst or **hematite/magnetite** to the affected areas. Drink a **scenic quartz** elixir or apply a brown banded aragonite elixir topically. *Marrow disease and disorders:* Carry or wear purple Mexican fluorite.

BOWEL INFECTION
Hold lithium quartz or **ruby and kyanite in fuchsite** to areas of distension or discomfort.

BRAIN
Injury: Hold cataclasite, chrome tremolite, epidote in quartz, green tourmaline in quartz, liddicoatite, microcline, nuummite, papagoite in quartz, petrified palm wood, scolecite, silver moonstone, stella beam calcite, or white chalcedony to the head. *Tumors:* Can be helped by holding **nuummite** or **white chalcedony** to the head.

BREAST
Hold lorenzenite or ritzullite to required area.

BREATHING
Wear a pendant or hold **blue aragonite**, blue john, **catlinite**, copal, green chalcedony, lepidocrocite, ritzullite, or Tanzanian aventurine. **Orange moss agate** can aid control of the breath.

BRONCHITIS
Wear a blue aragonite, blue john, catlinite, copal, **green chalcedony**, or Tanzanian aventurine pendant.

BULIMIA
Carry or wear **pink tourmaline and lepidolite in quartz** or stichtite and hold for one hour before meals.

BURNS
For mild cases, hold **golden healer quartz** or **rose quartz crystals** to affected area. In severe cases, place the crystals near the area but not in contact with damaged tissue. Also, if the skin is unbroken, gently bathe the area in a golden Lemurian quartz crystal elixir. You can work with either golden healer quartz or golden Lemurian quartz crystal to activate the area for maximum healing benefit.

CALMING
(physical) Hold blue mist Lemurian quartz crystal.

CANCER
Carry or wear amethyst, amethyst elestial crystal, **biotite**, **green jasper**, tangerine quartz, or yellow sapphire. Hold to any areas of discomfort for as long as possible and as many times as needed each day. You can also tape crystals to relevant areas. Blue spinel supports cancer treatment.

CARPAL TUNNEL SYNDROME
Hold ruby in fuchsite or ruby and kyanite in fuchsite to the wrist for minimum of 30 minutes daily.

CARTILAGE PROBLEMS
Hold benitoite, black septarian, gyrolite, hubnerite, infinite, **molybdenite**, **Tiffany stone**, or tugtupite to affected joint for a minimum of 30 minutes daily. For chronic cartilage pain, hold chevron amethyst to the joint as well.

CELL MEMBRANES
Carry or wear anthophyllite. Strengthening membranes can help to prevent viral infections taking hold when you're run down or post-operatively.

CHEMOTHERAPY
Keep uranophane on bedside table to help with side effects of chemotherapy and radiotherapy.

CHICKEN POX
Keep rosasite near and hold often.

CHILDBIRTH
Black onyx, cuprite, kimberlite, **rainbow moonstone**, and **white moonstone** can all ease the birthing process. Carry or wear continuously from four weeks before the baby is due and keep with you to hold during the birthing process. *Birth contractions:* Hold black onyx, cuprite, kimberlite, olive opal, **rainbow moonstone**, or **white moonstone** to belly to stimulate contractions.

CHILDREN
Babies: Place chalcosiderite in or under the baby's cot to aid physical development. *Growth:* Children should carry or wear **shungite** or tanzine aura quartz to promote healthy physical development. *With learning difficulties:* Keep **bustamite with sugilite** or stichtite around the child, in or under the bed and anywhere he/she spends a lot of time.

CHOLESTEROL
(high) Carry or wear strawberry aventurine.

CHROMOSOME DAMAGE Carry or wear cradle of humankind stone.

CHRONIC FATIGUE SYNDROME (CFS) Carry or wear brown banded aragonite, chrome tremolite, **girasol quartz**, **Lemurian quartz crystal**, **rhodonite in quartz**, and ruby in fuchsite 24/7. Work with other specific crystals to alleviate symptoms.

CHRONIC PAIN RELIEF Carry or wear amethyst zebra stone, blue jade, **chevron amethyst**, phillipsite, yin yang crystal 24/7 and hold to areas of pain.

COLON PROBLEMS Carry or wear anthophyllite, clear halite, or **papagoite quartz**. Hold to any areas of discomfort. *Colitis:* Carry or wear albite or **dumortierite in quartz** and hold to areas of discomfort until the discomfort eases.

COMMON COLD Carry or wear Andean opal, blue moss agate, chalcosiderite, hanksite, intrinsinite, jamesonite, leopard jasper, Navajo jasper, olive opal, opalized jasper, **phosphosiderite**, rose quartz crystals, Tanzanian aventurine, or yellow sapphire. Lithium quartz can pick you up when you're run down with cold symptoms.

CONSTIPATION Leave **copal** to stand in a glass of water for one hour and drink the resulting elixir. Hold dumortierite in quartz, green tourmaline in quartz, lepidolite in quartz, ruby and kyanite in fuchsite, or white moonstone to the abdomen. For chronic conditions, carry or wear these.

COOLING (hot climate) Carry or wear Andean opal, **cryolite**, brown banded aragonite, or purple ray opal and hold when affected.

COORDINATION Carry or wear lavender amethyst and hold for a few minutes before attempting complicated tasks.

CONNECTIVE TISSUE PROBLEMS Carry or wear green kyanite, **Hertfordshire puddingstone**, infinite, Kalahari picture stone, rose opal, or **yellow prehnite**.

CONVULSIONS Carry or wear **atacamite** 24/7 or keep **goethite on hematite** in your environment to reduce occurrences.

COUGH Carry or wear **erythrite, rose quartz crystals**, or yellow sapphire for a shallow, irritating cough.

CROHN'S DISEASE Carry or wear agnitite, dumortierite in quartz, ruby in fuchsite, **sunset aura quartz**, or **tourmalinated citrine** 24/7. Hold to any areas of discomfort.

CYSTITIS Carry or wear **buddstone** or olive serpentine and hold to areas of discomfort.

DEHYDRATION Hold blue moss agate, dragonstone, **Kambamba jasper**, or **Libyan gold tektite** and keep crystals around you until well.

DIABETES Carry or wear atlantisite, buddstone, girasol quartz, **Lemurian quartz crystal**, **nuummite**, olive opal, purple ray opal, or **quartz crystal** 24/7. Drink rose opal elixir daily.

DIARRHEA Carry or wear biotite, dumortierite in quartz, green tourmaline in quartz, or ruby and kyanite in fuchsite.

DIGESTION Carry, wear, or keep near you anthophyllite, Brandberg amethyst, brown banded aragonite, bubble gum tourmaline, bumble bee jasper, cuprite, dumortierite in quartz, green smithsonite, kimberlite, lepidolite in quartz, liddicoatite, llanite, purple ray opal, purple thulite, pyrolusite crystal, quantum quattro stone, steatite, tourmalinated citrine, yellow danburite, or yellow quartz. *Disorders:* Goethite on hematite, pink tourmaline in quartz, purple ray opal, and **Tibetan citrine** are helpful in the treatment of any and all affected or diseased areas. Carry or wear these or hold them to any area required or place them by your bed for all digestive disorders. To improve peristalsis, carry or wear ruby and kyanite in fuchsite.

DISCOMFORT Move a **Lemurian quartz crystal**, **Himalayan quartz crystal** point, or **quartz crystal** point clockwise over the affected area until the discomfort has gone; or hold or tape **snakeskin agate** to the area of discomfort; or place realgar in front of you on a table and, while looking at it intently, focus your mind on the area of discomfort.

DIZZINESS Hold **denim lapis** or doctor's stone until symptoms stop.

DYSLEXIA Carry or wear **bustamite with sugilite** or purple scapolite.

EAR *Ache:* Slowly move a **quartz crystal** point in small clockwise circles near the ear opening until discomfort stops. Hold black amethyst to the ear. **Disorders:** Hold blue apatite, blue quartz, nuummite, petrified palm wood, stella beam calcite, or white chalcedony to ear. Move **quartz crystal** point in clockwise circular motion over ear. Place goethite on hematite under your pillow. **Eustachian tube:** Hold **denim lapis** or petrified palm wood behind the ear for 10 minutes. Repeat as often as required. **Infection**: Slowly move a Lemurian quartz crystal or quartz crystal point in small anticlockwise circles near the ear opening for 2–5 minutes. Repeat at least twice daily and place the crystal under your pillow or on a bedside table at night. Hold petrified palm wood to your ear for a similar length of time and also place under pillow. **Inner ear infection:** Hold **elestial quartz crystal**, **lorenzenite**, moqui marbles, or petrified palm wood against ear. **Ménière's disease:** Hold elestial quartz to ear for 30 minutes or for as long as it is bearable. Repeat as often as possible, at least daily.

EMPHYSEMA Carry, wear, or tape to chest blue john, catlinite, copal, or rhodonite in quartz.

ENDOCRINE SYSTEM Place green quartz, tanzine aura quartz, or **Vera Cruz amethyst** on a bedside table at night. **Glands:** Hold **amethyst** or golden rod calcite to relevant area and keep near you or carry or wear during the day.

ENDURANCE (physical) Carry or wear **black onyx**, **Kambamba stone**, limonite, or scepter quartz crystal. Black septarian can be placed in training areas for athletes.

ENERGY Place olivine on basalt where you're working or training to boost all kinds of energy. **Blocks (causing physical dis-ease):** Carry or wear **golden healer quartz**, **kundalini citrine**, or spodumene. Hold to energy block if you know where it is. **Excess:** Hold double terminated quartz crystals, or for longer-term relief carry or wear them. **Physical:** Carry or wear and keep in your environment Alaskan garnet, almandine garnet in pyroxene, bumble bee jasper, catlinite, doctor's stone, harlequin quartz, kimberlite, Lemurian quartz crystal, limonite, orange mist aura quartz, quartz crystal, sunset aura quartz, or tangerine quartz. Realgar and celestite with sulfur can also help in work environment. **Storage for future use:** Carry or wear orange moss agate or place on your sacral chakra for 10–20 minutes daily.

EPILEPSY Carry or wear bustamite with sugilite or green kyanite 24/7.

ESOPHAGUS Carry or wear lorenzenite and hold to any painful area.

EXHAUSTION Hold yellow quartz; carry or wear for chronic symptoms.

EYE PROBLEMS All the following crystals can aid the eyes: almandine garnet in pyroxene, atacamite, blue apatite, blue moss agate, blue quartz, blue spinel, cat's eye, chevron amethyst, epidote in quartz, green chalcedony, green tourmaline in quartz, lepidocrocite, papagoite quartz, petrified palm wood, **scenic quartz**, and stella beam calcite. Place them on eyelids for 15–30 minutes and repeat until symptoms desist. Bathe eyes in an elixir drawn from an abalone shell. **Astigmatism:** Place blue apatite, lepidocrocite, nuummite, opalized white agate, purple ray opal, purple scapolite, **scenic quartz**, or Tibetan citrine on eyelid. Keep epidote in quartz or yin yang crystal on bedside table. **Cataracts:** Bathe eye in abalone shell (whole) elixir or hold purple scapolite to closed eye for at least 5–10 minutes. **Glaucoma:** Place purple scapolite on eyelid for short periods, but repeat often. **Infection of iris:** Place purple scapolite on eyelid for 5–10 minutes. Repeat as needed. **Sight**: Hold blue barite, epidote in quartz, scenic quartz, or Tibetan citrine to eyelids or bathe eyes in elixir. Place chrysotile serpentine or petrified palm wood on a table at a comfortable distance and focus your eyes on it regularly during the day. **Strain:** Place auralite-23 on eyelids.

FATIGUE (long-term) Carry or wear Andean opal, benitoite, infinite, or **yellow quartz**. Carry any of these with you, especially when driving through the night.

FEET Hold axinite, buddstone, elestial smoky quartz, **harlequin quartz**, microcline, pyroxene, scheelite, or Tibetan smoky quartz to affected areas. **Lava stone** relieves aching feet. Hold **doctor's stone** to the soles of your feet. **Bunions:** Hold blue aragonite, brown banded aragonite, or **lava stone** to the area. **Corns:** Soak feet in warmed lava stone elixir.

FERTILITY Women: Any of the following may help in different circumstances. Carry or wear blue mist Lemurian quartz crystal, brecciated jasper, bryozoan snakeskin agate, bubble gum tourmaline, chrysanthemum stone, cinnabar in quartz, colemanite, columbite, **cuprite**, **goddess stone**, golden feldspar, hanksite, honey calcite, lemon chrysoprase, lepidocrocite, Libyan gold tektite, pink tourmaline in quartz, purple ray opal, **rainbow moonstone**, **rose quartz crystals**, ruby and kyanite in fuchsite, silver moonstone, strawberry aventurine, tangerine quartz, tanzine aura quartz, **white moonstone**, or **yin yang crystal**, and hold to belly for at least 10 minutes each evening. Try meditating with **abalone shell** or realgar. *Men:* Keep a scepter quartz crystal in your trouser pocket.

FEVER Hold or place next to bed Andean opal, afghanite, bismuth, blue scheelite, brown banded aragonite, **cryolite**, jamesonite, kimberlite, Libyan gold tektite, **olive opal**, purple ray opal, or ruby and kyanite in fuchsite.

FIBROIDS Carry or wear **brecciated jasper**, chrysanthemum stone, or **cuprite**.

FIBROMYALGIA Carry or wear agnitite, brown banded aragonite, or **ruby in fuchsite** and hold to any areas of discomfort.

FIBROUS TISSUE GROWTHS Hold celestite with sulfur to affected area.

FLU Carry or wear **chalcosiderite**, hanksite, intrinsinite, lithium quartz, Navajo jasper, or opalized jasper. Hold leopard jasper or meditate with jamesonite to relieve symptoms.

FLUIDS (body) *Imbalance:* Carry or wear **molybdenite** or stromatolite. *Retention:* Carry or wear molybdenite or **orange selenite** and hold to areas of swelling.

FOOD POISONING (prevention) Carry or wear ruby and kyanite in fuchsite when eating out.

FREE RADICALS (combating) Carry or wear **tangerine quartz** or place where you spend most of your time.

FROZEN SHOULDER Hold intrinsinite or liddicoatite in the hand of the affected shoulder.

GALL BLADDER (pain) Carry or wear pink danburite, steatite, or **yellow sapphire**.

GASTROENTERITIS Place opalized white agate near bed and hold to areas of discomfort as required.

GENETIC DISEASES Carry or wear **cradle of humankind stone** or moqui marbles; hold or tape to appropriate areas.

GLANDS *Adrenal:* Hold a piece of **phosphosiderite** for at least 30 minutes each day. Actinolite in quartz, bustamite with sugilite, and rose quartz crystal, or a silver aventurine elixir may also be helpful. *Glandular fever:* See mononucleosis. *Pineal:* Lie down and place blue coral, **bustamite with sugilite**, or cataclasite on your brow or third eye for 30 minutes daily. *Pituitary:* Hold or place **blue coral** or bustamite with sugilite on the back of the neck near the top. *Swollen:* Carry or wear blue halite, denim lapis, **green quartz**, lazulite, scenic quartz, or **violet sapphire**. *Thymus (over/under active):* Place amethyst zebra stone, chevron amethyst, **green tourmaline in quartz**, peach aventurine, or Tibetan citrine on thymus (top of the chest) for 20–30 minutes daily. *Thyroid (over/under active):* Carry or wear dragonstone, **epidote in quartz**, golden feldspar, phosphosiderite, or Tibetan citrine and hold to the throat when needed.

GOUT Hold yellow prehnite to affected joints.

GUT HEALTH (increasing microbiota) These are good bacteria in the gut that may have many varied health benefits. Carry, wear, or place by your bed or on dining or kitchen table Hertfordshire pudding stone, steatite, or **tourmalinated citrine**.

HAIR *Healthy:* Carry or wear **dragonstone**, hanksite, hausmannite, hematite/magnetite, or silver moonstone. Massage a white moonstone elixir into the scalp. *Loss:* Carry or wear Andean opal, girasol quartz, golden selenite, grape chalcedony, phosphosiderite, or purple ray opal.

HANDS (dexterity) Hold **bumble bee jasper**, hematite/magnetite, lemon chrysoprase, or **microcline** each day for 20–30 minutes.

HAY FEVER Carry or wear **chalcosiderite** and meditate with it daily.

HEADACHES Can have many causes and therefore many remedies. Try holding **amethyst**, auralite-23, black amethyst, buddstone, bustamite with sugilite, cat's eye, champagne aura quartz, denim lapis, elestial quartz, Himalayan diamond, infinite, intrinsinite, olivine on basalt, peach aventurine, scenic quartz, tanzine aura quartz, Vera

Cruz amethyst, or vortex healing crystal to the area of pain. Double terminated quartz crystal placed on the crown chakra can also help alleviate headaches. *Chronic pain relief:* Try chevron amethyst. *Exacerbated by stress:* K2 jasper or stichtite are good. *Mild and recurring:* Opt for lavender amethyst. *Tension:* Amethyst zebra stone is preferred. *Unexplained:* Hold petrified palm wood to areas of concern.

HEARING *Long-term difficulties:* Carry or wear amethyst, blue apatite, buddstone, **Lemurian quartz crystal**, moqui marbles, **quartz crystal**, or Vera Cruz amethyst. Hold petrified palm wood to your ear for 5–10 minutes. Repeat several times during the day. *Temporary loss:* Carry or wear **denim lapis** or quartz crystal and meditate with it daily. *Tinnitus:* Move a **quartz crystal** point slowly in a clockwise direction pointing into the ear until symptoms improve. Repeat every time symptoms appear, and the frequency of events will slowly reduce. Also carry or wear elestial quartz, Lemurian quartz crystal, nuummite, quartz crystal, or tanzine aura quartz, and place under your pillow or on a bedside table at night.

HEART *General health:* Many crystals can assist the heart in different ways. Carry, wear, or hold the crystal. Lie down and place it on the center of your chest for at least 20–30 minutes. Repeat as often as needed. Try any of the following: Alaskan garnet, almandine garnet in pyroxene, amegreen, amethyst, black tourmaline with mica, blue mist Lemurian quartz crystal, bubble gum tourmaline, bumble bee jasper, colemanite, copal, diopside, golden Lemurian quartz crystal, green chalcedony, green kyanite, green selenite, green tourmaline in quartz, green zoisite, Inca jade, infinite, lemon chrysoprase, Lemurian black jade, lepidocrocite, lizard skin agate, piemontite, pink tourmaline in lepidolite, pink tourmaline in quartz, quartz crystal, rhodonite in quartz, ritzullite, rose opal, rose quartz crystals, ruby in kyanite, silver aventurine, spodumene, stichtite, Tibetan citrine, vortex healing crystal, or yellow prehnite. *Heart block, congenital:* Place agnitite or **ruby in fuchsite** above or below cot (out of the baby's reach). *Heart conditions:* Carry or wear chrome tremolite or keep it in or by your bed. *Heart disease:* Carry albite. *Heart rate:* Carry or wear blue aragonite. *Irregular heartbeat:* Carry or wear creedite or lepidolite in

quartz. Lie down and place the crystal on your chest for 20–30 minutes daily.

HEAT EXHAUSTION Sit quietly, hold petrified palm wood, and drink lots of water. (If you have heatstroke/sunstroke, which is more serious, seek immediate medical attention.)

HEMERALOPIA (inability to see clearly in bright light) Keep abalone shell near you. Gently bathe eyelids in water from the shell for five minutes or so first thing in the morning.

HEMORRHAGE Hold yellow sapphire to area.

HERNIA Hold or place atlantisite, rosasite, or stichtite on the area for 30 minutes daily.

HIP Hold or tape caramel calcite or pyroxene to point of discomfort. Scheelite can improve the blood flow to the hips.

HIV Carry or wear chevron amethyst.

HORMONES (imbalance) *Both sexes:* Carry or wear copal, golden calcite, golden feldspar, green quartz, limonite, **rainbow moonstone**, scheelite, spodumene, tanzine aura quartz, and **violet sapphire**. Blue mist Lemurian quartz crystal and lepidocrocite can help to balance hormone levels. *Female:* Carry or wear white moonstone.

HYPOGLYCEMIA Carry or wear atlantisite or hubnerite, or place next to bed.

HYPOTHERMIA Hold **Andean opal**, brown banded aragonite, **cryolite**, olive opal, **purple ray opal**.

IRRITABLE BOWEL SYNDROME (IBS) Carry, wear, and hold to areas of discomfort brown banded aragonite, dumortierite in quartz, opalized white agate, quantum quattro stone, or sunset aura quartz.

IMMUNE SYSTEM (support) Many crystals can support the immune system in different circumstances. Carry or wear any of these crystals and place them around your home and workplace: actinolite in quartz, aegerine, agrellite, amethyst zebra stone, Andean opal, black rutilated quartz, blue moss agate, blue quartz, blue smithsonite, Brandberg amethyst, cataclasite, chevron amethyst, chrome tremolite, creedite, denim lapis, dragonstone, dumortierite in quartz, golden feldspar, golden healer quartz, golden Lemurian quartz crystal, green selenite, green smithsonite, green tourmaline in quartz, Inca jade, indigo gabbro, Kalahari picture stone, Lemurian black jade, moqui marbles, olive opal, opalized jasper, prehnite with epidote, purple ray opal, quantum quattro stone, ruby in fuchsite, ruby in kyanite, scenic quartz, Sirius amethyst, and Vera Cruz amethyst.

INCONTINENCE Carry or wear libethenite or purple scapolite.

INDIGESTION Hold atlantisite, green jasper, mimetite, purple thulite, or yellow sapphire to area of discomfort. *Acid indigestion:* Hold **atlantisite**, **green jasper**, **mimetite**, purple thulite, or tangerine quartz to your chest just above the area of discomfort. As the discomfort reduces, lower the crystal until the discomfort has gone. Carry or wear atlantisite or green jasper to reduce or prevent recurrence. *Belching:* Carry or wear **green zoisite**, opalized white agate, pink thulite, or **purple thulite**. *Flatulence:* Carry or wear green zoisite, purple thulite, or yellow sapphire. *Wind pains:* Hold green zoisite, leopard jasper, opalized white agate, pink thulite, or purple thulite to area of discomfort. In chronic cases, carry or wear these crystals.

INFECTION *At first sign:* Golden calcite can be effective at the start of infections. *Diseases:* Keep chevron amethyst near your bed. *Wounds:* Carry or wear actinolite in quartz, agrellite, **amethyst**, blue scheelite, cinnabar in quartz, **copal**, indigo gabbro, kammererite, petrified palm wood, ruby in kyanite, Sirius amethyst, Tanzanian aventurine, or violet sapphire. Hold to the site of external infections for 30 minutes and repeat every few hours. **Celestite with sulfur** is particularly good for this.

INFLAMMATION Hold brown banded aragonite, indigo gabbro, peach aventurine, scenic quartz, or tanzine aura quartz to the site of swelling.

INSOMNIA Hold **pink tourmaline and lepidolite in quartz** or **pink tourmaline in lepidolite** for one hour before you want to go to sleep. Do all your normal ablutions and keep holding the crystal when you go to bed. Your sleep pattern will improve the first night and should return to normal over two weeks. Carrying or wearing afghanite, amethyst, amphibole in quartz, denim lapis, intrinsinite, nuummite, phosphosiderite, Preseli blue stone, ruby in fuchsite, scolecite, stella beam calcite, tanzine aura quartz, or vortex healing crystals in the evening can also help. Place goethite on hematite, **scenic quartz**, Vera Cruz amethyst, or **yin yang crystal** by your bed.

INTESTINAL DISORDERS Carry or wear amethyst zebra stone, chevron amethyst, green jasper, kimberlite, opalized white agate, purple thulite, ruby and kyanite in fuchsite, tangerine quartz, **tourmalinated citrine**, and white halite. Hold crystals to areas of discomfort. *Duodenum:* Carry anthophyllite 24/7. *Small intestine:* Carry or wear sunset aura quartz and hold to areas of discomfort.

JAUNDICE Carry or wear leopard jasper, **Tibetan citrine**, or yellow sapphire.

JAW (aching) Hold arsenopyrite to the skin by the affected area for 20–30 minutes. Repeat as required.

JET LAG Carry goethite on hematite.

JOINTS *Damaged/injured:* Hold ammonite, axinite, benitoite, **black rutilated quartz**, blue john, brown banded aragonite, bryozoan snakeskin agate, **chalcosiderite**, garden quartz, gyrolite, infinite, mimetite, molybdenite, **orange selenite**, scenic quartz, Tiffany stone, **tugtupite**, or yin yang crystal to affected joint. *Flexibility:* Carry or wear black septarian, hubnerite, polychrome jasper, or **silver leaf jasper** and hold to relevant joints. *Pain relief:* Carry, wear, or tape to the painful joint atacamite or **quantum quattro stone**; or hold celestite with sulfur to the site.

KIDNEYS (disease/dysfunction) Carry or wear the following crystals, and place larger ones around your home and workplace: abalone shell, ankerite, blue halite, cat's eye, clear halite, conichalcite, copal, cuprite, golden calcite, golden rod calcite, green jasper, Kalahari picture stone, leopard jasper, molybdenite, nuummite, olive opal, rainbow moonstone, rose quartz crystals, ruby in kyanite, ruby and kyanite in fuchsite, smoky citrine, Tibetan citrine, Tiffany stone, yellow aventurine, yellow calcite, and yellow prehnite.

KNEE (injury or stiffness) Hold **elestial smoky quartz**, harlequin quartz, **petrified palm wood**, pyroxene, or **Tibetan smoky quartz** to knee.

LEGS (aches/disease/injury) Hold axinite, elestial smoky quartz, **harlequin quartz**, pyroxene, **scheelite**, or **Tibetan**

smoky quartz to affected area. Also place in bottom of bed at night.

LETHARGY Carry or wear brookite, **green zoisite**, or polychrome jasper. Hold when feeling particularly tired.

LEUKEMIA Carry or wear cat's eye.

LIGAMENTS Hold ammonite, axinite, **black rutilated quartz**, bryozoan snakeskin agate, **faden quartz**, gyrolite, hubnerite, lepidolite in quartz, Tiffany stone, or **tugtupite** to injured ligament.

LIGHT SENSITIVITY Carry or wear petrified palm wood and **rhodonite in quartz**. **Angel wing selenite** can help with light-sensitive skin symptoms.

LIVER (diseases/overworked) Carry or wear Alaskan garnet, almandine garnet in pyroxene, amethyst, **amethyst zebra stone**, ankerite, blue coral, cat's eye, chevron amethyst, clear halite, creedite, golden calcite, green jasper, lazulite, leopard jasper, olive opal, **pink danburite**, rainbow moonstone, ruby and kyanite in fuchsite, scenic quartz, smoky citrine, steatite, Tibetan citrine, Tiffany stone, or yellow sapphire. Hold to liver to relive discomfort.

LONGEVITY Carry or wear angel wing selenite or **Himalayan diamond**.

LUMBAGO Tape harlequin quartz or scheelite to lower back at center of discomfort.

LUNG DISEASES Wear a pendant or carry amethyst zebra stone, blue aragonite, blue jade, blue john, blue mist Lemurian quartz crystal, catlinite, chevron amethyst, diopside, green chalcedony, green kyanite, green zoisite, lepidocrocite, orange moss agate, orthoclase, peach aventurine, pink tourmaline in lepidolite, pink tourmaline in quartz, ritzullite, rose opal, ruby in kyanite, scenic quartz, scolecite, silver aventurine, spodumene, or yellow sapphire. Choose peanut wood for fungal infection.

LYMPHATIC SYSTEM PROBLEMS Carry or wear ankerite, cat's eye, colemanite, opalized white agate, **rainbow moonstone**, ruby in kyanite, **smoky citrine**, or yellow prehnite. *Lymph disorders:* Carry or wear molybdenite or nuummite.

MALAISE (general) Carry, wear, or keep around you Lemurian quartz crystal or quartz crystal.

ME (MYALGIC ENCEPHALITIS) See CFS.

MEASLES Keep rosasite near and hold often.

MELANOMA Keep black septarian near you. Hold crystal to affected area for 30 minutes daily. Place crystals in any area where you spend a lot of time.

MENOPAUSE Carry or wear pink **tourmaline and lepidolite in quartz**, ruby in fuchsite, **white moonstone**, or cuprite 24/7. Hold **indigo gabbro** when symptoms are active.

MENSTRUAL CYCLE *Menorrhagia (heavy menstrual bleeding):* Carry, wear, or hold rainbow moonstone or goethite on hematite until bleeding subsides. *Pains and cramps:* Carry or wear **atlantisite**, buddstone, indigo gabbro, olive serpentine, **rainbow moonstone**, spodumene, or **white moonstone** and hold to area of discomfort until pain subsides. Carrying or wearing crystals 24/7 for three months plus will help to reduce the onset of pain. *Regulating:* Carry or wear **black moonstone**, blue scheelite, orange selenite, **rainbow moonstone**, **rose quartz crystals**, spodumene, or **white moonstone** 24/7 for three complete cycles.

METABOLISM Carry, wear, or place around you Andean opal, cuprite, Himalayan diamond, pyrolusite crystal, strawberry aventurine, or tanzine aura quartz.

MIGRAINE Hold the darkest purple **amethyst** or **black amethyst** as close as you can to the site of pain until relieved. Carry the same crystal with you 24/7 to reduce frequency of attacks; or carry or wear buddstone or peach aventurine and place olivine on basalt by your bed and in your workplace or any other area where migraine attacks are triggered.

MINERAL DEFICIENCIES *Calcium:* Carry or wear honey calcite or **yellow calcite**. *Iodine:* Keep blue halite with you, especially at meal times and for one hour after each meal. *Iron:* Carry or wear Andean opal or **tangerine quartz**.

MONONUCLEOSIS Carry or wear violet sapphire or place next to bed.

MOUTH (diseases/disorders in and around) Hold a washed Tibetan citrine or ruby in kyanite tumble polished stone in the mouth for five minutes or so several times a day; or carry arsenopyrite, petrified palm wood, or **stella beam calcite** and hold in hand while focusing your mind on the mouth. ***Gum discomfort/ disease:*** Gently hold blue spinel, petrified palm wood, **purple Mexican fluorite**, or stichtite to affected areas. Place next to bed at night.

MUCOUS MEMBRANE CONDITIONS
Carry or wear **blue coral** or petrified palm wood. Hold close to affected area as required.

MULTIPLE SCLEROSIS (MS)
Carry or wear hematite/magnetite, **Lemurian quartz crystal**, leopard jasper, or quartz crystal. Hold to areas of discomfort and work with any other crystals to relieve specific symptoms. Place goethite on hematite by the foot of your bed.

MUSCLES
Carry or wear atacamite, atlantisite, axinite, benitoite, bismuth, bryozoan snakeskin agate, ferberite, gyrolite, hubnerite, infinite, lavender amethyst, papagoite quartz, **peach aventurine**, ritzullite, ruby and kyanite in fuchsite, silver aventurine, silver leaf jasper, Tiffany stone, or tugtupite. Hold to injuries or areas of discomfort. A black septarian elixir can also help. Yellow aventurine will help with problems associated with the core. ***Aching:*** Hold **auralite-23** or **peach aventurine** to the aching muscle for at least 30 minutes. Carry bustamite with sugilite during the day. Opalized jasper and polychrome jasper can also help, or try a brown banded aragonite elixir. If the symptoms persist, place a piece of phillipsite near the muscle overnight. ***Cramps:*** Hold **lepidolite in quartz** to affected muscle while stretching. Carry or wear **auralite-23**, blue jade, infinite, leopard jasper, lepidolite in quartz, or **stibiconite** and hold to affected muscles. **Champagne aura quartz** can be effective for cramp in the arms and legs. At night, place **goethite on hematite** at the foot of the bed. ***Spasms:*** Hold atlantisite to affected muscle. For persistent conditions, carry or wear atlantisite. ***Torn:*** Hold creedite to damaged muscle for 20–30 minutes. Repeat often during the day.

NAILS
For stronger nails and to combat unhealthy nails, hold dragonstone to them for 20–30 minutes daily.

NAUSEA
Hold dumortierite in quartz, orange selenite, olivine on basalt, **Tibetan citrine**, or violet sapphire until feeling desists. Place **double terminated quartz crystal** on the solar plexus. Consider emotional as well as physical causes. See also Travel sickness.

NERVE PROBLEMS
Carry or wear **amethyst**, bumble bee jasper, chevron amethyst, golden rod calcite, leopard jasper, lepidolite in quartz, or vortex healing crystal; hold to affected areas. ***Connecting to senses:*** If any one of your five senses seems deficient, hold **kammererite**, **purple chalcedony**, or **stella beam calcite** to the area concerned; and hold one of these to restore your sense of environment. ***Damage:*** Carry or wear creedite and hold to affected area for at least 30 minutes daily. ***Erratic nerve impulses:*** Carry or wear chevron amethyst and hold to affected areas. ***Nervous system (disorders)*** Carry or wear amethyst, black rutilated quartz, **Brandberg amethyst**, brown banded aragonite, **chevron amethyst**, epidote in quartz, ruby and kyanite in fuchsite, or **super seven**. ***Central nervous system (CNS):*** Carry or wear dragonstone or **nuummite** 24/7. ***Neurological pathways (resetting)*** Carry or wear Brandberg amethyst or chevron amethyst and hold to specific areas as required. ***Neuropathic pain (burning or shooting pain)*** Carry or wear **chevron amethyst**, kammererite, or phillipsite and hold to painful areas until pain eases.

NOSE
(disorders) Hold blue apatite, blue quartz, goethite on hematite, lorenzenite, petrified palm wood, ruby in kyanite, or **stella beam calcite** to nose. For long-term conditions, carry or wear these. ***Nasal passage:*** Hold **lorenzenite** or petrified palm wood to nose. ***Nose bleed:*** Hold ruby in kyanite to nose until bleeding stops.

NUTRIENTS
(malabsorption) Carry or wear anthophyllite.

OBESITY
See Appetite (excessive). Also, carry or wear black onyx, **blue apatite**, **Lemurian quartz crystal**, or **white chalcedony + quartz crystal** 24/7. Place a quartz crystal cluster next to the bed at night. Sit quietly and hold your crystals, focusing your thoughts on them, for at least 30 minutes daily. Also look at crystals in the emotional section of this book to see if any resonate with underlying causes.

OLD AGE
(degeneration) Carry **cradle of humankind stone** or **phosphosiderite** and hold it when you feel "old." Carry or wear Himalayan diamond, silver moonstone, or violet sapphire. See also Youthful appearance.

OSTEOPOROSIS
Carry or wear ammonite, green smithsonite, or orange selenite. Hold to painful areas for 30 minutes each.

PANCREAS (disease/disorders) Carry or wear Alaskan garnet, almandine garnet in pyroxene, amethyst zebra stone, chevron amethyst, green zoisite, opalized white agate, pink tourmaline in quartz, purple ray opal, yellow calcite, or yellow sapphire and hold to area of discomfort.

PARASITES *External:* Place olive serpentine in rooms and carry a piece with you. *Intestinal:* Hold scolecite to areas of identified infestation.

PARKINSON'S DISEASE Carry or wear **black rutilated quartz**, **epidote in quartz**, or nuummite 24/7.

PHOTOSENSITIVITY (sun allergy) Carry lazulite during daylight hours.

PNEUMONIA Carry or wear orthoclase or place next to bed.

POLLUTION EFFECTS Carry or wear spodumene.

POST-OPERATIVE ISSUES *Healing:* Place Alaskan garnet, almandine garnet in pyroxene, **blue jade**, cacoxenite in amethyst, copal, **kundalini citrine**, and purple scapolite next to the bed. Play with any of these in your hands and hold to areas of discomfort. *Pain:* Play with phillipsite in your hands and hold to areas of discomfort.

POSTURE Carry or wear amethyst.

PREGNANCY Carry or wear rainbow moonstone to promote a healthy pregnancy and Kambamba stone or **white moonstone** to relieve uncomfortable symptoms.

RADIATION Carrying or wearing **lion skin stone** can be protective. Wear or carry blue barite 24/7 or place uranophane near you for 30 minutes daily.

RECTAL PROBLEMS Carry or wear Tibetan citrine or **papagoite quartz**.

RED BLOOD CELLS (RBC) Carry or wear strawberry aventurine, **tangerine quartz**, or yellow prehnite.

REPRODUCTIVE SYSTEM (disorders) *Both sexes:* Carry or wear bubble gum tourmaline, caramel calcite, colemanite, honey calcite, pink tourmaline in quartz, ruby and kyanite in fuchsite, tangerine quartz, or yin yang crystal and hold to areas of discomfort. *Female (whole system):* Hold, carry, or wear abalone shell, bryozoan snakeskin agate, chrysanthemum stone, cuprite, goddess stone, hanksite, orange moonstone, rose quartz crystals, or silver moonstone to help with most conditions. *Fallopian tubes and womb disorders (such as fibroids):* Hold **brecciated jasper** or abalone shell to area of discomfort. *Ovaries:* Carry or wear brecciated jasper or orange selenite, or place larger pieces and abalone shell around your bed. *Male:* Hold, carry, or wear blue jade, kammererite, Lemurian black jade, limonite, scepter quartz crystal, or scheelite to help with most conditions.

RESTLESS LEG SYNDROME Place champagne aura quartz or blue jade at the bottom of the bed. If symptoms persist, carry or wear crystals 24/7.

RHEUMATISM (rheumatoid arthritis) Hold atacamite, blue john, cuprite, **grape chalcedony** (especially knees), gyrolite, indigo gabbro, or **scenic quartz** to affected joints. Carrying or wearing may also help.

SCARS Hold golden feldspar to site.

SCIATICA Carry or wear doctor's stone. Hold to areas of pain.

SCURVY Carry or wear lemon chrysoprase.

SENSES To enhance, help, boost, or repair, carry or wear intrinsinite or white chalcedony.

SEX Place cryolite, golden selenite, **kundalini citrine**, realgar, tangerine quartz, tanzine aura quartz, Tiffany stone, and white moonstone around the room to improve the sexual experience. *Sexual dysfunction:* Carry or wear orange moonstone or tangerine quartz 24/7 *Sexual energy:* Opalized white agate and rose quartz crystals help to control an excess of sexual energy. Angel wing selenite, blue mist Lemurian quartz crystal, **kundalini citrine**, realgar, sunset aura quartz, and Tiffany stone all boost sex drive and can revive your interest.

SINUSES Meditate with olivine on basalt and hold to sinuses if required.

SKIN *General health:* Carry or wear amethyst, columbite, hematite/magnetite, Kalahari picture stone, kammererite, silver moonstone, spodumene, stichtite, tanzine aura quartz, or white topaz. Hold to required area and place crystals next to bed at night. Apply topically elixir of **white moonstone**. *Complexion aid:* Try washing your face in a rose quartz crystals elixir daily.

Damage (such as from burns or eczema): Hold golden healer quartz about ½in (1cm) or so above the wound for 2–5 minutes and repeat as often as possible. **Eczema:** Hold **angel wing selenite** or **K2 jasper** to the worst affected area for 30 minutes each day. Don't be concerned that one area will get better while another gets worse—just pick the worst spot each day. After two weeks the condition should have noticeably improved. Also try washing with a strawberry quartz topical elixir. **Elasticity:** Carry, wear, or hold to skin atlantisite, **grape chalcedony**, phosphosiderite, or stichtite. **Inflammation (rashes and swelling):** Hold peach aventurine to the inflamed area. **Oily:** Gently rub a **violet sapphire** crystal against your skin for a few seconds to help close the pores. **Psoriasis:** Hold **angel wing selenite**, **K2 jasper**, quantum quattro stone, or strawberry aventurine to the worst affected area for 30 minutes daily. Put **brown banded aragonite** in your bath water to create a giant topical elixir. Also look at possible emotional causes. **Sensitivity:** Drink rose opal elixir daily. **Skin (conditions/disorders)** Hold albite, blue smithsonite, or K2 jasper to the affected area and apply a topical elixir of blue moss agate, rosasite, strawberry aventurine, or yellow sapphire. **Smoothness:** Carry or wear dragonstone 24/7. **Stress-related disorders:** Hold angel wing selenite to the worst area for 10–30 minutes daily.

SMELL (loss of) Carry or wear blue apatite or white chalcedony.

SPEECH IMPEDIMENTS Carry or wear cryolite or nuummite.

SPINE Alignment: Place scolecite under your mattress. **Damage:** Lie down and place axinite, blue spinel, **Lemurian quartz crystal**, orthoclase, quartz crystal, or snakeskin rock on or under back for at least 20 minutes or overnight. For chronic conditions, carry or wear these crystals.

SPLEEN (diseases/disorders) Carry, wear, or hold to the spleen cat's eye, golden rod calcite, green zoisite, lemon chrysoprase, leopard jasper, pink tourmaline in quartz, rose opal, rose quartz crystals, white chalcedony, yellow aventurine, **yellow calcite**, or yellow sapphire.

SPOTS Hold blue smithsonite or cinnabar in quartz to each spot for 10–15 minutes daily.

STAMINA Carry, wear, or place around you atlantisite, benitoite, bismuth, black onyx, blue spinel, dumortierite in quartz, hubnerite, lion skin stone, olive opal, prehnite with epidote, ruby in fuchsite, silver aventurine, and strawberry aventurine. Kimberlite is particularly helpful for athletes.

STOMACH PROBLEMS Hold or place on stomach amethyst, atlantisite, leopard jasper, phosphosiderite, purple thulite, **sunset aura quartz**, **Tibetan citrine**, violet sapphire, yellow aventurine, yellow danburite, or yellow quartz. For chronic conditions, carry or wear these 24/7. **Stomach cramps:** Brecciated jasper is helpful. **Upset stomachs:** Hold diopside or **vortex healing crystal**.

STRENGTH Carry or wear **black onyx**, **black rutilated quartz**, ferberite, llanite, peanut wood, prehnite with epidote, or scepter quartz crystal, and meditate with the crystal before preforming arduous tasks.

SWELLINGS Hold agrellite, **blue jade**, celestite with sulfur, jamesonite, Kalahari picture stone, phillipsite, scenic quartz, stromatolite, tugtupite, or white moonstone to affected area.

SUN BURN Hold golden healer quartz to affected area, or if this is painful, hold just above the skin for 5–20 minutes.

TASTE (loss of) Wash a few of the following crystals and place them on the tongue for five minutes daily until sense returns: blue apatite, elestial quartz, petrified palm wood, or purple ray opal. You can also carry or wear these 24/7.

TEETH/TOOTHACHE Carry or wear amethyst, black amethyst, **blue john**, blue spinel, brown banded aragonite, lazulite, orthoclase, **purple Mexican fluorite**, stibiconite, or stromatolite. Hold to skin near painful teeth. Try black septarian elixir as a mouthwash. Place arsenopyrite next to bed.

TEMPERATURE (control/balance) Carry, hold, or wear **Andean opal**, brown banded aragonite, cryolite, or purple ray opal.

TENDONS Injury: Hold or tape **faden quartz**, gyrolite, hubnerite, Tiffany stone, or **tugtupite** to the affected area. **Tendonitis:** Hold lepidolite in quartz or Tiffany stone to affected tendon.

TENSION (physical) Carry or wear amethyst zebra stone or hold abalone shell at night for 10 minutes and then place next to the bed before going to sleep.

THROAT *General health:* There are many crystals that will help the throat in different circumstances. Carry or wear albite, Argentinian blue calcite, blue apatite, blue aragonite, blue quartz, blue scheelite, copal, doctor's stone, gem silica, goethite on hematite, green kyanite, intrinsinite, lorenzenite, mimetite, nuummite, papagoite in quartz, petrified palm wood, quantum quattro stone, ritzullite, ruby in kyanite, or yellow sapphire. Hold to throat as required. For long-term problems, place crystal on throat for 30 minutes daily. *Infection:* Place **actinolite in quartz**, **Argentinian blue calcite**, or rhodonite in quartz on throat for 30 minutes daily until symptoms desist. *Laryngitis:* Hold actinolite in quartz, **Argentinian blue calcite**, **blue scheelite**, gem silica, petrified palm wood, or quantum quattro stone to throat for 20–30 minutes as required. *Pharyngitis:* Hold actinolite in quartz, Argentinian blue calcite, blue scheelite, gem silica, petrified palm wood, or quantum quattro stone to top of neck. *Sore:* Hold **gem silica** to throat for a few minutes until it eases. *Tonsillitis:* Place **blue scheelite** or petrified palm wood on throat for 30 minutes daily until symptoms clear.

TIREDNESS (short-term) Carry or wear golden selenite or yellow quartz.

TIRING EFFECTS OF COMPUTER SCREENS

Place lion skin stone or purple Mexican fluorite between you and the screen or on your desk near the screen.

TISSUE REGENERATION (after injury or surgery) Carry or wear **aegirine**, afghanite, anthophyllite, **cacoxenite in amethyst**, cinnabar in quartz, **earthquake quartz crystal**, Hertfordshire pudding stone, **malacholla**, moqui marbles, phillipsite, **shungite**, or **Tibetan citrine**. Hold any of these to required area.

TOES Hold Tibetan smoky quartz to painful or damaged area. *Ingrown toe nail:* Hold or tape lava stone to nail for 20–30 minutes daily.

TRANSPLANTS Carry or wear phillipsite to help avoid tissue rejection.

TRAVEL SICKNESS Carry or wear **chalcosiderite**, goethite on hematite, or tugtupite. In case of severe symptoms, hold until they cease. *Air:* Carry **hematite + turquoise** stones and play with them, getting as much skin contact as possible. *Sea:* Carry or wear chalcosiderite or **tugtupite** to prevent it or hold goethite on hematite to ease symptoms.

TUBERCULOSIS (TB) Carry or wear orthoclase and place next to the bed.

TUMORS Carry or wear amethyst elestial crystal, biotite, tangerine quartz, or yellow sapphire. Hold to areas of discomfort. Place uranophane by the bed. *See also* Cancer.

ULCERS (mouth, skin, stomach) Hold diopside close to ulcerated area. In severe cases carry or wear these crystals.

ULCERATIVE COLITIS Carry or wear albite and hold to areas of discomfort.

UROGENITAL SYSTEM (disorders) Carry or wear peach aventurine or silver aventurine. Hold to, or place on, areas of discomfort.

VEINS To improve vascular health, carry or wear goethite on hematite, green smithsonite, papagoite quartz, purple scapolite, or **vortex healing crystal**, or hold or tape to affected area. *Varicose veins:* Hold or tape opalized white agate or rose quartz crystals to affected areas. *Vascular disease:* Carry or wear vortex healing crystal.

VERTIGO Carry or wear buddstone, cuprite, denim lapis, doctor's stone, **elestial quartz**, **golden Lemurian quartz crystal**, or **rose quartz crystals**.

VIRAL INFECTION Hold or place amethyst to or on affected area.

VITAMIN DEFICIENCIES Carry or wear tangerine quartz.

VITALITY Carry or wear any of the following: almandine garnet in pyroxene, amethyst elestial crystal, angel wing selenite, biotite, black rutilated quartz, blue spinel, bustamite with sugilite, caramel calcite, cuprite, denim lapis, ferberite, golden rod calcite, green smithsonite, green zoisite, harlequin quartz, Lemurian quartz crystal, nuummite, opalized white agate, orthoclase, pink tourmaline in quartz, polychrome jasper, ruby in fuchsite, scheelite, sunset aura quartz, white chalcedony, white moonstone, or yellow sapphire. Choose whatever combination you are drawn to.

VOMITING Hold Tibetan citrine until symptoms stop.

VOICE Carry or wear gem silica. Hold to, or place on, throat.

WEIGHT *To gain:* Carry or wear **blue apatite**, goethite on hematite, **pink danburite**, or **Sirius amethyst**. *To lose:* Carry or wear **blue apatite**, blue spinel, green tourmaline in quartz, Lemurian quartz crystal, mimetite, quartz crystal, **Sirius amethyst**, **tangerine quartz**, or white chalcedony. Hold the crystal for 30 minutes each evening, focusing your mind on the benefits of losing weight. Drink a large glass of **blue apatite** elixir each morning.

WOUNDS Hold Alaskan garnet, almandine garnet in pyroxene, golden feldspar, mother of pearl, quartz crystal, ruby in fuchsite, scolecite, vortex healing crystal, or white topaz to the wound. Wash wound with pyrolusite crystal elixir. *Cuts and grazes:* Hold faden quartz or **golden healer quartz** to the injury.

WRINKLES Carry or wear angel wing selenite or rinse your face with a rose quartz crystal elixir.

YOUTHFUL APPEARANCE Carry or wear **rose quartz crystals** and add them to your bath. Also try carrying or wearing angel wing selenite, phosphosiderite, silver moonstone, spodumene, and white moonstone. Rinse your face with an olive opal elixir. To look and feel rejuvenated, carry or wear **almandine garnet in pyroxene**.

DETOX

This is a vital part of the healing process. As toxins, pollutants, and other substances are released from the body, your natural relaxation response kicks in and tension flows away. Your skin improves and many physical conditions, ailments, illnesses, and diseases, even long-term chronic ones, seem to ease or disappear completely. No one "magic crystal" does this for everyone, but from the many listed below, one could be your "magic crystal." Try one or two of them, whichever ones you are drawn to. Keep them with you 24/7. Place them under your pillow or on a bedside table at night. Hold them and play with them and see what happens over two weeks. Persist with these and add others from the list. Some, like friends, will be needed for a short time, while others will stay with you forever.

Abalone shell (whole), agrellite, albite, amethyst, amethyst zebra stone, Andean opal, ankerite, arsenopyrite, blue barite, blue moss agate, blue scheelite, cat's eye, chevron amethyst, clear halite, colemanite, conichalcite, copal, creedite, dragonstone, golden rod calcite, golden selenite, green chalcedony, green jasper, green selenite, Himalayan diamond, jamesonite, kundalini citrine, malacholla, nuummite, olive opal, olive serpentine, piemontite, pink danburite, prehnite with epidote, quantum quattro stone, rainbow moonstone, rose quartz crystals, ruby in kyanite, ruby and kyanite in fuchsite, smoky citrine, Tibetan citrine, and Tiffany stone. You can also try elixirs of shungite or yellow sapphire.

REMEDIES FOR EMOTIONAL ISSUES

For all emotional conditions, carry or wear the crystals. Hold them and play with them as much as possible. Keep them around you 24/7. Place larger crystals in any room where you spend a lot of time, including the bedroom, living room, and workplace. Follow any specific instructions given.

Health is maintained when physical, mental, emotional, and spiritual energies are in balance, those within us and around us in our environment. We are inescapably linked to the world around us. When the various energies are balanced, we are in a state of well-being. When unbalanced, we are in a state of dis-ease and become more and more susceptible to illness. Amegreen, **amethyst, calcite (all varieties)**, **double terminated quartz crystal**, **grape chalcedony**, lemon chrysoprase, mimetite, moqui marbles, orange moonstone, **quartz crystal**, ruby and kyanite in fuchsite, Vera Cruz amethyst, and **yin yang crystal** all help in diverse ways to effect this balance, thereby removing dis-ease and maintaining health.

Be aware that any of the conditions listed below can be linked to current or past stresses or trauma. Current trauma can be relieved with abalone shell, Alaskan garnet, amegreen, **cataclasite, orange mist aura quartz**, orthoclase, purple ray opal, **tanzine aura quartz**, and tangerine quartz. Trauma and issues going back into the past, from yesterday to birth, can be helped with **angel wing selenite, biotite, doctor's stone, earthquake quartz crystal**, quantum quattro stone, realgar, **scenic quartz**, and **sunset aura quartz**. Experiences you have in childhood can affect you either consciously or subconsciously for all your life. **Scenic quartz** helps to bring these experiences to the fore, allowing you to recognize them, release the bad ones, and use the good ones, understanding the spiritual lessons they may have brought. **Stella beam calcite** and **scenic quartz** can also help you to unlock trauma from past lives.

Emotional conditions are often so upsetting that they require something that will calm you down before you can even consider what it is that concerns you or give any thought to healing. A few quick go-to calming crystals are any variety of tourmaline for the mind or calcite for emotions, green quartz for nerves, Argentinian blue calcite for spiritual wobbles, amethyst for passion, and Tibetan citrine for anger. Blue quartz quells fear. Silver aventurine will help to keep you stress free and promotes a sense of tranquillity. Try drinking a daily glass of rose opal elixir, too!

ABUSE Whether physical, sexual, or verbal, the emotional scars can run deep. It may take many months or years for these to heal. Hold **angel wing selenite**, **cataclasite**, or **green tourmaline in quartz** for 30 minutes each day. Continue daily, even if you feel upset as hidden emotions begin to flow. Copal, Inca jade, and ruby and kyanite in fuchsite can also help. **Lemurian black jade** can provide protection against predators and **scenic quartz** can help calm trauma from childhood abuse.

ADDICTIVE BEHAVIOR Pink tourmaline and lepidolite in quartz, Sirius amethyst, and white chalcedony are good for emotional addictions that create unhealthy behavior patterns. **Skeletal quartz** can release addictions to people and caramel calcite can set you free from an addictive personality. **Amethyst** is helpful for addictive behavior generally.

AGGRESSION Blue apatite, jamesonite, and **pink tourmaline and lepidolite in quartz** dispel aggressive feelings. **Amethyst** and realgar can stem violent tendencies. **Agrellite** can lessen bad temper.

AGING **Himalayan diamond** and violet sapphire can help mental and emotional symptoms associated with old age. Also try a **rose quartz crystal** bath. Place several crystals into your normal bath and relax in it. Dim the lights or light a candle and put on some gentle music or a spoken meditation album for added benefit. **Silver moonstone** allows you to age gracefully and **olive opal**, olivine on basalt, and phosphosiderite can all promote a youthful attitude to life.

AIMLESSNESS Purple thulite can help you find direction in life.

ANGER/RESENTMENT Whether slight annoyance or total rage, the following crystals will reduce these feelings: agrellite, **amethyst**, auralite-23, blue apatite, bustamite with sugilite, cinnabar in quartz, gem silica, grape chalcedony, hematite/magnetite, jamesonite, lava stone, **lithium quartz**, realgar, **rose quartz crystals**, Tanzanian aventurine, **Tibetan citrine**, and **vortex healing crystal**. **Indigo gabbro** releases blocks that cause anger. **Girasol quartz** can slow explosive anger, avoiding unnecessary rage. **Papagoite quartz** and **purple ray opal** change anger into peaceful, loving calm, creating an optimistic outlook.

ANXIETY Many crystals can help in diverse ways. See which ones you are drawn to in this list, or ask your pendulum which of them are best for you. Check how they interact with you in other ways by consulting their entries in the Crystal Finder (chapter 3). All of these can calm anxiousness: amegreen, amethyst zebra stone, Argentinian blue calcite, black onyx, black tourmaline with mica, blue apatite, blue aragonite, blue moss agate, blue scheelite, caramel calcite, green jasper, green quartz, hanksite, harlequin quartz, hausmannite, intrinsinite, Kambamba stone, lazulite, lemon chrysoprase, lepidocrocite, lepidolite in quartz, lion skin stone, lithium quartz, lizard skin agate, molybdenite, orange moonstone, orange moss agate, pink tourmaline and lepidolite in quartz, pink tourmaline in lepidolite, prairie tanzanite, Preseli blue stone, rhodonite in quartz, Tanzanian aventurine, vortex healing crystal.

APATHY Brookite can revive interest in everyday life.

ARGUMENTATIVE TENDENCIES Amblygonite and green smithsonite reduce quarrelsome tendencies. Candle quartz brings healing energy to any room.

BROKEN HEART Brandberg amethyst, **golden Lemurian quartz crystal**, and lemon chrysoprase help to mend a broken heart. Mother of pearl gives a gentle, nurturing energy to bathe the heart center and hold it in a sea of loving energy.

BURDEN If you feel like you're carrying the world on your shoulders, **purple scapolite** can help lift the weight. **Amethyst** helps you cope with feelings about responsibilities.

CENTERING This is the feeling of stillness within, centered in the middle of your physical body around your solar plexus; the knowledge that the center is there and the outside world is all around you. K2 jasper, lavender amethyst, libethenite, orange selenite, and spodumene help to bring you to this point of inner stillness. These crystals are beneficial for people who feel they are always on the go and can't stop. Centering doesn't stop you from doing anything; it simply allows you to relax while you go about your daily life. Continue working with these crystals to find a deeper meaning to life.

CLARITY Blue halite helps you to be under no illusions and to see things as they really are.

CONCENTRATION Harlequin quartz, lion skin stone, and Tanzanian aventurine help you to be attentive and concentrate.

CONFIDENCE As with anxiety, crystals can help in many ways. See which ones you are drawn to in this list, or ask your pendulum which of them are best for you. Check how they interact with you in other ways by consulting their entries in the Crystal Finder (chapter 3). All these crystals boost confidence: aegirine, albite, almandine garnet in pyroxene, atacamite, black onyx, blue mist Lemurian quartz crystal, blue moss agate, bryozoan snakeskin agate, bubble gum tourmaline, bustamite with sugilite, chrome tremolite, doctor's stone, dumortierite in quartz, goddess stone, golden feldspar, golden labradorite, golden Lemurian quartz crystal, golden rod calcite, grape chalcedony, hausmannite, Hertfordshire puddingstone, Kambamba stone, lion skin stone, malacholla, mimetite, molybdenite, olivine on basalt, orange moss agate, orange selenite, peach aventurine, phosphosiderite, pink thulite, polychrome jasper, rainbow moonstone, ruby in kyanite, scepter quartz crystal, smoky citrine, spodumene, strawberry aventurine, sunset aura quartz, tourmalinated citrine, white chalcedony, white moonstone, white topaz, and yellow quartz. Bumble bee jasper washes away self-doubt and opalized white agate creates an energy shield around you, allowing your confidence to grow.

CONFUSION Intrinsinite clears disorder in your mind. Black onyx, elestial quartz, lorenzenite, prairie tanzanite, rhodonite in quartz, and tanzine aura quartz provide help for those times when you are simply perplexed with life, the universe, and everything.

COURAGE Blue apatite, buddstone, bustamite with sugilite, conichalcite, dragonstone, goethite on hematite, golden feldspar, golden Lemurian quartz crystal, green jasper, hematite/magnetite, Inca jade, Kambamba stone, Lemurian black jade, lion skin stone, piemontite, Preseli bluestone, Sirius amethyst, and tangerine quartz can give you the strength to be brave. Indigo gabbro supports the underdog.

CRISIS Gyrolite is a good friend to have around when all else is going wrong.

CYCLES AND REPEATED PATTERNS Many things seem to go around and around in our lives—careers, relationships, events. Sometimes we find ourselves repeating these cycles over and over again. Sooner or later, we must break them to move on. Angel wing selenite, ammonite, blue scheelite, golden selenite, indigo gabbro, and peanut wood are all helpful in this respect. *Behavioral:* The measure of acceptable behavior is set by the society we live in and varies from one culture to another. In western culture, actinolite in quartz, auralite-23, black onyx, bubble gum tourmaline, chrysotile serpentine, golden feldspar, golden healer quartz, golden selenite, lithium quartz, pink tourmaline and lepidolite in quartz, rainbow moonstone, sieber agate, sunset aura quartz, and Tiffany stone can help you to alter unhelpful patterns. Ankerite helps you to see and break these patterns.

DARK SIDE Alaskan garnet, arsenopyrite, cacoxenite in amethyst, colemanite, and indigo gabbro all help you to see, face, and deal with your own dark side.

DEATH AND DYING PROCESS Alaskan garnet, almandine garnet in pyroxene, amegreen, hanksite, lepidolite in quartz, olivine on basalt, orpiment, peanut wood, and rainbow moonstone promote acceptance and can ease the passing of spirit from the physical body to the next world.

DEMENTIA Blue barite, bryozoan snakeskin agate, buddstone, grape chalcedony, green chalcedony, purple chalcedony, silver moonstone, and white chalcedony can help slow deterioration of the condition. They are most helpful at the beginning of illness.

DEPRESSION The following crystals can all help: amegreen, amethyst zebra stone, atlantisite, black rutilated quartz, blue aragonite, blue spinel, brown banded aragonite, bumble bee jasper, creedite, denim lapis, dumortierite in quartz, golden selenite, grape chalcedony, jamesonite, kimberlite, lemon chrysoprase, lepidolite in quartz, limonite, lion skin stone, lithium quartz, orange mist aura quartz, orange moonstone, piemontite, pink tourmaline and lepidolite in quartz, pink tourmaline in lepidolite, smoky citrine, spodumene, tourmalinated citrine, violet sapphire, vortex healing crystal, yellow danburite, and yellow sapphire.

DESPAIR These crystals can alleviate despondency about a situation, the feeling that there are no answers and you have nothing left to give: black rutilated quartz, blue aragonite, bustamite with sugilite, grape chalcedony, and lithium quartz.

DISTRESS Bubble gum tourmaline and green jasper can ease concern and suffering.

EATING (disordered) Hold some crystals of **blue apatite**, **green tourmaline in quartz**, **pink tourmaline and lepidolite in quartz**, Sirius amethyst, or stichtite for one hour before eating. Keep them with you, preferably on the table, while you eat. Over a few weeks you will find that your eating pattern begins to return to normal. (*See also* Anorexia and Bulimia in Remedies for Physical Ailments.)

EMOTIONS *Balance:* When you feel highly emotional, **bubble gum tourmaline**, **caramel calcite**, cat's eye, columbite, diopside, **golden healer quartz**, golden Lemurian quartz crystal, **honey calcite**, ruby in fuchsite, **shungite**, and **yellow calcite** bring stability. Almandine garnet in pyroxene and golden rod calcite can help you hold it all together. Lorenzenite helps to stabilize emotional wobbles. *Blockages:* Copal helps release blocked feelings. *Control:* K2 jasper and **spodumene** help you keep control of your emotions when needed. This is just a short-term fix and can cause emotional blockages, which sooner or later you are going to have to release. *Energy:* Amethyst gives your emotions a boost. **Olive opal** gives you strength to get through breakup, lost love, and relationships. **Pink tourmaline in quartz** can help you get your mojo back. *Endurance:* Silver aventurine helps you to keep going when life is tough. *Expression:* Agnitite and **ruby in kyanite** help you to express your feelings. *Release:* Ankerite allows you to be brave and let your feelings out. *Strength:* Almandine garnet in pyroxene, golden feldspar, and **Preseli bluestone** keep you going, even if you feel you're being emotionally battered. **Cryolite**, lemon chrysoprase, and tangerine quartz help when it's all just too much. *Pain relief:* Blue mist Lemurian quartz crystal, blue scheelite, hausmannite, realgar, and **shungite** can ease emotional suffering. *Wounds:* Orange mist aura quartz, piemontite, and **rose quartz crystals** help to heal the feeling of being wounded emotionally. **Preseli bluestone** can soothe the emotions after a relationship breakup. **Abalone shell** and **Tibetan citrine** cleanse the hurt you feel from other people's words and actions, washing away issues that may pollute your feelings.

EMPATHY Afghanite, **blue aragonite**, **bubble gum tourmaline**, green selenite, K2 jasper, and rhodonite in quartz promote compassion, sympathy, and understanding.

ENDINGS Any ending may be difficult to cope with, as even the smallest one represents all the other big ones every time. Lemurian black jade, rainbow moonstone, and tourmalinated citrine soothe emotions tied up with the physical world, such as relationships, people, and property. White moonstone helps new beginnings and endings of relationships that don't support your ongoing development.

ENERGY *Blocks:* Place bustamite with sugilite, indigo gabbro, spodumene, and Tiffany stone on the area of the body where you "feel" the block is for 30–60 minutes. This may relate to physical symptoms or be intuitive. Carry the crystal with you and repeat daily. You will notice when the block has cleared. Physical symptoms may clear up—you feel either re-energized or simply calm and peaceful, but you will recognize the change in yourself. Bismuth and nuummite are good for energy blocks that you put in your own way. *"Vampires":* Some people have a natural tendency to draw energy from others. Most of us know someone like this. They are draining, and you always feel tired or exhausted after seeing them without knowing why. Infinite and **yellow aventurine** will help stop others leeching your energy.

EXAMS Intrinsinite will calm the nerves, ease the heart and physical tension, and clear the mind, allowing you to study and to stay focused during the exam itself.

FAILURE Rose quartz crystals soothe feelings of inadequacy.

FEAR/APPREHENSION The sensations experienced are very similar to those of excitement. Many people cannot differentiate between the two and often mistake excitement for apprehension before the start of a journey, interview, or date. **Purple ray opal** can transform fear into positive feelings and actions, such as love and compassion. **Blue quartz**, **blue coral**, cinnabar in quartz, **goddess stone**, **grape chalcedony**, jamesonite, Kalahari picture stone, lava stone, and yellow calcite alleviate the feeling of being scared. *Phobias:* **Doctor's stone** relieves acrophobia (fear of heights) and, along with afghanite and libethenite, conquers fear of the unknown. Cuprite, Preseli bluestone, and rose quartz crystals help to dispel irrational fears.

FEELINGS Biotite, blue aragonite, and scenic quartz make you more aware of how you actually feel about an issue or person without the interference or judgment of the outside world.

FEMININITY Malacholla, rainbow moonstone, and rose quartz crystals bring out your softer, nurturing side.

FORGIVENESS Lepidocrocite, quantum quattro stone, and tangerine quartz promote a forgiving attitude.

GRIEF Amegreen, **amethyst**, **black onyx**, dragonstone, golden feldspar, hanksite, infinite, piemontite, **pink danburite**, quantum quattro stone, **rose quartz crystals**, and vortex healing crystal can ease the pain of bereavement. **Amphibole in quartz** offers empathy for grief or loss. **Hematite/magnetite** can help you to see the positives and **Kalahari picture stone** allows you to release trapped emotions.

GROUNDING When you feel you need to get your feet back on the ground, the following crystals can help: Andean opal, black onyx, black septarian, brecciated jasper, champagne aura quartz, cradle of humankind stone, cuprite, doctor's stone, harlequin quartz, hematite/magnetite, honey calcite, Kalahari picture stone, lava stone, lepidocrocite, libethenite, limonite, moqui marbles, pyroxene, quantum quattro stone, strawberry aventurine, and Tibetan smoky quartz.

GUILT Blue jade, golden feldspar, **rose quartz crystals**, and vortex healing crystal can help reduce feelings of guilt.

HOMESICKNESS Amethyst and green selenite relieve the longing for home. They can help you to remember that home is where you are at this moment. You carry a little bit of it in your heart always.

HOPELESSNESS Brookite, girasol quartz, Kalahari picture stone, phosphosiderite, and **yellow sapphire** inspire optimism when all else fails.

HOSTILITY Bustamite with sugilite allows you to let go of this feeling.

INFERIORITY COMPLEX Lemon chrysoprase can be helpful in overcoming this.

INHIBITIONS Rose opal can reduce shyness and help you to lose any hang-ups that may be holding you back. Tangerine quartz can help relationships, boosting passion and emotional connection, eliminating inhibitions, and releasing the desire for physical contact and sexual freedom.

INNER PEACE Chrome tremolite and prehnite with epidote promote feelings of peace and tranquillity within you.

INNER STRENGTH In times of need, you have an amazing capacity to achieve unlikely success. Almandine garnet in pyroxene, blue john, blue spinel, bryozoan snakeskin agate, chrome tremolite, columbite, conichalcite, **goddess stone**, **golden Lemurian quartz crystal**, golden rod calcite, **lion skin stone**, **pink tourmaline and lepidolite in quartz**, pink tourmaline in quartz, ruby in kyanite, **tourmalinated citrine**, and yellow aventurine can help you connect to this power inside you.

INSECURITY **Blue coral** and ruby and kyanite in fuchsite promote a feeling of security and safeguard your emotions.

INTIMACY Girasol quartz and orpiment promote closeness between people, helping a relationship to grow.

IRRATIONALITY Biotite, cuprite, **lepidocrocite**, and phillipsite enhance rationality and reasoning.

IRRITABILITY When you get that edgy feeling you can't quite place—you just know everything annoys you—grape chalcedony, green chalcedony, and pink tourmaline and lepidolite in quartz can help.

JEALOUSY/ENVY Blue apatite, bustamite with sugilite, green selenite, quantum quattro stone, and **rose quartz crystals** allow you to understand that you neither want nor need everything that you haven't got.

LAZINESS/LETHARGY Brookite, green zoisite, **lion skin stone**, and polychrome jasper can give you a boost and get you moving!

LONELINESS When you are alone and feeling isolated, leopard jasper helps you to cope with your feeling of seclusion.

LOSS Amphibole in quartz, **dragonstone**, golden feldspar, infinite, Kalahari picture stone, and **vortex healing crystal** help to ease feelings of loss. **Blue apatite** gives you the strength to carry on.

LOVE This comes in many guises—erotic love between lovers; affectionate love between friends; familiar love between parents and children and between siblings; physical, emotional, and spiritual love. We need self-love to care for ourself first so that we can help others— the Buddhist philosophy of self-compassion, and an unconditional and universal love for everyone and everything. All these crystals promote love. Keep those you are drawn to on you and around your home and workplace. If in doubt, ask your pendulum which would be best for you at any specific time: almandine garnet in pyroxene, amphibole in quartz, atlantisite, blue barite, **bubble gum tourmaline**, chrysanthemum stone, dumortierite in quartz, **goddess stone**, green quartz, lepidocrocite, **liddicoatite**, **olive opal**, phillipsite, **pink tourmaline in quartz**, Preseli bluestone, **purple ray opal**, realgar, rhodonite in quartz, **rose opal**, **rose quartz crystals**, scolecite, spodumene, stichtite, **super seven**, tugtupite, and white topaz. *Expressing love:* Use conichalcite and stichtite to help you. *New love:* To attract new love, try meditating with goethite on hematite or **hematite/magnetite**. *Self-love:* Carry or wear bryozoan snakeskin agate, opalized white agate, phosphosiderite, **pink tourmaline in lepidolite**, stichtite, or **sunset aura quartz** to boost self-love. *Separation:* Each of you should carry a double terminated quartz crystal or Himalayan diamond (Himalayan diamond is a variety of quartz DT) to enhance the energetic bonds between you. *Sharing love:* Use actinolite in quartz and **pink danburite**. *Unrequited love:* Agnitite helps to heal the heart when your feelings are not returned.

MANIC BEHAVIOR Black rutilated quartz, jamesonite, and **lepidolite in quartz** are helpful for treating the extreme emotional swings experienced.

MASCULINITY Limonite and scepter quartz crystal bring maleness to the fore.

MENTAL *Balance (health and healing):* Amblygonite, **amethyst**, black rutilated quartz, celestite with sulfur, champagne aura quartz, **elestial quartz**, epidote in quartz, green chalcedony, **lemon chrysoprase**, **lepidolite in quartz**, **lithium quartz**, pink tourmaline in lepidolite, **purple chalcedony**, and **tourmalinated citrine** all help to maintain mental well-being. *Blockages:* For those times when nothing comes to mind, try intrinsinite to let your thoughts flow freely. *Breakdown:* If it feels like your life is falling to pieces, black rutilated quartz can gently bring you back to the world. *Clarity:* Black onyx dispels confusion, promoting clear thoughts, allowing ideas to surface, and removing the restrictions you place on your own mind. Your mind is thus freed and open to new and potentially amazing levels of inspiration. *Energy:* Golden rod calcite gives a jump start to your brain to get your mind working again. *Fortitude:* Denim lapis helps you to keep thinking and functioning when challenged by extreme stress. *Pain relief:* When your head hurts from stress, hold, or meditate with, chevron amethyst.

MOOD SWINGS Black rutilated quartz, clear halite, **golden selenite**, limonite, **malacholla**, **orange mist aura quartz**, **pink tourmaline and lepidolite in quartz**, tanzine aura quartz, and **vortex healing crystal** can calm the emotional pendulum.

NEGATIVITY This is a state of mind that is highly susceptible to the environment around you. When you feel negative, you draw negativity to you—and when the atmosphere around you is full of negative energy, you are easily brought down. Protect yourself from negativity with **bumble bee jasper**, columbite, copal, **golden Lemurian quartz crystal**, **green tourmaline in quartz**, green zoisite, lava stone, **Lemurian quartz crystal**, lion skin stone, **mother of pearl**, **quartz**, **spodumene**, and **Tiffany stone**. They help you to release negative energy held in your aura and lift your sense of well-being. *Emotions:* Piemontite dispels these into positive feelings and Himalayan quartz protects you from their influence. *In rooms:* Larger harlequin quartz or quartz crystal clusters can remove negativity.

NERVOUSNESS/TENSION Amethyst, amethyst zebra stone, **Argentinian blue calcite**, auralite-23, **blue moss agate**, chevron amethyst, **golden Lemurian quartz crystal**, Himalayan diamond, **lepidolite in quartz**, **lithium quartz**, mother of pearl, **orange selenite**, prehnite with epidote, **rose quartz crystals**, ruby and kyanite in fuchsite, tangerine quartz, Tanzanian aventurine, and yellow sapphire calm the nerves and reduce the feeling of tension.

NERVES *Calming:* Carry or wear Argentinian blue calcite, golden calcite, or green quartz. *Exhaustion:* Orange mist aura quartz works well.

NIGHTMARES Place K2 jasper, lizard skin agate, or **pink tourmaline and lepidolite in quartz** under your pillow to stop bad dreams.

OBSESSION Fixation on anything or anyone is damaging and leads to sacrifices in your personal everyday needs. This is deleterious to your state of well-being, resulting in a general running down of health that eventually leads to disease. White chalcedony reduces obsessions. *Obsessive behavior:* Micalated quartz can reduce this. *Obsessive compulsive disorder (OCD):* Treat with amethyst, **black rutilated quartz**, orthoclase, or **white chalcedony**.

OPPRESSION Place olivine on basalt around the home to alleviate the feeling of being persecuted.

OVERATTACHMENT/LETTING GO Hematite/magnetite reduces overattachment and neediness, leading to clearer energy around you. Once you let go of people, issues, and things, the ones you really need will still be there. The others will be gone, creating space for new encounters to come into your life. The following crystals help you to let go of old "stuff" and move on in life—for example, at the end of a relationship or a job, or moving house: atacamite, **black moonstone**, black onyx, blue moss agate, bustamite with sugilite, cacoxenite in amethyst, **chalcosiderite**, chrysotile serpentine, elestial quartz, epidote in quartz, indigo gabbro, molybdenite, mother of pearl, **olive serpentine**, orange selenite, phosphosiderite, **purple chalcedony**, purple scapolite, rose opal, **shungite**, Sirius amethyst, skeletal quartz, **smoky citrine**, stibiconite, **tangerine quartz**, **tourmalinated citrine**, **tugtupite**, white moonstone, yellow prehnite. **Sieber agate** promotes your ability to accept situations, further facilitating release. Hausmannite and **scenic quartz** reduce dependence and the need to hold on.

OVERSENSITIVITY Amethyst, angel wing selenite, mother of pearl, stella beam calcite, and white moonstone all help to thicken a thin skin.

PANIC ATTACKS As soon as you feel an attack coming on, hold blue apatite, **blue aragonite**, **caramel calcite**, harlequin quartz, lazulite, lizard skin agate, **pink tourmaline and lepidolite in quartz**, pink tourmaline in lepidolite, Preseli bluestone, or vortex healing crystal. Look at the crystal. Imagine the fear starting to disperse and little blobs of it flowing into the crystal. You will start to feel calm. Breathe.

PASSION Agnitite, atlantisite, bumble bee jasper, polychrome jasper, **rainbow moonstone**, **sunset aura quartz**, tangerine quartz, **Tiffany stone**, and **white moonstone** boost passion and allow it to flow. **Amethyst** calms.

PATIENCE Amethyst, black septarian, **blue aragonite**, buddstone, colemanite, cradle of humankind stone, double terminated quartz crystal, **dragonstone**, **dumortierite in quartz**, **elestial crystal**, hanksite, and Kambamba stone can promote patience.

PERSONALITY BLOCKAGES We can stop our true character from showing, sometimes deliberately and sometimes on an unconscious level. Scenic quartz removes the blocks, either self-imposed or from your upbringing, allowing your personality to shine. Indigo gabbro helps alter detrimental traits.

PESSIMISM Argentinian blue calcite, atacamite, **blue aragonite**, brookite, dragonstone, **papagoite quartz**, **peach aventurine**, **rainbow moonstone**, and Tiffany stone give you a more optimistic outlook on life.

PMS/PMT (PREMENSTRUAL SYNDROME/TENSION) Changes in hormones during the menstrual cycle can cause emotional as well as physical upset. There are many and various symptoms, ranging from annoying to debilitating in effect. Carry or wear blue scheelite, olive opal, **orange moonstone**, **rainbow moonstone**, spodumene, or **white moonstone** 24/7 for three months. Hold these when you notice symptoms.

PREJUDICE Bustamite with sugilite, **kammererite**, and **micalated quartz** help to reduce prejudice and promote tolerance. Judgmental attitudes are softened by **brown banded aragonite**, conichalcite, elestial quartz, **lemon chrysoprase**, and quantum quattro stone. General bigotry and narrow-mindedness can be diminished with **violet sapphire**.

PROCRASTINATION If you tend to put off taking action, libethenite or **lion skin stone** will help you to see that what you are actually doing is trying to avoid the issue, whatever it may be. The action represents the issue in your subconscious mind.

POST-TRAUMATIC STRESS DISORDER (PTSD) Blue scheelite, orthoclase, and **pink tourmaline and lepidolite in quartz** can help to give calm relief.

RESTLESSNESS Brown banded aragonite and hanksite calm restlessness. Green smithsonite promotes peacefulness. *Restless mind:* **Black tourmaline with mica, green tourmaline in quartz,** Preseli bluestone, and white moonstone still the brain, promoting peace of mind.

SADNESS White topaz and vortex healing crystal help to relieve sorrow and lift melancholy. Andean opal, benitoite, cat's eye, chrome tremolite, **doctor's stone,** dragonstone, **girasol quartz, golden rod calcite, papagoite quartz,** pink tourmaline in lepidolite, prehnite with epidote, **Preseli bluestone, rainbow moonstone,** ruby in fuchsite, silver aventurine, **sunset aura quartz,** violet sapphire, and yellow danburite all promote happiness.

SCHIZOPHRENIA Work with **black rutilated quartz + copal + lemon chrysoprase + lepidolite in quartz.**

SELF-ACCEPTANCE Aegirine, **cataclasite,** and lemon chrysoprase help you to see yourself as you are. They blow away the clouds covering your heart and let you look into your soul. *Eccentricity:* Bustamite with sugilite helps you accept your eccentricities and live with them.

SELF-ESTEEM Actinolite in quartz, aegirine, amethyst, cat's eye, doctor's stone, golden feldspar, **golden healer quartz,** olive opal, **orange moonstone,** orange selenite, rhodonite in quartz, and **Tibetan citrine** boost your sense of worth.

SELF-IMPORTANCE Purple thulite helps you to find a balance between thinking too much and too little of yourself.

SEX (balance of energies) All of us have a feminine and a masculine side. Sometimes, because of life's events, we lose the balance between them. Circumstances may require us to take charge more often or we become more nurturing and homey. Almandine in pyroxene, **amegreen,** blue scheelite, bumble bee jasper, copal, denim lapis, golden healer quartz, hanksite, **hematite/ magnetite,** honey calcite, indigo gabbro, leopard jasper, Libyan gold tektite, lion skin stone, peach aventurine, ruby in kyanite, Tibetan citrine, yellow aventurine, **yellow calcite,** and **yin yang crystal** can help to restore the balance. (See *also* Femininity and Masculinity.)

SEXUALITY Mother of pearl and spodumene enhance a positive attitude to sex. *Sexual frustration:* Orange

selenite and rose quartz crystals can improve your outlook.

SHOCK Purple ray opal and **tanzine aura quartz** are very soothing, helping to restore your equilibrium. Alaskan garnet, **angel wing selenite,** ankerite, and orange mist quartz help to soothe emotional shocks. Carry, wear, or hold earthquake quartz crystal for mental trauma.

SHYNESS Blue barite and peach aventurine help you to overcome timidity and promote a sense of boldness.

SPONTANEITY Himalayan diamond encourages you to go with the flow.

STUBBORNNESS Celestite with sulfur reduces headstrong, obstinate behavior.

SUPERIORITY COMPLEX Lemon chrysoprase helps you to be humbler.

SUSPICIOUS MIND Blue apatite reduces obsessive suspicion and allows you to be more trusting.

TRAVEL ANXIETY Mother of pearl calms concerns associated with journeys.

UNCARED FOR FEELINGS Black moonstone, goddess stone, green chalcedony, green selenite, Lemurian black jade, opalized jasper, opalized white agate, **orange moonstone,** phosphosiderite, and **rainbow moonstone** promote the feeling of being nurtured.

UNDERSTANDING *Between partners:* Harlequin quartz supports the energy connection between partners. *Yourself:* Orpiment and tangerine quartz open your mind to your inner self.

UNFOCUSED Andean opal, anthophyllite, blue aragonite, brecciated jasper, bumble bee jasper, columbite, conichalcite, **dumortierite in quartz, Lemurian quartz crystal,** purple scapolite, quantum quattro stone, **quartz crystal,** realgar, Tanzanian aventurine, **yellow quartz,** and **yellow sapphire** all help you to concentrate for longer and keep your mind focused. **Mother of pearl** and **white topaz** help you to notice detail.

VICTIM MENTALITY Black tourmaline with mica, diopside, and papagoite quartz give you a feeling of protection, allowing you to be less defensive and thereby stop blaming everyone else for your troubles.

WILL TO LIVE Ammonite, colemanite, cuprite, **earthquake quartz crystal**, and **libethenite** can all promote survival instincts, and this can make all the difference in critical conditions. **Pink tourmaline in quartz** boosts your natural survival skills.

WORRY When you have thought of and done everything you can about a situation, worry has no point. It is a senseless state of mind. Albite, **blue jade**, brookite, **columbite**, cuprite, infinite, **lazulite**, **lepidolite in quartz**, peach aventurine, prairie tanzanite, **rhodonite in quartz**, and vortex healing crystal help you to stop worrying. **Chalcosiderite** is good for therapists and anyone in the caring professions who worries excessively about clients/ patients. **What others think:** Libethenite, mimetite, and purple scapolite give you a feeling of protection and inner strength, allowing you to live your life freely without being concerned about how others see or judge you.

CRYSTALS FOR SPIRITUAL ENHANCEMENT

We all follow our own unique path through life. Whether this is predestined or created by our own actions does not alter the fact that when we stay on the path, energy flows, life moves forward, and we feel healthy and happy. When we stray from it, energy stagnates, life moves sideways or back, and we feel stressed and tense. Blue apatite, **blue barite**, purple thulite, and spodumene help you to find your path and discover your life purpose. Once you see it, catlinite, **cradle of humankind stone**, **hausmannite**, kundalini citrine, lepidocrocite, malacholla, **manifestation quartz**, polychrome jasper, scheelite, **stella beam calcite**, stibiconite, **vortex healing crystal**, **yellow danburite**, and yellow prehnite point out the signposts for you to follow along the way. Blue spinel, creedite, green zoisite, liddicoatite, and orange mist aura quartz are good to work with when you face delays and obstacles along your journey. **Black amethyst**, **blue quartz**, and **spodumene** will help you to understand it all. **Amphibole in quartz**, **papagoite quartz**, violet sapphire, and yellow sapphire can help you to see the beauty in everything.

AKASHIC RECORDS Ankerite, axinite, **candle quartz**, **cathedral quartz**, chrome tremolite, **golden Lemurian quartz crystal**, K2 jasper, lazulite, **stella beam calcite**, and violet sapphire help you to gain access to this mystical knowledge.

ANGELS AND GUARDIAN SPIRITS Amethyst elestial crystal, amphibole in quartz, angel wing selenite, auralite-23, blue aragonite, blue barite, blue scheelite, Brandberg amethyst, cryolite, dumortierite in quartz, golden selenite, Himalayan quartz, infinite, lepidocrocite, olive serpentine, pink danburite, purple ray opal, ruby and kyanite in fuchsite, and Vera Cruz amethyst enhance your connection to the angelic realms.

AURA The aura holds a record of everything that has happened in our life. Sometimes dark energy, which represents illness and stress, groups together into a mass. Naturally, energy flows through our aura all the time and sometimes these dark areas just dissipate. At other times they don't, and over a prolonged period of time this can lead to disease in the area of the body close to where they are massed. Carry or wear **blue halite**, **champagne aura quartz**, **golden healer quartz**, **orange mist aura quartz**, **sunset aura quartz**, or **tanzine aura quartz**. Work with **candle quartz** or **stella beam calcite** to brush down the aura (see page 37), as an alternative to a selenite aura wand. Amegreen, amethyst, blue quartz (Brazil), blue spinel, faden quartz, gyrolite, infinite, kammererite, kundalini citrine, leopard jasper, nuummite, purple chalcedony, ruby in fuchsite, stromatolite, super seven, and Tibetan citrine may all be beneficial. *Protection:* Blue apatite, **double terminated quartz crystal**, and purple ray opal protect the aura. *Stabilization:* If you're feeling wobbly, carry or wear **amegreen** or leopard jasper. *Strength:* Black amethyst, Navajo jasper, opalized white agate, and pyrolusite crystal strengthen your aura and boost your energy field.

CEREMONY Promote a sense of ceremony and ritual by carrying or having within the sacred circle or ceremonial area abalone shell, golden Lemurian quartz crystal, green chalcedony, green selenite, Inca jade, Navajo jasper, or scepter quartz. Green kyanite and **Himalayan diamond** amplify the attunement process.

CHAKRAS All crystals work on your energy system, while specific crystals affect all the chakras or energy centers: quartz crystal and super seven balance them; kundalini citrine is for detox; golden healer quartz removes blocks; double terminated quartz crystal promotes energy flow in between chakras.

CLEANSING Carry or wear golden selenite, green jasper, malacholla, **olive opal**, smoky citrine, or **yellow sapphire** to cleanse spiritual energy within you.

COMMUNICATION Tune in to the spirit world with blue halite, **golden selenite**, **quartz**, ruby and kyanite in fuchsite, and **scolecite**. *Psychic readings:* blue coral, blue smithsonite, and **indigo gabbro** all help when using tarot cards, a crystal ball, and other psychic means.

CONNECTION *To ancestors:* abalone shell, ammonite, catlinite, cradle of humankind stone, and elestial quartz link you to your roots. *To God, or whatever you choose to call a higher being or energy:* Quartz crystal connects you to any godly energy, yellow sapphire to the Hindu deity Ganesh, goddess stone to the sacred feminine, and selenite in all its forms (angel wing, green, orange) to the moon goddess Selene. *To spirit:* Work with cryolite, phosphosiderite, purple ray opal, steatite, and super seven to sense spirit guides and the essence of all living things.

CRYSTAL CHILDREN Bustamite with sugilite and **K2 jasper** are beneficial for the development of the crystal child.

DISTANT HEALING Benitoite, **cathedral quartz**, **double terminated quartz crystal**, hanksite, **Himalayan diamond**, jamesonite, **kammererite**, and **Libyan gold tektite** enhance absent healing. **Stella beam calcite** directs it to its target.

DREAMS Actinolite in quartz, amphibole in quartz, Andean opal, Argentinian blue calcite, bismuth, blue quartz, buddstone, celestite with sulfur, double terminated quartz crystal, girasol quartz, grape chalcedony, green kyanite, Hertfordshire puddingstone, indigo gabbro, lavender amethyst, Lemurian black jade, lithium quartz, microcline, orpiment, rosasite, scenic quartz, scolecite, sieber agate, sunset aura quartz, tanzine aura quartz, Tiffany stone, yellow prehnite, and yin yang crystal help you both to have and remember your dreams. Blue jade guides your understanding. Problem solving in dreams is promoted by colemanite and olive opal. See *also* Nightmares in Remedies for Emotional Issues.

HIGHER SELF/INNER SELF Some people call this the soul, spirit, chi, life force, or essence. Work with these crystals to increase your awareness and insight and help you to connect to and explore that deep, innermost part of you that you know is the true you: **amegreen**, blue halite, **blue mist Lemurian crystal**, **elestial quartz**, **green zoisite**, **kammererite**, Lemurian black jade, **liddicoatite**, **manifestation quartz**, micalated quartz, Navajo jasper, **phillipsite**, **pink thulite**, **purple thulite**, **ritzullite**, **prehnite with epidote**, **skeletal quartz**, and snakeskin agate. **Colemanite** illuminates any darkness in your soul and **Sirius amethyst** and **piemontite** help you to understand your inner self.

INDIGO CHILDREN Keep bustamite with sugilite or K2 jasper around the home for the continued benefit of the indigo child or adult.

KARMA Ankerite, **auralite-23**, and **super seven** help you to understand karmic issues. **Elestial quartz**, quantum quattro stone, and uranophane speed the process of karma so you don't take it into your next lifetime.

LOVE Spiritual love is enhanced by phosphosiderite. Brandberg amethyst and golden Lemurian quartz crystal promote universal love.

PAST LIVES Abalone shell, **ammonite**, ankerite, **Argentinian blue calcite**, atlantisite, **auralite-23**, blue mist Lemurian quartz crystal, blue moss agate, **candle quartz**, catlinite, chrysotile serpentine, **cradle of humankind stone**, **doctor's stone**, **elestial quartz**, golden Lemurian quartz crystal, K2 jasper, olive serpentine, phosphosiderite, realgar, sieber agate, **skeletal quartz**, and **super seven** facilitate access to past-life experiences. **Amphibole in quartz** aids recall. **Stella beam calcite** releases trapped energy from past lives and **Sirius amethyst** helps you to understand it.

PURITY Himalayan quartz enhances spiritual purity and orpiment personal purity.

SOUL MATES This may or may not involve a physical relationship. Dumortierite in quartz can help you to find and link with your spiritual partner.

SPIRITUAL DEVELOPMENT Aegirine, diopside, **golden Lemurian quartz crystal**, grape chalcedony, and **yin yang crystal** boost your spiritual growth.

SPIRITUAL DETOX Himalayan diamond clears unwanted energies, releasing fear, stress, and tension and opening the spirit to spontaneity and new possibilities.

TOTEM ANIMALS Identify and connect with your spirit animals through green quartz, **Himalayan quartz**, **Inca jade**, **purple ray opal**, ruby in fuchsite, and **scenic quartz**.

WISDOM Almandine garnet in pyroxene, **cathedral quartz**, **green kyanite**, jamesonite, white moonstone, and **yellow sapphire** promote insight, knowledge, understanding, and good judgment.

Blue barite can help you to find your path and discover your life purpose.

PROTECTION

Our energies are zapped daily. Deliberate psychic attacks as well as everyday unkind words and thoughts can bring you down. The streets aren't safe. Crime, violence, and even bad spirits may be out to get you. But it's not even that obvious. Therapists and carers pick up empathic pains and sometimes symptoms from their patients/clients. The neighbor who pops in for a cup of tea stays for an hour during which she dumps her troubles on you. She may leave feeling greatly relieved, but you just feel exhausted. Unknowingly, she has taken your energy and you feel tired and drained.

Certain crystals stop this happening. Try any of the following: abalone shell, aegirine, amethyst, amethyst elestial, amethyst zebra stone, ammonite, amphibole in quartz, black moonstone, black onyx, black septarian, brecciated jasper, **bubble gum tourmaline**, cat's eye, chevron amethyst, doctor's stone, goddess stone, green kyanite, Himalayan quartz, kimberlite, lepidocrocite, **liddicoatite**, lion skin stone, malacholla, olive serpentine, phillipsite, **pink tourmaline in lepidolite**, **pink tourmaline in quartz**, prehnite with epidote, Preseli bluestone, purple Mexican fluorite, quantum quattro stone, shungite, spodumene, Tibetan smoky quartz, tourmalinated citrine, Vera Cruz amethyst, or yellow sapphire.

Tangerine quartz brings a sense of spiritual security and **smoky citrine** offers protection in spiritual work. If you feel your energy is being sucked out of you by an energy vampire, go for **yellow aventurine** while **Lemurian black jade** protects against predatory people. Carry **nuummite** to protect you or leave it by a door or window to look after family and home while you are away. **Black amethyst**, **columbite**, and **Inca jade** support physical protection, helping you to avoid accidents. Whether you are fighting for a principle or your struggle is personal, **copal** is one of the traditional stones to protect warriors in battle. **Black rutilated quartz** makes you aware of danger so you can avoid it and **black tourmaline with mica** acts as an energetic mirror, sending negative energy back to its source, so whoever sent it will get it right back, speeding up the laws of karma!

From top to bottom: bubble gum tourmaline, liddicoatite, tangerine quartz, smoky citrine, yellow aventurine, Lemurian black jade, nuummite, and Inca jade.

CRYSTALS FOR LIFESTYLE ENHANCEMENT

ABUNDANCE/PROSPERITY/MONEY/WEALTH
Black rutilated quartz, blue coral, blue spinel, **Brandberg amethyst**, chrysanthemum stone, **goddess stone**, golden healer quartz, green quartz, **green tourmaline in quartz**, Lemurian black jade, lion skin stone, **manifestation quartz**, orange moonstone, pink tourmaline in lepidolite, and realgar can all be helpful in the acquisition of both wealth and material items. **Citrine**, known as the money stone, attracts riches. All the varieties of citrine work well, including kundalini, smoky, Tibetan, and tourmalinated. Keep a crystal in your pocket, purse, or wallet.

ACCIDENTS (prevention) Inca jade protects the accident prone.

ACTIVITY (increase) Carry or wear amethyst zebra stone, blue scheelite, buddstone, silver leaf jasper, or **snakeskin agate**, or place some of these and/or benitoite and/or gyrolite in your workspace.

ANIMALS Blue aragonite and diopside soothe distressed animals.

APPRECIATION Lemurian black jade allows you to realize the value of everything around you. and promotes gratitude.

AMBITIONS/DREAMS/GOALS/IDEALS Infinite, violet sapphire, and yellow sapphire help you to fulfill your ambitions. Auralite-23, chrysanthemum stone, copal, Hertfordshire puddingstone, leopard jasper, limonite, Preseli bluestone, purple scapolite, and super seven are all helpful in your quest for a more fulfilled lifestyle. Amethyst, atacamite, atlantisite, buddstone, colemanite, green quartz, green selenite, green tourmaline in quartz, honey calcite, peach aventurine, phillipsite, pink tourmaline in quartz, and tourmalinated citrine promote success.

BRAIN (left/right balance) This is the place where intellect meets intuition and science and magic converge. **Golden labradorite**, phillipsite, snakeskin rock, Vera Cruz amethyst, white chalcedony, and **yin yang crystal** aid a state of equilibrium. **Steatite** boosts brain power.

BURN OUT **Brown banded aragonite**, kimberlite, and yellow quartz alleviate symptoms and get you back on your feet.

CHALLENGES Blue spinel, **bubble gum tourmaline**, infinite, **orange mist aura quartz**, **orange moss agate**, and strawberry aventurine help you to face new challenges, giving you feelings of strength and courage. They will open your mind to the positive benefits of the test and help you to see the way forward.

CHANGE Many crystals promote and support change in different ways. See which ones you are drawn to, ask your pendulum for help and guidance, and then check the detailed description in the Crystal Finder (chapter 3). **Hausmannite**, **manifestation quartz**, and **sunset aura quartz** let you see the changes you need to make in your lifestyle and facilitate the transformation within you that change brings. Golden healer quartz, purple thulite, and stella beam calcite ease the process of change and soothe your emotions, gently bathing your heart center in healing energy. Alaskan garnet, almandine garnet in pyroxene, amegreen, amethyst, anthophyllite, atlantisite, black amethyst, black septarian, blue apatite, blue john, blue scheelite, buddstone, bumble bee jasper, caramel calcite, chrysanthemum stone, colemanite, conichalcite, green jasper, green selenite, Lemurian black jade, lepidolite in quartz, libethenite, nuummite, olive serpentine, orange selenite, petrified palm wood, pink tourmaline and lepidolite in quartz, polychrome jasper, Preseli bluestone, purple scapolite, rainbow moonstone, Sirius amethyst, stibiconite, stichtite, tangerine quartz, tanzine aura quartz, white moonstone, and yin yang crystal also promote change. **Cataclasite**, **girasol quartz**, pyrolusite crystal, **Tiffany stone**, and uranophane bring the really big shifts in your life, and **purple ray opal** can ease the pain of the largest changes. Dragonstone gives the strength and courage needed to change. Elestial quartz supports change through life's natural phases.

CHILDREN Bustamite with sugilite is good for all children's development and together with K2 jasper can be beneficial for development of the indigo or crystal child. **Blue coral**, traditionally a child's first stone, helps protect kids in the great adventure playground called life.

COMMUNICATION/EXPRESSION

All these crystals enhance the exchange of information, whether spoken or written: albite, Andean opal, Argentinian blue calcite, auralite-23, blue scheelite, denim lapis, gem silica, girasol quartz, K2 jasper, lavender amethyst, libethenite, mimetite, olivine on basalt, phillipsite, purple Mexican fluorite, ruby in kyanite, sieber agate, and spodumene. Biotite improves communication skills. Carry or wear **cryolite** or libethenite and hold when you need to say important things. *Communicating calmly:* In sticky situations, look to blue quartz or golden calcite for help. *Explaining ideas:* Blue apatite, blue aragonite, blue barite, doctor's stone, dumortierite in quartz, and microcline assist with this. *Expressing emotions:* Actinolite in quartz, agnitite, chalcosiderite, conichalcite, harlequin quartz, malacholla, and quantum quattro stone all help you to speak from the heart. *Expressing profound thoughts:* This is promoted by creedite, intrinsinite, Preseli bluestone, purple chalcedony, and vortex healing crystal. *Public speaking:* Blue moss agate and chalcosiderite make this easier.

CREATIVITY

Use your intuition or ask your pendulum to help you select the right crystals for you from this list: amblygonite, amegreen, Andean opal, blue jade, blue john, Brandberg amethyst, bubble gum tourmaline, bumble bee jasper, bustamite with sugilite, doctor's stone, girasol quartz, golden calcite, golden labradorite, golden rod calcite, golden selenite, green quartz, green tourmaline in quartz, Kambamba stone, kundalini citrine, Libyan gold tektite, liddicoatite, manifestation quartz, molybdenite, opalized jasper, orange mist quartz, peach aventurine, pink tourmaline in quartz, polychrome jasper, rainbow moonstone, rose quartz crystals, scenic quartz, scheelite, smoky citrine, snakeskin agate, strawberry aventurine, sunset aura quartz, super seven, tangerine quartz, Vera Cruz amethyst, vortex healing crystal, white chalcedony, white moonstone, yellow aventurine, and yellow sapphire. Libyan gold tektite can inspire artistic creativity.

DECISIONS

Choices are made easier with **actinolite in quartz**, amegreen, **amethyst elestial crystal**, anthophyllite, blue john, bumble bee jasper, cacoxenite in amethyst, green selenite, K2 jasper, **Tibetan citrine**, and yellow aventurine. **Cataclasite** and conichalcite can help with the really major decisions in life. **Lepidocrocite** helps you find answers to life's problems. To aid business decisions, turn to **buddstone**.

DESIRE

Amphibole in quartz, jamesonite, kimberlite, and realgar bring desires to the surface and allow them to manifest. Catlinite promotes the desire for freedom, while violet sapphire helps to control desires.

DIVORCE

Black amethyst, **blue jade**, girasol quartz, and pyrolusite crystal can ease this tough time and help you to remain rational and composed through the process. **Vortex healing crystal** helps you to release post-relationship sadness and guilt. **Scenic quartz** or **tugtupite** will help you to find new love.

ENVIRONMENTAL ISSUES

Black septarian, **black tourmaline with mica**, blue aragonite, green selenite, Inca jade, Kalahari picture stone, and Kambamba stone increase your awareness of green issues. **Shungite** is the go-to crystal for geopathic stress. Black tourmaline with mica and **stella beam calcite** enhance your connection to nature. *Practical:* Use copal elixir to disinfect household surfaces. Several celestite with sulfur crystals in a room will act as a fumigant. Get rid of any fungal infestations by washing down affected areas with peanut wood elixir and drying thoroughly.

FLOW

Axinite, **blue scheelite**, champagne aura quartz, clear halite, **conichalcite**, **golden selenite**, **papagoite quartz**, steatite, stichtite, and yellow prehnite make everything flow better in life. Things that were stuck become fluid. Your life moves forward, and if you need it, doctor's stone can get you going.

FRIENDSHIP

Axinite, **blue barite**, **blue jade**, green jasper, green selenite, and pyrolusite crystal help you to make new friends.

FUN/HUMOR

Benitoite, goethite on hematite, piemontite, **Preseli bluestone**, **rainbow moonstone**, silver aventurine, snakeskin agate, violet sapphire, and **yellow quartz** help you to see the funny side of situations and life in general. **Strawberry aventurine** helps to restore a lost sense of humor.

GETTING BACK INTO THE WORLD

Bismuth and **pink danburite** help you after absence through breakdown, drugs, hospitalization, unemployment, grief or any other reason.

HOUSE If you are selling your home, place a **Tibetan citrine** crystal in each room to speed the sale. The experience of moving is made easier with **girasol quartz**. Placing strawberry aventurine in a grid around your house can encourage family harmony and heal domestic rifts.

INSPIRATION Cataclasite, celestite with sulfur, cryolite, **golden calcite**, golden labradorite, lavender amethyst, **nuummite**, **orange mist aura quartz**, **rainbow moonstone**, scenic quartz, **Sirius amethyst**, sunset aura quartz, **tanzine aura quartz**, and yellow aventurine free your mind, allowing the brainwaves and flashes of genius to appear. **Conichalcite**, **mother of pearl**, and **rose quartz crystals** allow your imagination to flow freely. **Olive serpentine** encourages inspiration from guides. **Smoky citrine** grounds your inspiration into reality. *Blocks:* Blue scheelite removes writer's and other creative blocks. *Individuality:* Uniqueness is supported by **blue apatite** and **hubnerite**. *Invention:* Blue john, **bubble gum tourmaline**, Kambamba stone, and **liddicoatite** inspire this. *Lateral thinking:* Manifestation **quartz** can help.

LEADERSHIP Golden Lemurian quartz crystal, green smithsonite, peach aventurine, and violet sapphire promote leadership. **Amethyst elestial crystal**, **blue coral**, and **blue quartz** aid organizational skills and can help bring order out of chaos.

LEARNING/STUDY Argentinian blue calcite, **diopside**, dumortierite in quartz, Kambamba stone, prehnite with epidote, purple Mexican fluorite, and **Tibetan citrine** all aid the pursuit of knowledge. **Amblygonite** can improve the classroom environment. Chrysotile serpentine and **yellow quartz** help you to learn from experience. Spiritual learning is promoted by **skeletal quartz**. White chalcedony supports learning languages.

LIVING IN THE MOMENT The past has gone and the future isn't here yet, so don't let yourself dwell on them. Kimberlite helps you to stay in the present. Chrysanthemum stone helps you to seize the moment!

LUCK Black rutilated quartz, **cat's eye**, chrysanthemum stone, copal, **liddicoatite**, orange moonstone, **peach aventurine**, realgar, white moonstone, and **yellow sapphire** can tip the scales in your favor.

NEGOTIATION SKILLS Amethyst helps you to reach agreement.

NEW BEGINNINGS The start of anything new—projects, relationships, jobs—is helped with **black moonstone**, **bubble gum tourmaline**, **doctor's stone**, **dumortierite in quartz**, **garden quartz**, **goddess stone**, **golden labradorite**, green smithsonite, **hausmannite**, **lava stone**, **Lemurian black jade**, malacholla, **orange selenite**, Preseli bluestone, **rainbow moonstone**, **smoky citrine**, stibiconite, **Tibetan citrine**, **tourmalinated citrine**, **white moonstone**, and yellow sapphire.

POSITIVE OUTLOOK Snakeskin agate helps you to make the best of the world around you.

RELATIONSHIPS *Attract a new partner:* Try **actinolite in quartz**, albite, axinite, blue barite, **blue scheelite**, denim lapis, **garden quartz**, **golden healer quartz**, Inca jade, lavender amethyst, papagoite quartz, **pink tourmaline in quartz**, ruby in fuchsite, stibiconite, **Tibetan citrine**, **Tiffany stone**, or white topaz. *Faithfulness:* Olive opal and **opalized white agate** promote faithfulness in marriage or partnerships. *Increase your sexual attraction:* Work with **kundalini citrine**, **orange selenite**, realgar, or **tangerine quartz**. *Moving on:* Black onyx, conichalcite, **earthquake quartz crystal**, mimetite, phosphosiderite, pyrolusite crystal, ritzullite, **rose opal**, and **white moonstone** all help you to let go, release, and break free of old relationships. *Renew/repair relationship:* Blue jade, green jasper, Hertfordshire puddingstone, and lithium quartz can help. *Romance:* Bring this out with rose quartz crystals. *Sexuality:* Liberate with kundalini citrine.

SMOKING CESSATION Black onyx, blue spinel, **caramel calcite**, and orthoclase help you to quit the habit.

SPEAKING YOUR TRUTH All these crystals help you to live your life in your own spiritual way. Andean opal, blue moss agate, chalcosiderite, creedite, doctor's stone, girasol quartz, green kyanite, intrinsinite, papagoite quartz, phillipsite, ruby and kyanite in fuchsite, and sieber agate help you to talk your talk. Catlinite, doctor's stone, golden healer quartz, orange moss agate, and sieber agate inspire you to walk your walk. Piemontite encourages you to walk your talk and practice what you preach.

TEAMS Be they sport, work, or any group, albite, **auralite-23**, black septarian, **bumble bee jasper**, girasol quartz, **grape chalcedony**, Hertfordshire puddingstone, K2 jasper, kundalini citrine, microcline, pyrolusite crystal, scolecite, and **stromatolite** promote teamwork.

TIME MANAGEMENT Blue coral, honey calcite, and scheelite help you to organize your time effectively.

TRAVEL A journey can be a walk to the corner shop, a trip around the world, or following your path through life. Whatever it is, abalone shell, albite, **chalcosiderite**, faden quartz, garden quartz, green selenite, **Himalayan diamond**, Inca jade, mother of pearl, and **white moonstone** will keep you safe. **Lava stone** holds your connection to home.

WELL-BEING Diopside gives you a general sense of health and happiness.

WORK/LIFE BALANCE Kimberlite, Lemurian black jade, libethenite, orange moonstone, **phosphosiderite**, and **yellow quartz** can all help to restore equilibrium.

ZEST FOR LIFE Lemurian quartz crystal, orthoclase, peach aventurine, and strawberry aventurine boost your enthusiasm to live life to the full.

Sunset aura quartz lets you see the changes you need to make in your lifestyle and facilitates the transformation within you that change brings.

GLOSSARY

Acicular Needle-shaped.

ADHD Attention deficit hyperactivity disorder.

Adularescence The appearance of a milky glow from below the surface of the crystal, caused by light diffraction between layers of the mineral. Also known as a schiller effect.

Aggregate A mixture of minerals combined in a geological process; resembles a solid rock.

AIDS Acquired immune deficiency syndrome.

Akashic records A library of spiritual information that exists on another plane.

Alluvial Made from sediment in riverbeds, which produces "river-tumbled" crystals.

Astral travel The ability to send a part of the astral/spirit body to travel outside of the physical body (while remaining connected to the physical body).

Aura The subtle energy field (qv) around the body.

Bladed A crystal that resembles a flat knife blade.

Bodymind The body's energy system, which links mind, body, and spirit.

Botryoidal Describes bulbous minerals that resemble a bunch of grapes.

Brecciated Describes rocks formed from clastic (rock formed from broken pieces of older rock) angular fragments in a matrix of smaller stones and mineral cement.

CFS Chronic fatigue syndrome, also known as myalgic encephalitis (ME).

Chakra The Sanskrit word for "wheel." Chakras are the energy centers of the body, appearing as wheels to people who see energy.

Channeling The communication of messages or information from the spirit world via a medium.

Chatoyancy An optical effect, also known as "cat's eye" (see page 75), found in some polished crystals. Chatoyant crystals bring good luck, happiness, and serenity. They raise intuition and awareness, provide protection, and can help with disorders of the eyes, night vision, and headaches.

Chi In Chinese medicine and philosophy, chi is the energy or life force of the universe, believed to flow round the body and to be present in all living things. Other cultures call chi by different names. For example, ki (Japan) and prana (India).

Clairaudience The ability to hear psychic information.

Clairsentience The ability to feel psychic energies.

Clairvoyance The ability to see psychic information.

Clast A fragment of geological debris—a chunk or smaller grain of rock which has broken off another rock due to physical weathering or seismic activity. Clasts often recombine in another concretion material to form a clastic rock.

Columnar Stout parallel clusters with a column-like appearance.

Concretion Hard, compact mineral mass, often spherical.

Crust The top or outer layer. Crystals occurring as crusts are growing on the surface of a rock or mineral. *See also* Druse.

Cryptocrystalline Microscopic crystalline structure.

Crystal children Children with special abilities, often psychic. A further development, or the next stage, from indigo children. *See also* Indigo children.

Crystal system A classification of crystals according to their atomic structure, describing them in terms of their axes (imaginary straight lines through the center, around which they are symmetrically arranged). The systems are hexagonal, isometric, monoclinic, orthorhombic, tetragonal, and triclinic (qqv).

Cubic Describes a cube-shaped crystal, with six square faces. The three axes are the same length and are at right angles to one another.

Dis-ease A state of unsoundness on any level (physical, emotional, mental, or spiritual), which may weaken the body's natural defense systems and increase the risk of illness or disease. It relates to underlying causes and not a specific illness or disease.

Distant healing The process of sending healing energy, good thoughts, or prayers to a person who is not physically present. Also known as absent healing or remote healing.

Dodecahedral Describes a crystal having 12 pentagonal (five-sided) faces meeting in threes at 20 vertexes.

Druse A surface crust of small crystals on a rock of the same or a different mineral.

Earth healing Sending/directing healing energy to the planet.

EMF Electromagnetic fields.

Energy A supply or source of power: electrical, nuclear, mechanical, or subtle (*qv*), such as chi (*qv*).

Enhydro Water bubble(s) trapped in air pocket(s) inside a crystal as it was forming. The water and air inside may be hundreds of millions of years old.

Equant Having different diameters approximately equal, so as to be roughly cubic or spherical in shape.

ESP Extra-sensory perception.

Feldspar A group of silicate minerals.

Fibrous/fiber A rock made up of roughly parallel fine threads.

Fire A play of color caused by dispersion of light within a crystal, such as that shown by diamonds. Fire opal does not necessarily exhibit fire, but occurs in colors of fire—reds, oranges, yellows. Opal does not display true fire but a play of light caused by the scattering of light by microscopic silica spheres in the opal structure.

Globular Globe-shaped/spherical.

Granular A mineral composed of grains. May be formed with rounded, semi-rounded, or angular grains or can be massive (see Mass).

Hexagonal Describes a crystal system having four axes, of which the three horizontal axes are equal in length and cross at 120° angles, and the vertical axis is a different length and at right angles to the others. A hexagonal crystal has eight faces.

HIV Human immunodeficiency virus.

IBS Irritable bowel syndrome.

Inclusion A mineral found within the structure of a different mineral.

Indigo children Children with special abilities, often psychic. Most indigo children are now grown adults and are at the forefront of the human consciousness movement. See *also* Crystal children.

Iridescence Colors appearing inside a crystal due to either the diffraction or refraction of light within the crystalline structure.

Isometric Describes a crystal system having three axes that are all equal in length and at right angles to one another.

Karma/karmic process/karmic healing Karma equals action or deed. Also refers to cause and effect and specifically to how the actions of an individual can/will affect his/her future. Karmic healing is about healing karma from past lives or this life so you do not take it with you into the next life, meaning it cannot influence the next life.

Kundalini energy Kundalini is the source of primal energy (chi (*qv*), prana, ki, etc.) and consciousness that we are born with. It comes coiled like a serpent at the base of the spine and can be awakened/raised using various methods such as yoga and crystal healing.

Lamellar Scaly. An aggregate of scales.

Lemuria According to legend, Lemurian civilization was a highly advanced ancient society that pre-dates Atlantis. Priests of Lemuria are believed to have worked extensively with crystals, especially quartz crystals. In the final days before catastrophic destruction, they programmed quartz crystals with the knowledge of their society, sealing them in caves to protect them until the time was right for rediscovery.

Macrocrystalline/macrocrystalline quartz Having crystals large enough to be seen with an unaided eye. This term is used to contrast cryptocrystalline/microcrystalline, where the crystals are too small to be visible to the naked eye.

Manifestation The bringing of your dreams, desires, or goals into physical reality.

Mass Matter that has no definable crystalline structure. When the term massive is used, it refers to this rather than to the size of the crystal.

Matrix A rock or mineral that has an embedded crystal or crystals growing from it, or on it.

ME Myalgic encephalitis, also known as CFS (chronic fatigue syndrome).

Meridian An energy pathway through the body. Meridians carry chi in the same way that veins and arteries carry blood.

Mica Individual member of the mica group of related aluminum silicate minerals that are soft and have perfect basal cleavage (when a mineral has only one cleavage plane), which allows individual members to be "peeled."

Monoclinic Describes a crystal system having three unequal axes, only two of which are at right angles.

MS Multiple sclerosis.

NLP Neuro-linguistic programming.

Nodule A form of mineral that is massive (see Mass) with a rounded outer surface.

OCD Obsessive compulsive disorder.

Octahedral Describes a crystal having eight faces that are all equilateral triangles; resembles two four-sided pyramids joined at the bases.

Opalescence Color effect, typically found in opals, which causes a play of light when moved and viewed from different directions.

Orthorhombic Describes a crystal system having three axes of unequal lengths that cross at right angles.

Phantom When a crystal, typically quartz, stops growing and another mineral is deposited on the surface of the facets making the termination. Sometime later, possibly millions of years, the quartz starts to grow again, growing faster than the other mineral, covering it and leaving a ghostly shape within the crystal.

Plagioclase A series of feldspars, including labradorite and sunstone.

Plate A crystal that has grown flattened and often thin.

PMS Premenstrual syndrome. Also known as PMT (premenstrual tension).

Polymorph/polymorhpic Two or more minerals that are made from the same chemical composition but differ in their crystal structure. Well-known examples are diamond and graphite, which are two different minerals composed of the exact same substance, but forming very different crystals.

Prismatic Describes a crystal having faces that are similar in size and shape and that run parallel to an axis; the ends are rectilinear and similar in size and shape. For example, a triangular prismatic crystal has two triangular ends joined by three rectangular faces, while a hexagonal prismatic crystal has two hexagonal ends connected by six rectangular faces.

Pseudo- (before a shape, for example, pseudocubic, pseudo-octahedral, or pseudo-orthorhombic) Assuming a false shape; the crystal is apparently this shape, but not actually so.

Pseudomorph A mineral that replaces another within the original's crystal structure. As a result, the new mineral has the external shape of the departed one.

Psychic abilities These include intuition or gut feelings, channeling (qv), clairaudience (qv), clairsentience (qv), clairvoyance (qv), sensing energies and auras (qv), seeing auras, interpreting auras, telepathy, extrasensory perception, and increased insight into divination and tarot card readings.

Psychic surgery A technique used to enter the physical body with psychic fingers to remove unhealthy energy.

PTSD Post-traumatic stress disorder.

Pyramidal Describes a crystal in which the base is a polygon (i.e. with at least three straight sides) and the other faces are triangles that meet at a point.

Quartzite Non-crystalline or cryptocrystalline variety of quartz, also known as snow quartz or milky quartz.

RBC Red blood cell count.

Reiki A form of hands-on healing that originated in Japan and now has millions of practitioners worldwide. The Reiki healing ray is the frequency of Reiki energy as it is transmitted in healing.

Remote viewing The ability to see places and events at a distance. *See also* Astral travel.

Reniform Kidney-shaped.

Rhombic Describes rhomboid crystals, i.e. those with a parallelogram shape (a parallelogram has four equal sides and oblique angles).

Rhombohedral Describes crystals having six faces, each of them a rhombus (which has four equal sides, with opposite sides parallel, and no right angles). A rhombohedron resembles a cube that is skewed to one side.

RSI Repetitive strain injury.

Scalenohedral Describes crystals having 12 faces, each of them a scalene triangle (which has three unequal sides).

SAD Seasonal affective disorder.

Scaly Describes an aggregate of scales, which are small, flattened, overlapping crystals.

Schiller effect, also known as shiller effect (see Adularescence).

Scrying Looking into a crystal ball (or obsidian mirror) to see images to predict the future, or to view the past or present.

Shamanic healing An umbrella term covering a multitude of ancient forms of healing, all of which are linked to nature. One of the oldest forms of traditional healing.

Skeletal Crystals with gaps in their structure due to periods of unstable growth.

Spirit guides The beings or energies of departed souls who impart information, knowledge, and wisdom to help you on your path.

Stalactites Mineral formations descending from the roof of caverns, created as mineral-rich water drips down, facilitating the mineral to deposit over thousands or millions of years.

Striated Describes crystals having parallel grooves or markings along their length.

Subtle energy Energy that is outside of the known electromagnetic spectrum and therefore not easily detected.

Tabular Describes crystals that are broad and flat; sometimes shortened to "tabby."

TB Tuberculosis.

Termination The end of the crystal formed by the facets or faces making up the point. Note that a few varieties of crystal have flat terminations, such as some tourmaline and spodumene crystals.

Tetragonal Describes a crystal system having three axes, of which only the two horizontal ones are equal, and all three axes are at right angles. It resembles a cube that has been stretched vertically.

Tetrahedron A triangular pyramid with four triangular faces.

Totem animals Animal spirits or characteristics that help to guide you on your path in life.

Triclinic Describes a crystal system having three axes, none of them equal in length or at right angles.

INDEX

Page numbers in **bold** refer to main entries. Please note that ailments and other conditions are listed in alphabetical order on p122–53.

NOTES

1. (p. 14) phys.org, Physics, General Physics, February 27, 2014, "Glimmer of light in the search for dark matter," Leiden University

2. (p. 15) https://home.cern/about/physics/dark-matter

3. (p. 15) Bessel van der Kolk, *The Body Keeps The Score*, Viking Penguin 2014

4. (p. 17) Institute of Medicine Report from the Committee on Advancing Pain Research, Care, Education and Research, The National Academies Press, 2011

ACKNOWLEDGMENTS

I would like to thank my wife, Lyn, for her support, and my friends, clients, and students, who inspire me and provide a wealth of experience for me to share with you. All the people at CICO Books for their input—especially Carmel Edmonds (a very patient lady), Sally Powell, and particularly Cindy Richards for the good sense to publish this book. Finally, but perhaps most importantly, the people who inspired me to write: my father, Cyril, American crystal healer Melody, and Ian, who knows why.

Philip Permutt's website, with an online crystal shop and details of his workshops, classes, and courses, is found at www.thecrystalhealer.co.uk.

You can also follow him on Facebook (facebook.com/TheCrystalHealer), Twitter (@1CrystalHealer), and Instagram (@thecrystalhealer).